CLASS
ACT

BENITA EISLER

CLASS ACT

AMERICA'S LAST DIRTY SECRET

A GROLIER COMPANY

FRANKLIN WATTS 1983
New York   Toronto
London   Sydney

Library of Congress Cataloging in Publication Data

Eisler, Benita.
Class act.

Bibliography: p.
Includes index.
1. Social classes—United States.
2. Social mobility—United States.   I. Title
HN90.S6E37   1983   305.5′0973   83-12420
ISBN 0-531-09802-8

CONTENTS

**TO THE
MEMORY OF
MY FATHER**

CLASS
ACT

INTRODUCTION

This book is about Americans who are in the process of changing their lives.

Since the 1960s, *changing* our bodies, our attitudes, our personal relationships, our sexual behavior, or *coping with change* such as divorce, parenthood, mid-life crises, aging and death have been our central preoccupations. But in the rush to improve our personal lives, we have largely ignored the most dramatic transformation of all, one affecting millions of Americans—social mobility, or the experience of changing class.

By mobility, social scientists mean those changes in education, occupation and income which allow us to say—of ourselves or others—that we have risen or fallen in social class, rank and status relative to our parents' position.

As a child of the middle class, I had been blind to class structure. Being poor had never occurred to me as a possibility. Still my failure of imagination was more than youth. On the social map of America in the 1950s, even the margins of the middle class were hard to see. Great wealth and poverty alike had not been tabulated* and remained invisible, hidden

---

*Until 1960, the highest bracket of family income published by the IRS was "over $25,000." Only in 1964, when Mollie Orshansky, an HEW statistician, established a measure of poverty (based on food costs for a "non-farm family of four"), were the poor counted.

behind the walls of estates, tenements or tar-paper shacks. But the mystery of the missing extremes was, as Marxists say, no accident. Without a top and bottom, distance up and down was hard to define and impossible to measure. This distance is social class.

By the 1970s, class had definitively come out of the closet. The agonies of the 1960s had demonstrated that racial and ethnic conflict were also about class. The angry, competing claims of that decade were based upon assumptions of plenty. The Great Society and its successors had mobility to spare. Ten years later, this optimism had vanished. Growing drug traffic, ever younger "career criminals," younger and poorer teenaged mothers, and the abandoned elderly pointed not only to "intractable" social ills but to the fact that the Great American Pie was shrinking. We were no longer a "people of plenty,"[1] but an aging population where pensioners would soon outnumber employees, while jobs of millions of other workers disappeared, as factories closed or moved to lands of cheap labor.

For the first time since the 1950s, upward mobility itself is regarded as a declining possibility for Americans at every level. The causes are complex, ranging from the demographic "crowding" of young adults of the baby-boom generation competing for jobs, to structural problems of the economy summed up by the term "stagflation": the combination of double-digit inflation, high interest rates and steadily climbing unemployment which, for a decade, have stymied all attempted solutions. For alarming numbers, the economic bad news of the late 1970s and early 1980s meant more than a brake on mobility or a leveling off of the expected rise in our standard of living. Moving up was not just "on hold." For the first time since those "hard times" half a century ago, fear of falling has become a reality for many middle-class Americans. And for the first time since the New Deal, an administration has served notice that it is not the government of those unable to help themselves. Social policies aimed at fostering mobility for individuals and families who might make it—with help— are fast disappearing.

Why then a book on mobility *now*?

Because in periods of flux, like the present, individual social and economic behavior becomes more crucial to life chances. This is not a truth to cause most of us to rejoice, still less those who hold to the Marxist view that the few rise at the expense of the many—but it is a truth nonetheless. When a rising tide no longer lifts all boats, the characteristics of the crafts and the choices of the skippers become the determinants of who capsizes, who keeps afloat, who darts ahead.

As I began research on this book, I talked with a noted sociologist about those choices made by the poorest Americans. When I mentioned Susan Sheehan's portrait of a New York City welfare mother,[2] he was horrified. There was no reliable evidence to be gathered from such a book because, he explained, the subject "was only a sample of one." In the course of a year, I interviewed hundreds of men and women, from welfare mothers to self-made millionaires. They are, all of them, only samples of one, but they represent, nonetheless, attitudes, values and aspirations of many other mobile Americans. Each individual exists; each was the only source for the "telling life" that was shared with me. Only names, communities, and in some cases the specifics of jobs or business have been changed. The people who talked to me live in Chicano slums and blue-collar suburbs, "gay ghettos" and gilded ones, in Soho lofts and "landmark" country houses, in shiny Sun Belt cities where the poor are carefully hidden, and in dying urban centers where only the poor live.

My interviews with these men and women could be described as structured lack of structure. That is, I began by asking my respondents standard "demographic" questions about their parents' education and occupation, the number of siblings, the material circumstances of their early years, their schooling and employment history. As they moved in their narrative toward their own adulthood (the youngest of my respondents was twenty-four, the oldest fifty-eight), I let them tell me about the factors that seemed to propel them upward or downward, and what part choice played in moving them from there to here.

I found my subjects through a method known as "snowball sampling." Social agencies, schools and "interest groups" provided initial contacts. The payoff of snowball sampling, though, is usually not the first "referral," but the "someone-else-you-should-really-talk-to" syndrome. There were two categories of people I avoided—acquaintances and celebrities. The first because of the obvious restraints that friendship places on the candor of both subject and researcher; the second, because the very phenomenon of fame encourages self-mythologizing. Some readers may wonder at the absence of any "new immigrants": Chinese, Koreans, Vietnamese. With their fierce work ethic, entrepreneurial skills, the "over representation" of their children in elite schools and colleges, many of these new citizens have already reenacted the success story of earlier immigrant groups. Of those I met, the language barrier meant that the complexity of their thoughts and feelings would have to be imagined or "fictionalized"; their lives told by me, not them.

To the extent that my respondents are a "self-selecting" group, volunteering their time and experiences *because* of the social-class change evident in their lives, and not a random or representative sample, they present no hard data about the extent of social mobility in America.

Neither the men and women in this book, nor the author, makes any moral or ideological case for or against those who move up or down. But nonideological doesn't mean unbiased. Some of my biases are classically middle class, others are personal. Some were confirmed, others challenged. I have a mystical belief, for instance, in the virtue of education. I use the word *mystical* because a growing body of evidence suggests that education does less for mobility than it used to. Yet my bias is shared by millions who consider education the way up for those who aim higher or as a "good" in itself. Equally, I have an "old" middle-class faith in the redeeming power of work. So, I learned, do millions of Americans.

Initially, I assumed that my categories would derive from the class structure itself. From working poor to skilled worker, white collar to professional, I would "track" the process of class change through life choices in an orderly fashion. But social mobility, I should have guessed, like life, is a disorderly affair. Class and status discrepancies abound. Values, aspirations and actuality pull us in opposite directions.

One of the most startling lessons I learned was the pervasive influence of television on the values and goals of many Americans. From commercials to family sitcoms to the "style" of anchorpersons, the prevailing picture on the screen is America as a one-class society. Even more startling is the way these images are "read" as mobility directives. I was not prepared for the attachment of lower-income viewers to favorite programs and characters. Social scientists and television marketing analysts have documented this as a demographic phenomenon.[3] As I listened to the people behind the statistics, the potency of television in shaping social goals became palpably real.

In researching *Class Act*, I found that I wanted to learn and write about precisely that which social science isn't equipped to measure and which fiction rearranges as art. I wanted to explore the dynamic between the individual and society, the people and the process behind the quintessentially American journey: social-class mobility.

1

MIDDLE-CLASS
COUNTRY:
ARRIVING . . .

CHAPTER ONE

CLASS IN AMERICA: OUR LAST DIRTY SECRET

Class is America's last dirty secret. Accustomed as we are to chatter into every stranger's ear and every microphone about every sexual experience and problem, such as impotence and orgasm, abortions and sperm counts, coming out or staying chaste, we blush, cough and cover children's ears at the mention of class. Sometimes, even covering young ears is not enough.

The "first and only" time her grandmother ever slapped her, recalls Marietta Tree, an irrefutably upper-class citizen, related by ties of blood and marriage to almost every great New England family, was when, as a young girl, Marietta referred to an acquaintance as "middle class."

"There are no classes in America—upper, lower or middle," was the explanation for the severity of the lesson. "You are never to use that term again."[1]

But refusal to admit the existence of class in America simply means it's the subject on everyone's mind, even as they say it isn't so.

Like M. Jourdain, Molière's hero who discovered to his amazement that he had always spoken in prose, most Americans, without being aware of it, describe themselves, their neighbors and the larger community in terms of class. Constantly.

"They're the kind of people who would be on the symphony board." "She married beneath her." "My brothers have low-level ambition and jobs to match." "You can tell immediately from their accent that they're upper class."

How could it be otherwise? As one researcher recently noted: "People observe the fact that some have more of what everyone values than do others, and begin to build theories to account for it."

"Social arithmetic"[2]—the way in which people formulate a sense of their place and the place of others—in the class structure contains calculations that are made at every level.

The question of who gets what and how—otherwise known as social ranking—is discussed, argued and explained by everyone in America, from black out-of-work teenagers on street corners to retired millionaires in Palm Beach, not forgetting enough social scientists to fill a hundred convention centers (with a hundred more needed to house their writings on the subject).

Until I went off to a New England women's college in 1954, I had never met an upper-class American—or indeed, anyone very rich (as opposed to well-to-do, which to use Katherine Mansfield's nice distinction, is "stuffy and sounds like one's grandparents"). During my second year of college, there was an epidemic of Asian flu and the entire school was quarantined for spring vacation, only a few weeks away. Waiting in the outer office of the class dean, I overheard an astonishing snatch of conversation. One of my classmates was explaining to the dean why—contagious or not—she had to be allowed to go home to Winnetka for her coming-out party. "You don't understand," the sobbing undergraduate told the apparently unyielding administrator, "It's not a party, it's a social obligation."

I was mystified. I had never heard this expression before in any context. And its application—by a studious young woman, no less—to a dance was incomprehensible.

This painless instruction into the mysteries of upper-class "values" was nothing compared to the principal culture shock of college: my discovery that all of upper middle-class America was suburban.

To be Jewish was to be a well-represented minority in my new surroundings, but being urban middle class placed one in the same category of exotica as the few students strolling around in saris. My classmates' prosperous professional (or self-made rich) parents had formed the flying wedge of the "flight" to the suburbs, just then gaining momentum for the middle-middle classes.

With marriage, I acquired another perspective on the paradox of class in a classless society.

A refugee from Nazi Germany, my husband arrived here with his family in 1940 when he was nine years old. Scholarships were arranged for him and his brother at a famous progressive private school in New York. Here, following the social and educational precepts of John Dewey, the grandsons of John D. Rockefeller learned to scour pots and pans alongside the children of black dancers, Reform rabbis and radical editors. Students were taught black history, and were "guided" toward independent research projects on migrant workers and the destruction of the native American Indian. In fact, as one of my husband's classmates, now a psychoanalyst, once noted waggishly, it was only when he got to college that he learned white people had problems, too.

The elder émigrés were ecstatic. In curriculum and student body, here was democracy in action. Just what America was supposed to be about.

But a few years later, far from this "laboratory" of democracy, in his first days at a large public high school in Berkeley, California, the new arrival was helpfully provided with an essential piece of advice: merely to be seen *speaking* to one of the few Chinese-American students would be a cause for instant and permanent social ostracism.

Fifteen years after my discovery of coast-to-coast suburbia, the social obligations of the American upper class, followed by my husband's European perspective, came the real shock. With the rest of a shamed America, I confronted for the first time—then intimately and regularly—lives bounded by poverty.

To the children I tutored in East Harlem and their parents, living on or near what was described as the "worst block

—11—

in New York," life was an obstacle course unimaginable to any middle-class American. Simply to stay in school, for a fifteen-year-old boy whose two sisters were prostitutes and drug addicts by the age of sixteen, whose only brother had been killed by a policeman's bullet during a holdup, called for effort, will and discipline of a heroic order. It was outrageous, unforgivable that, daily in America, such demands be made of adolescents—just to survive. The high of self-righteous anger soon gave way to the discomforts of shame. Why had it taken me so long to learn about the lives of fellow New Yorkers living less than twenty blocks away from my home? Sooner or later, the city—where we are all variously, and sometimes interchangeably, neighbors, oppressors and victims—imposes this lesson. In the older urban centers of the Frost Belt, where neighborhoods are not flung apart by freeways, races and classes cannot remain invisible or even inaudible to one another.

I was reminded of a lunch, some years ago, where the host, a Texan of fabled millions and art treasures to match, raged and sulked, more than a dozen floors above Fifth Avenue. All the costly soundproofing efforts hadn't been able to shut out the sounds of the Puerto Rican Day Parade, breaking in waves from the avenue below. On at least one day a year, he was forced to contemplate his Vermeer and Watteau to the accompanying sounds of the celebrating poor.

In the early 1970s, like many women recycled back into the labor force when their children finally graduate from pre-school half days, I went to work again.

From the familiar world of print, I plunged into the newer, if not braver, world of television; "the oldest girl reporter in the Western world," as I used to joke. And appropriate to my age, the relatively peaceful pastures of the Arts were my beat.

Most of my colleagues in production, alumni of the student movement of the 1960s, were ten years my junior. With incredible dedication and energy, they were investigating and exposing every social ill within striking distance of a camera; dropping through roofs of nursing homes, standing in freezing dawns on welfare and unemployment lines, they tracked the far-from-hidden injuries of class in hospital wards, prisons, foster care agencies. Evasive bureaucrats writhed under their implacable questions. The inarticulate poor became all the more eloquent for their groping phrases and broken English. In admiration, I sat in editing rooms and watched the raw material of abuse and suffering take accusing shape. And yet, something was missing. Was it the futuristic setting of monitors and flashing computer digits that seemed to reduce angry black kids yelling "Motherfucker!" at the police to an interlude of local color? Or some unbridgeable distance between the reporters, former student activists from Princeton, Notre Dame, Yale Law School, and their subjects?

For much of American history, the class system has been in place. Yet, despite the undeniable hardening of class lines, we were also, it seemed, a highly mobile society. If Horatio Alger was indeed a myth, fostered by the dime novels and penny papers that were also American inventions, the reality of rags to riches was exemplified by a well-publicized few— and witnessed by many more.

As the granddaughter of an immigrant peddler and daughter of privilege, I saw the myth and was proof of the reality.

So I began to read about class and mobility, starting with the meaning of *class* itself, which is no simple matter in a country that professes it isn't so.

The classic Marxist definition of class—an individual or group's relationship to the means of production—only took care of the factory owner at the top and his wage slaves at the bottom, with the petty bourgeoisie, like small shopkeepers, being the "swing vote," so to speak.

But this model became increasingly irrelevant to postindustrial societies where many people at or near the top controlled no means of production except what emanated from their own heads. In any case, ownership was often diffuse, as in publicly held corporations where major stockholders may well be union pension funds, where most workers themselves labored in offices, not factories.

The other classic formula for assigning class membership retains something of the mechanistic Marxist flavor: punch in a person's income, education and occupation and the printout will tell you everything you ever wanted to know about his/her class.

Disparities create problems with this tidy triad. Recently, I met a young man in his late twenties, an aspiring novelist who announced: "I never graduated from high school. I've never earned more than four thousand dollars a year, my ex-wife and kids are on and off public assistance. But I can never be anything but upper class, because that's what my parents and my grandparents are."

Is he right? (And what about *his* children?) Most Americans don't like to think so. Even less do we like to believe that his contemporary, a great-grandson of slaves, grandson of sharecroppers and son of a kitchen worker, can never climb out of the lower class. These notions of class immobility—inheriting class and status—go against the American grain. In fact, as every survey of attitudes, beliefs and even experiences of representative Americans shows, most of us know many people whose present class or social standing is far removed from their origins.

The German sociologist Max Weber differentiated between *class* and *status*. Class, he held, meant a category of people with common economic opportunities and—to use one of his two famous phrases—common "life chances." Status, on the other hand, described intermingling and intermarrying social groups who shared a common "life-style"[3]—Weber's other famous phrase.

Strangely enough, while most Americans found the notion of class to be shamefully un-American, status has been a much more "salable" concept. Every real estate developer, automobile manufacturer and jeans company has been paying hordes of people to "sell" it on a vast scale, since the 1950s—when Vance Packard and others identified us as a nation of status seekers.[4]

The more available connotations of status, suggesting *things* anyone could buy, like the home abutting the golf course and the tailfin car, made this notion more democratic, more palatable than class, with its Anglo-European legacy of inherited advantages, and fixed position in the social pecking order. Indeed, indigenous American sociologists such as W. Lloyd Warner had insisted that class in America really *was* status: how others saw and ranked us (which might or might not be directly correlated with income, education or occupation). In a given community, class could be anything anybody said it was. Like beauty, it existed in the mind of the beholder.

To a nation of pragmatists, what you saw was what you got, in class as in other choices, like political candidates. And what people saw was status: class made visible, audible, palpable—and best of all for those who aspired to move up—attainable.

So if Americans weren't going to buy class without status, researchers bowed to the inevitable. They combined the two to arrive at: *social standing.*

Social standing accounted for class and status. That skeleton in the class closet, rattling the bare bones of job, income and education, was now fleshed out by the way he/she was likely to live, eat, play, mate, rear children, dress and vote; and also by the equally "distinct reality" that this "blend"[5] of activities and attributes, values and experience conferred membership in a "large group of families approximately equal to each other and clearly differentiated from other families,"[6] in other words, a social class.

But how "fixed" is this "distinct reality" of social standing for most Americans, this composite picture of "life chances" and "life-styles," and what happens between one and the other? How do people play that class hand they are dealt?

From magazines, newspapers and television screens, the terms *upward* and *downward mobility* hail the viewer and reader. *Cosmopolitan*'s guide on schussing into Mr. Right at the "in" ski resorts advises the uninitiated on "How to Be Upwardly Mobile on the Downhill Slopes,"[7] while a television program ponders the problem of "Downward Mobility and the Baby Boomers: How America Has Let Them Down."[8]

Upward and downward relative to what?

Our parents, of course.

Mobility, I learned, was in effect measured by a series of stills which, like the earliest films, were designed to give the illusion of motion.

Click goes the camera at birth, recording that Morton Mobile was born into a stable working-class family in 1937. Another click for Morton Mobile, B.A., the first of his family to graduate from college. The happy photograph with Morton shaking hands with his company president on the day of his promotion in 1967 to regional vice-president for marketing, is another milestone of Morton's ascent into the middle class.

But his son, Morton, Jr., does not have the "orderly career" which elates both parents and sociologists. Stuck at the rank of assistant manager, he is the victim of that generational glut known as the baby boom. Too many Mortons mean not enough places in that narrowing pyramid for all who would and could have moved beyond their fathers' attainments. Another album snapshot might show Morton, Jr., the Merry Moving Man, at the wheel of his freshly painted truck. He's turned his back on overwork and ulcers and weekends spent poring over company reports. Mort, Jr., packs it in when he garages the van for the day.

Multiply the snapshots, the albums, and we have rates of mobility.

The big picture—like a panoramic summer camp photo—tells us that, for the whole "cohort of Americans who were in the thirty-two to sixty-four age group as of the early 1970s: 42–44 percent were upwardly mobile by one or more class levels, 48–50 percent stayed in their social class of origin, and 8–10 percent moved down. In the period between 1940 and 1970, the three half-classes at the top—lower and upper middle class and upper class—accepted the most new members. Middle class and upper class increased their 'share' of the population from 38.5 percent to 45.0 percent, while the percentage of working-class Americans dropped slightly and those at the bottom declined most sharply, from 22.5 percent to 17.5 percent."[9]

As the camera pans slowly along the serried ranks, grouped by height, we get stratification studies, libraries and data banks full of them, concerning the mobility of blacks, Irish, Italians, Jews and Chinese. Who gets ahead and who doesn't. What education accomplished and in what ways it now seems to be failing. What happens to assembly-line workers and secretaries. The fate of families with two paychecks and families with none; of couples with 5.0 kids and couples with 0.0. The effects of inflation and migration, unemployment and self-employment, more and fewer social programs. The role of brains, looks and luck. These studies evoke no mere polite disagreements among authorities; rather, they are bloody battlegrounds, in which the first engagement is about turf.

Social psychologists see class and social mobility as shaped more by personality structure, in which the individual "actor's" attitudes, values and motivation are the determinants of who gets ahead. Sociologists, on the other hand, have a vested interest in explaining even individual class position by the structure of *society*, not the self. People may indeed erect barriers to their own mobility, but complex industrial societies have evolved a system of differential opportunities and rewards, based upon their own needs.

The vexing question, of course, is: how accessible are these opportunities and rewards? On what basis is access accorded—or denied—to higher education, desirable jobs and finally—the question which entices economists into the fray—are the numbers of coveted positions so "fixed" that only a fraction of those who are qualified will secure them?

Enter politics and ideology.

Conservative-leaning writers, like sociologist Seymour Martin Lipset and economist Morton Paglin, find a flexible structure "out there" which yields to different kinds of social and economic behavior on the part of individuals and families.[10] They point to the unhappy effects of Americans' tendency to split up families, thereby swelling the ranks of the immobile poor. The same family, Professor Lipset points out, that in Japan will stay together and be well off, will, in the

United States, have spun off its oldest and youngest adult members who—by no coincidence—are the poorest Americans.[11]

The aged pensioner and teenaged mother living alone in poverty are simply the extremes of the alarming American impulse to atomize our collective assets—an impulse which those on the right judge to have been reinforced instead of restrained by past "liberal" government policy.

Researchers on the left, though, see a very different picture, a negative image in which large social and economic forces—manipulated by those who have already made it (or whose grandfathers did all the work)—restrict the mobility of those further down the scale. In the view of sociologists on the left, inflation,[12] income distribution (who gets taxed and how), the disparity between the highest salaried work and the lowest, are the real roadblocks to individual mobility. They remind us that for the last thirty years the richest 0.5 percent of the population has consistently held about 22 percent of all personal wealth,[13] exercising a disproportionate influence on who receives the other 78 percent.

The Great Mobility Debate has a lot in common with the old distinction between the optimist and the pessimist; in this case, those on the right cheerfully behold the donut while those on the left gloomily describe the hole.

To those in the conservative camp, whether Old Guard or Neo-Conservative, there are enough donuts to insure that the most able, ambitious, talented and persevering on all levels will have plenty. Especially if those who already control the distribution of dough are helped to acquire more. They will in turn supply the rest of us with more goodies.

Another slant on this sunny view also justifies the persistence of those at the bottom. A complex technological society must offer differential rewards and opportunities to fulfill its specialized needs. To each according to his function, argue the functionalists.[14] Fewer of us are qualified to be surgeons, corporate lawyers or even sociologists, so the talent and lengthy training required for such work must be encouraged and rewarded.[15] Merit—as defined by these kinds of abilities—means more donuts.

—18—

The liberal-to-radical side of the spectrum challenges, first, this view of merit. A corporate manager is no more "meritocratic," no more useful to society than a donut seller—or a kindergarten teacher. Further, they argue, even if we accept such "elitist" views of merit, access to these desirable, highly competitive and highly rewarded positions is determined by what one writer has called "a shrewd birth certificate."[16] The "wrong" race, sex, geographical region or neighborhood, early schooling and parental education, effectively imposes handicaps on professional achievement. Social programs, those that "enable" people to help themselves—job training, family planning, Head Start and student aid—are the favored liberal means of fostering mobility.

The arguments that raged throughout the 1970s over equality of opportunity and equality of result, on quotas and busing, and on the "forgotten" blue-collar majority, were, besides being debates about race and ethnicity, also debates about social-class mobility. Who was being helped to move up—and at whose expense?

Who *does* move up or down? Why and how do they move? How do individuals negotiate that birth certificate, as well as the structure "out there"? How do we play the "class" hand we are dealt? Do the movers change values *before* they change class? And what happens to people as they move up or down?

"You're talking about process," said social psychologist Melvin L. Kohn. "Social science just isn't equipped to measure that. Our tools are too crude. These are really questions of individual history. Unfortunately, social scientists tend to be ahistorical."[17] The drama, the individual history of class and change, has been left to the novelist and autobiographer.

Indeed, for a country that has so persistently denied the existence of a class system, there is hardly a work of fiction or memoir which does not deal with its effect on individuals and families. Virtually all American novelists of the last two centuries—Henry James, Herman Melville, Edith Wharton and William Dean Howells—documented the "hazard of new fortunes," both to the upwardly mobile and those left behind.

Even more inescapably in our own century, heroes and

antiheroes alike have also tended to be the victims or victors of social mobility, its seductive myths and realities, cruel or benevolent. From *An American Tragedy* to *The Great Gatsby*, Sammy Glick and Scarlett O'Hara, *Princess Daisy* and *Portnoy's Complaint*, serious and popular fiction all chronicle the conflicts of individual aspirations and the complex social forces that shape or distort them. Certainly the greatest comic creators, including Mark Twain and Charlie Chaplin, have scored the most laughs on the ludicrous antics of upwardly mobile strivers. After all, what could be funnier than changing class in a classless society? Most American autobiographies, whether by Andrew Carnegie, Jane Addams, Richard Wright or Lauren Bacall, focus on the discovery of class—that sense of measured distance between where others are, where you are and where you want to be—as a central event in their lives. Chronicling the first of many changes in his life, Norman Podhoretz, in *Making It*, describes the move from his working-class Jewish family in Brooklyn to membership in the Manhattan intelligentsia as nothing less than a change of citizenship. To those who remained behind, he now inhabits a "country as foreign as China..."[18] In *Growing Up*, humorist Russell Baker attributes his own "change of citizenship" to a single crucial event: his mother's remarriage to a man who rescued the family from a life of marginal poverty.[19] Some writers look back on a cheerful journey from the "old neighborhood," relishing every step of the trip that replaced egg creams, *zeppole* or chitlins for champagne and caviar. Most recently, of course, the search for roots, the nationwide nostalgia for past privations, has increased the present prosperity of skillful storytellers.

The men and women in this book will confirm what we all know from our own lives: the definition of mobility changes as it rises. When people make choices and act on them with the hope of providing a decent job for themselves, better housing and more "life chances" for their children, we are really witnessing the "class struggle" in action. Moving out of poverty is no joke; nor is getting stuck in a well-paid, but back breaking, blue-collar job with no future. As soon as our creature comforts are taken care of, "opportunities" for ourselves and our kids assured, when we start wanting what we don't need—more "status," social skills, friends of a higher class, culture, the envy and admiration of others—we enter the domain of satire. In fact, middle-class aspirations to gentility, nobility or more "class" have comprised the stuff of comedy since Chaucer. Audiences still shriek at Sheridan and Congreve. Readers laugh with Trollope and Jane Austen, at the pretensions of the parvenu.

These "disparities" of evolving needs, of aspirations that zigzag between the serious and frivolous, worthy and unworthy, describe all of us. They are the untidy, irrational conflicting claims of our humanity. And the subject of that ongoing tragedy, drama and comedy: changing class in America.

CHAPTER
TWO

THE MOBILE
MIDDLE

Mobility, as hope or realization, is the measure of middle-class membership. Rising from poverty to self-sufficiency, or from unskilled to skilled labor, may constitute quantum leaps of a heroic order. But it is movement into our largest and most influential class, especially from its lower to upper ranks, that defines America as an open society.

In the period between 1940 and 1970, the middle classes, upper and lower, increased their "share" of the population from 38.5 percent to 45 percent.[1] The era that began when a wartime economy "put America back to work" was followed by the boom years of postwar expansion and growth.

Moreover, the mushrooming mobility rate of Americans during this thirty-year span was the happy result of *both* supply- and demand-side economics. This unprecedented prosperity, according to demographer Richard A. Easterlin, caused the rush to fertility known as the baby boom. Seeing no limits to growth, the new middle class reproduced itself with optimistic abandon.[2] Growing, getting and spending began to characterize so many American families, that upwardly mobile and middle class appeared to describe most of us. "New" home owners drove their shiny new Detroit cars along new highways to new jobs in new or expanding plants and offices. Optimistic observers came up with a theory of class convergence:[3] as in "everything that rises (like standard of living) must converge."

Shiny new possessions (encouraged by low interest mortgages for veterans and guaranteed cost-of-living increases in new union contracts) multiplied, were replaced, traded in or traded up to the siren song of the media. We were all rapidly becoming, if we weren't already, middle class. Consumer solidarity forever!

The turbulence of the late 1960s cured most of our myopia. Any lingering symptoms of blurred vision would be dispelled by the "stagflation" of the following decade, when rising unemployment and continuing inflation eroded many of the assumptions and expectations of the past thirty years.

Climbing into the middle class was suddenly difficult; staying there now meant two-paycheck households. Moving up within the middle class was ever more problematic. And for the first time in a generation, passing on the entitlements of parental upward mobility such as more and better schooling, housing and career opportunities was no longer taken for granted.

Still, the era of middle-class expansion had not been an optical illusion. And its legacy has been the identity problem that often accompanies growth. As the bulge in the center of our social pyramid widened, criteria of middle-class membership became fuzzier. Education—once the indisputable yardstick of occupational and social mobility—was proving an unreliable indicator of class. In 1974, one-third of the children of blue-collar workers were college graduates. By 1980, close to 16.3 percent of all Americans had graduated from college. But among these were many examples of an immobile "pen-and-pencil proletariat."*[4] In 1981, the supervisor of a General Motors auto assembly plant in Westchester County (New York) could report that more than 75 percent

---

*Whose ranks were swelled by the "best-educated generation in history:"[5] the 44 percent—25 million Americans born in 1946–60, who have had at least four years of college.

of the 1,200 most recently hired workers had at least two years of college.*[5]

Money doesn't clarify matters, either. If earnings alone are considered a measure, the Congressional Budget Office now uses a $15–30,000 range to describe the middle class, because one-third of our incomes are higher, one-third lower than the median 1982 family income of $21,020.[6] Using income as a yardstick, other estimates identify three-fifths to one-half of all Americans as middle class.

These elastic measures do not take into account regional or tax differences, or how many paychecks it takes to arrive. In an eloquent defense of his striking rank and file, the leader of a large service workers union noted that the average salary of his membership, $10,000 a year, placed most of his workers dangerously close to the poverty line. Asked by someone in the audience how many members had spouses whose earnings moved them into the middle-income category, he snapped: "That's not my business." Even for the disinterested researcher, though, the business of assigning class to a two-paycheck family is a tricky one—especially when each spouse wears a different-colored collar to work.

Middle class, argues Joseph Minarik of the Brookings Institution, is less the cash flow than its source.[7] Until unearned income from investments tops take-home pay, you are still in the struggling center. Since an interesting life "on interest" alone is hard to swing until total earnings exceed $200,000, those high-level managers or dual-career couples searching for bargain shelters against tax-bracket creep at $150,000 are still "just folks."

But when wealth (which includes property, savings, insurance policies, investments, government transfer payments and employer-paid benefits) rather than earnings is the criterion of middle-class membership, 70 percent of us qualify.

---

*Increasingly, "years of college" and even a degree have less meaning in terms of job and income, than *which* institution issues the diploma. The gap between a community college and an elite institution translates into far more than prestige.

Possession of assets harkens back to an earlier ascertainment of middle-class status: when a "man of property" needed no other credentials (certainly not a framed sheepskin hanging on his library wall) to establish himself as a solid and respectable citizen—a bourgeois, if not a gentleman. Since our beginnings, property has focused on home ownership. A house, "typically a single family detached dwelling standing on its own plot of land," notes one study, "symbolizes the independent self-sufficiency so central to the American dream and permits much of that dream to come true."[8] Significantly, the bill that President Lincoln signed into law in 1864, giving free land to those willing to settle the West, was titled the Homestead Act.

In the century preceding the Great Depression, home ownership was a long and unstable process. With the New Deal, the National Housing Act created government agencies with the power to buy mortgages that were in trouble, thereby rescuing families for whom loss of their home was imminent. Going further, the Federal Housing Administration made mortgage financing readily available, bringing home ownership within reach of millions of American families. These millions, by 1946, still translated into only 30 percent of us. It took the Veterans Mortgage Guarantee Program of the GI Bill to extend the deed of property to millions more young families who would help expand the mushrooming middle class. Recent critics have judged that postwar housing subsidies aided those already in the middle—in class, if not cash. Although no returning veteran needed a dollar of his own for the down payment, high carrying charges meant that low-income families couldn't take advantage of this opportunity—or soon defaulted when they tried. Others have pointed out that the legal right to buy and sell government-subsidized mortgages, along with the incentives to trade up, created a new generation of upwardly mobile real-estate entrepreneurs—at taxpayer expense!

Tax policy, as economist Robert Lekachman reminds us, is social policy.[9] The creation of the suburbs and of the "homeowner advantage" became and remained public policy for thirty years.* By 1982, 65 percent of Americans owned their own houses—up 35 percent from 1946.

In the wake of providing stability *and* mobility for millions there came the inevitable unintended consequences. Following World War II, one-house, one-plot grids covered America with development tracts, even as they covered developers with money. However, the "view from the picture window" was not of democratic vistas. One-child, one-wading-pool was the vision of the good life that came to pass for a generation of upwardly mobile Americans. But the legacy to their children is fear of sinking. Many of the youngsters who, twenty-five years ago, splashed securely while Mom kept a weather eye out from the kitchen, now fret that they and *their* kids have been priced out of their middle-class birthright.

Mourning their inability to afford that first house, one young Houston couple, parents of a two-year-old daughter, admitted, "Our greatest fear is that Chelsea will never have a yard of her own to play in." A father says, "I can't see a kid with his tricycle in a hall that he has to share with somebody."[11] These unlovely examples of second-generation middle-class "status panic," the "me generation" agonizing over the awful possibility that their kids might have to share a hallway or a yard, are not what the planners of upward-mobility-through-home-ownership had in mind.

The class and racial isolation fostered by suburbs zoned to exclude all but single-family property owners has been challenged everywhere—from Beverly Hills to Forest Hills—on issues as diverse as school financing, busing, multifamily occupancy, and public housing, by plaintiffs ranging from vagrant men to millionaire Moonies.

How could it be otherwise? Give people property and they have to defend it. And defending anything always requires an adversary. We defend against... "them," other classes, lowering the value of "our" investment.

---

*So entrenched is the belief in home ownership as entitlement, that the 1968 National Commission on Urban Problems declared flatly that recipients of public assistance should be given the choice of whether they would like to rent or own their dwellings.[10]

The paradox of home ownership, reaching well into the working class, now priced out of the present reach of young middle-class families, illustrates the unreliability of property as a measure of class. Assets may not only be frozen, they can put a freeze on mobility. Counting the numbers of the immobile "equity-poor," some would claim that middle class begins only when discretionary income starts jingling a little loose change in our pockets. But how much?

Common sense tells us that, depending on family size, as we move up from the median figure, discretionary and disposable incomes are apt to be counted in larger coin: by the instant disappearance of what once seemed quantities of cash; by the slight squeak of plastic in the credit card machine or the silent writing of checks whose amounts often include interest on debts incurred. Middle-class status itself, the white-collar job, the bank references, is a prerequisite for discretionary spending based on revolving credit.

Discretionary dollars and how they get spent tell us more about this amorphous middle. Disposable income describes a middle class in the process of making very particular choices, such as spending, saving or investing the money left after paying the mortgage or supermarket bills. The very term *discretionary* implies a way of life where choice becomes operational and is expressive of aspirations and expectations, of what we want for ourselves and our children, of what we are willing to forego and for how long—in order to buy what we want.

For behind the numbers, that slippery three-fifths, one-half, one-third or 70 percent of us earning between $15,000 and $140,000, behind the 49 percent of us who have had several years of college, the more than 60 percent who are white-collar workers—lies the realm of values. As students, workers, voters, consumers, patients, parents and sexual partners, we inherit values from our family.* These values, in turn, are retained, modified or traded in entirely, as life experiences and goals dictate. Yet, the dominance of middle-

*Freudians, to be sure, interpret the same data altogether differently.

class values has proved strangely enduring. Even when re-christened "bias," and challenged by social upheaval, sexual revolution, or the generation gap, the beliefs-become-behavior of our most numerous class have remained the measure for other Americans of where they are and where they want to be.

The American middle class, at all levels and in every period, have shown themselves to be *planners*. And anxiety, defined as the quintessential middle-class malaise, has made them, first, experts in preventive planning. Insurance empires flourish on the faith (shared by an aspiring working class) that by investing now to protect against disaster later, we still come out ahead. Insurance premiums are a propitiatory offering of the middle class against the possibility of downward mobility. Thus we insure against loss of assets, livelihood and loved ones—especially when the latter are also providers.

The philosophy of preventive medicine addresses another very middle-class concern: maintenance. The antithesis of the fatalism of the poor, the ounce of prevention invested in our bodies, our cars, our houses and gardens, has psychic rewards beyond saving the costlier pound of cure. Prevention reinforces the middle-class need to control the future. By following certain measures, buying specific products, the middle-class consumer runs less risk of falling victim to disease, dry rot or crabgrass. Careful stewardship of ourselves and our possessions holds the chaos of nature at bay.

Consumers of contraceptives are overwhelmingly middle class. The prime example of preventive medicine—successful birth control—as one researcher noted, requires the rational and consistent perception that one does *not* want a child.[12] And although many reasons contribute to this decision, a constant remains (as we will examine later)—the typically middle-class calculation that children must be "affordable," which is another way of stating that their cost should not adversely affect their parents' chances for moving ahead.

"Middle-class morality"—a phrase that once described puritanical views (and implied hypocritical posture) about sex—was largely based on the disastrous social and economic consequences for middle-class aspirations, of sex unsanctified by marriage. Once contraception and abortion became legal and widely available, middle-class morality was no longer needed to maintain status or to move up. Subsequently, as growing numbers of affluent college-educated middle-class Americans exalted the value of the therapeutic above all else, self-denial in matters of sexual behavior was considered undesirable and even deviant.

Predictably, the backlash came with the next wave of arrivals to the middle class. Based largely in newly prosperous areas of the nation, the Moral Majority quickly made themselves heard. As the collection plates of the New Christian Right remind us, the ranks of reaction include the little old lady from Pasadena, brown-bagging Texas millionaires bent on reclaiming middle-class morality, *and* a growing number of affluent mainstream Americans. Nor is their notion of how respectable citizens should behave quite as archaic as their liberal critics suggest.

Until the 1960s, discipline and self-denial—even sacrifice—were the salient middle-class characteristics. A decade later, these hard-core principles had vanished. In fact, researchers were beginning to suggest that other values and experiences were more crucial to mobility than the much-heralded virtue of deferring gratification. The securely middle class were more and more to be observed eating their dessert before they finished their spinach. And their children were usually encouraged to question received wisdom on principle.

Working on the hypothesis that most child rearing equips children for assuming their parents' station in life, social psychologist Melvin L. Kohn persuasively demonstrated that middle-class parents who value self-direction rather than conformity to external authority, inculcate this value in their young. Praised and encouraged for qualities of curiosity, initiative and independence, the middle-class child, Kohn notes, "is able to develop a perspective on the world which translates into effective ways of going about important activities like school tasks, and later on, to the self-directed work which describes most middle class occupations."[13] The emphasis is not upon renunciation and sacrifice, but upon the individuality and expressiveness which foster the full development of talent, intelligence, and achievement.*

Yet even as middle-class children are rewarded for initiative and independence, it is apparent that their parents' authority does not rest on these qualities alone. They have mysterious access to information and knowledge which they use to negotiate the outside world with competence. Their promises and plans, more often than not, become realities.

Gavin Mackenzie, a Cambridge University sociologist, studied American class differences by comparing the values of managers, clerks, skilled and unskilled workers in Providence, Rhode Island. Where aspirations for children were concerned, the British scholar was surprised to find that all levels of workers shared a historically American goal: over 80 percent in all four occupational groups felt "very strongly" that one or more of their children should attend college. However, even taking into account the fact that lower-paid workers and clerks can rarely afford to save toward that goal, Mackenzie was struck by the inability of the best-paid skilled craftsmen to "translate this concern into action—even where financial sacrifice was not the issue." It was not lack of sincerity or even means, he concluded, that explained the gap between values and behavior of different classes. Exposure to higher education itself, and information about savings, investments, loans and scholarships made the difference.[14]

Ability to translate concern into effective action is nothing less than power: the real subject of middle-class instruction. A sense of power leads to the conviction that one's decisions and actions are consequential. Thus middle-class

*That these notions of the desirable in child rearing always reflected middle-class values is demonstrated by the fate of the Progressive Education Movement. Envisioned by John Dewey as a democratic force to eradicate class barriers, the child-centered curriculum was gradually abandoned by local public school districts, to remain the province of a few upper-middle-class independent schools. And a recent minirevival, in the form of the "open classroom," was greeted by working-class and minority parents with outright hostility.

participation in political life, their overwhelming presence at the polls (and the underrepresentation of the poor—especially the minority poor) underline the belief on the part of the citizen pulling the lever that he or she counts.

Empowerment is the link between the self-definition encouraged from childhood and the self-improvement of middle-class adults; indeed, it is the meaning of all those ugly hybrid words that begin with SELF. And the process of this empowerment, however arduous, is also liberating.

The education of young middle-class adults is often the happiest experience of their lives. Private institutions of higher learning would never have survived without the conviction of their graduates that those bright college years were a largely pleasurable preparation for a life of well-rewarded work. Even professional training supposes one of the significant privileges of middle-class empowerment: choice of work, a choice signifying the match of individual interests, learned skills and the demands of a specific occupation.

That "room for advancement" promised by "learning and working one's way up" may have shrunk, the result of baby-boom adults crowding career ladders made already precarious by a shaky economy. However, even with the highest unemployment rate since the Great Depression, entry-level options were not lacking for middle-class college seniors in 1982, trying to decide among training programs in banking, retailing or marketing.[15] The major difference between this generation and their predecessors of more prosperous years is that graduate school was unaffordable for many. Lean times had led many more to "position" themselves early—in marketable fields, such as computer science and accounting. "Getting a job" is the first career goal for greater numbers of graduating students in the 1980s.

Middle-class values instilled early will enshrine the ideal of work as its own reward. Even as they "adjust" their interests to market demand, these young adults will continue to require work with satisfactions beyond a decent paycheck and Christmas bonus. (Those who reject these values are the subject of another chapter.) "Work with larger meaning," "a job where

I can use all my abilities," "I need to feel I'm making a contribution"—these are all middle-class requirements. As criteria for choices, values may have to be put on "hold," but they are unlikely to disappear.

Even more likely to survive economic swings is a peculiarly middle-class avidity for experience, along with the belief in its transforming powers. Somewhere between faith and expectation is the certainty that art, travel, psychotherapy, tennis, sex and diet are more than improving, broadening or thinning. By these experiences, we will have become more *valuable*, regenerated by looking, listening, feeling or winning, through knowledge of ourselves, and our children.

The six Americans in this chapter share basic middle-class characteristics; yet, they differ dramatically in income, education, and work; in the way they vote, where and whether they worship; and how they have fun. They have all traveled far, with gains and losses along the way.

A NEW TRADITIONALIST

Ray Billings doesn't like to pigeonhole people in any particular class because all that tells him is "how much money have they got?" Not that he is naive about money. He knows, for example, about the very rich people who live in mansions on the bluffs, and about the many more poor people, blacks and Appalachians mostly, who are crowded in the same part of town where Ray's family used to live and where he was born. Most people, nowadays, Ray guesses, live in communities pretty much like his own—a subdivision of trim ranch houses and lovingly tended yards where sprinklers turn in the summer heat. Feeling a part of this majority allows Ray to feel that instead of belonging to a class, "We're all just Americans."

His Catholic forebears landed in Maryland or Georgia "back when our country was founded." As far as he knows, they were people who had little to leave their children but the religion that has been practiced in his family through the generations.

He is a large freckled man whose extra pounds and thinning red hair conspire to add ten years to his age of forty. Ray's father was a lathe operator, then a cab driver, and finally owner of a small junkyard. But he couldn't seem to make a go of anything. Partly it was the "fear" the Great Depression left with so many people, but mostly, Ray says soberly, his father was such a Christian that everyone took advantage of him. Ray hopes the example of his father's charity is a force in his own life, but free of his parents' fear, he has been able to move far beyond them.

After graduating from high school in 1959, Ray went to work delivering milk for a dairy. Then Ray discovered he had that particularly American talent, a "real knack for selling," that resulted in several promotions. Eventually, he was promoted to sales manager for the two principal cities in the state. Beyond the recognition and the rewards, though, Ray loved the work, "especially the challenge. I need goals, and I enjoy attaining those goals, then resetting them to a higher level. That's what motivates me." When the company was sold to a conglomerate five years ago, retail sales and home delivery were phased out, and Ray Billings had to find other work. His present job, production supervisor for a large furniture manufacturer, seemed at the time "a fine opportunity." But since then, Ray has had many occasions to reflect on that phrase.

Although he had to take a slight cut from his salary of $26,000 at the dairy, he now receives 49 percent of his take-home pay in benefits, along with overtime, and including cost-of-living increases. Among the benefits he mentions is the interest-free company loan that secured his new house with its tree-shaded back yard for the kids, front lawn for Ray's rose garden, and perhaps the most important measure of middle-class attainment for Americans living in the southern half of the United States: central air-conditioning.

Ray's income dictates that parents and children do things together. A meal out means hamburgers for the whole family. Yet, he doesn't mourn unaffordable dinners downtown or the price of two tickets to a touring Broadway musical. What he does lament, though, is the scarcity of movies that qualify as "family entertainment," however they may be officially rated. Ray used to enjoy "taking in a show." Nowadays, either the sex is "way too explicit" or the language is offensive. The content of most movies—in the post-Breen Office era—has changed from family to "adult." And that definition of adult is younger, more affluent, college educated, probably more urban, and certainly more liberal in both life-style and political beliefs than Ray and his wife, Noreen.

For the Billings, athletic events at the girls' school are the family's central recreation. An ex-basketball player himself, Ray is immensely proud of his oldest daughter's starring role. Fourteen-year-old Rose Marie is headed for interstate competition and Patty, at ten, is already a runner to watch.

Social scientists are often baffled by the passion that Americans invest in high school athletics—especially those living in smaller cities and towns. Dr. Theodore Caplow, continuing research begun by the Lynds on "Middletown, U.S.A.," confessed that after eight years he still couldn't understand the mania of Muncie, Indiana—the real "Middletown"—for its two basketball teams. All observers agree that the involvement of smaller communities in their homegrown young athletes embraces black and white, working-class through middle-middle-class citizens. As Dr. Caplow noted, if the Muncie Symphony—the cultural pride and pleasure of the upper middle class—were to disappear overnight, hardly anyone would notice. With the loss of the two championship teams, though, the town would fall apart.[16]

For American men, "following" our national sports pastimes on television is a form of male bonding that transcends class. (Women appear to lack those shared rituals that dissolve class lines.)

For sports-fan Ray Billings, the work place is a source of much less satisfaction. Selling, with its "goals and challenges," has been replaced by the frustrations of the supervisor. And these frustrations have much to do with the mixed blessings of mobility. For Ray Billings, a new member of the middle class, is also a man caught in the middle. As production supervisor, Ray is a "superforeman" who will never be a manager. Because of his age and lack of education credentials, he will always report to "kids with MBAs." Even at his present level, Ray knows, he is already a rarity. "I'm the last generation of front-line management to have only a high school diploma."

But if Ray Billings gets impatient with the "guys on top who think that degrees solve all the problems," he is saddened and perplexed by the attitude of the people below him—people who are, after all, very much like Ray. "They just don't care," he says, and Ray is inclined to lay part of the blame for this on what he calls the "union environment." If someone isn't good at their job, "you have to go through so many procedures to correct the problem," that it's almost "hopeless." Ray doesn't think anybody has ever been terminated at the plant—not even for repeated failure to show up.

The union rule book alone, though, doesn't explain to Ray why employees don't care anymore, why pride in the job well done—the source both of his self-esteem and his material rewards—is disappearing. And like many Americans, casting about to explain changes that threaten and diminish values by which they live, Ray Billings points to "humanization."

Humanization, as he defines it, is close to the narcissism others have described, both cause and symptom of the "me generation" in which the demands of the self threaten the "integrity" of all the institutions that claim Ray's loyalty: family, church, work place. It explains boredom and drug abuse in kids, the cynicism of their elders, whether union or management, "right up to the loss of our markets to Japan, because our efficiency has just dropped so dramatically." In fact, Ray thinks this humanism is "what's wrong with America."

As a Catholic, Ray Billings is a member of a religious minority. But his traditional conservative Catholicism does not separate him from his Protestant neighbors, whether they call themselves a Moral Majority, or simply Baptists or Methodists. Like his neighbors, Ray and his family attend church regularly, and like them, he is skeptical about the new forms of religious observance. About Charismatic Christians or

Evangelical Catholics, Ray wonders what they are looking for that traditional churches don't provide, and especially why these younger people need to define their faith by "forming sects, like Moonies or hippies."

If Ray Billings is discomforted by the mystical—the transcendental movements which, since the 1970s, have attracted so many young white adults, from middle- to upper-middle class—it is because his faith joins him to a secular and social tradition that has long characterized our mainstream denominations: Jewish, Catholic and Protestant.

Nevertheless, in important ways, Ray exemplifies what one historian has called the "New Traditionalism," whose larger discontents fuel the New Christian Right. For the New Traditionalists, antihumanism is a reaction against the "fun morality"[17] of modernism, the if-it-feels-good-it-is-good culture. But to thoughtful and concerned men and women like Ray Billings, humanism describes deeper ills than can be cured by banning books or sex education in schools. Theirs is a judgment, notes church historian Martin Marty, on the "moral anomie" of a pluralistic society, and especially upon its "apparent inability to generate positive values for common action."[18]

New Traditionalists like Ray are seekers, not mindless zealots. Their "wholeness hunger," unlike the yearnings of many of their contemporaries, does not focus on personal transformation, but upon nostalgia for a "simpler, ordered homogeneous" world. And a particularly crucial task for New Traditionalist parents is the recreation of this lost Eden for their children. In it, the authority of the family and school will reflect divine authority (and depose that of "liberal" government, regarded as remote, bureaucratic, interfering and permissive, at the same time).

Both Ray and his wife attended local public schools, but they have chosen parochial school for their daughters, to be followed, he hopes, by Catholic colleges later on. "Not for the Godly nature of it, but for the moral." And moral, for Ray Billings, is the reassuring knowledge that "there are restrictions, there is discipline, that you do it, or you're out."

There is a crucial difference between New Traditionalists like Ray and Americans who held similar values in the past. That difference is upward mobility. Those who once hungered for authority, favoring in Robert Jay Lifton's phrase, the "restrictive" over the "protean" personality style, were also those least favored by society: underclass, ethnic or marginal Americans. In contrast, new adherents of that old-time religion are no longer those left behind. They do not all reside in humble dwellings; indeed, as Marty points out, many of them are moving into the higher social classes. Like Ray Billings, they have made the big jump from blue collar to middle class, taking some of their traditional values with them. Further, new upper-middle-class constituents have swelled the ranks of denominations once associated with less-educated, less-prosperous Americans. The pastor (a former Quaker) of an evangelical congregation in Illinois noted that his membership had grown 48 percent in three years, raised almost $600,000 in one year, and that many of these affluent newcomers were couples in their early thirties with Ph.D.s.[19]

Politically, upwardly mobile New Traditionalists have swelled the conservative ranks. In 1981, for the first time since the New Deal, the liberal consensus of younger, more affluent Americans seemed to have dissolved: of those surveyed under age forty-four, 43 percent claimed Republican affiliation,[20] while fully one-third of all adult Americans told pollsters they were conservatives. Like many New Traditionalists, Ray defines conservative in terms of past values: "We have to get back to how we started," when opportunity meant "getting out there and making it happen," not, as Ray defines liberalism, "sitting around waiting for that check."

For his children, Ray harbors large ambitions. "I would like for them to be professional people," he says, articulating the dream of millions of American parents. That is the opportunity he would have liked more than anything else, the chance he still misses most. Ray assumes his daughters will not choose "a traditional family life-style." As he sees it, by the time they're of age, the full-time housewife-and-mother role won't be traditional, "it will just be old-fashioned," and if inflation continues, "it may not even be possible anymore."

"They've got the capability," he says proudly. "That's the big thing. They're both at the top of their class. They've got all the potential. I just don't want to see it go undeveloped. Because that's the tragedy, isn't it? Talent gone to waste."

THE URBAN STRIVERS

Early each morning, Rebecca Lacey and her ten-year-old son Nelson set out from their public housing project in the South Bronx for the long subway ride to central Harlem, where Nelson goes to school. As soon as Nelson races to join the bottleneck of small jostling bodies at the door, his mother rushes for the bus that takes her to Manhattan's West Side, where she works as a telephone switchboard operator in a drug counseling program.

Now a fourth-grader, Nelson's school is all black and private, a school where parents, many of them single mothers, like twenty-nine-year-old Rebecca Lacey, pay fees on a sliding scale for the kind of education they want for their children. "I knew what I *didn't* want for Nelson, and that was the unhappiness I had in public school."

The second in a family of six children, Rebecca, her mother, five brothers and sisters lived "on and off the welfare" in a mixed black and Italian neighborhood in Brooklyn. In her school, "integrated" meant that whenever there was a problem, especially if it had to be settled by the white principal, the black child was always the one who got punished. When she recalls the pain of those years, Rebecca Lacey's dazzling smile disappears. If you had a mother on welfare, brothers and sisters with different fathers, "they just assumed you were some kind of delinquent," she says. Even if, like her mother, Celena, you also had two jobs, cooked every meal "including baking the bread, and made all our clothes."

But it isn't only the racism she remembers. "Nelson is so high-spirited and full of energy, I knew he'd always be in trouble with a teacher or principal in one of those sit-down-and-be-quiet kind of classrooms." Rebecca had better experiences in mind for her son, so she "shopped around." A black education was high on her list, but it had to be a special kind; if old-fashioned religion was out, so was revolution. "I didn't want a militant kind of thing, and no black English, either."

The Hughes School was just what she was looking for. "The teachers are *real* pros. This school is about directing the child's energy and curiosity, first into the basics... then beyond, into his own interests and talents."

Rebecca Lacey's energy and curiosity are moving her beyond the basics, too. A community college dropout, she moved from job to job, for ten years: switchboard operator, receptionist, typist, bookkeeper. "I always learned a lot and then I moved on," but although she earned a little more with each change, "I really wasn't going anywhere."

The drug counseling program has given her some ideas about her future. When the switchboard closes for the day, Rebecca helps out with the evening therapy sessions. The center is understaffed and she gets a chance to be part of the entire sequence of activities, recording intake interviews, videotaping the group meetings, fielding calls on the emergency hotline. The counseling process and the kind of work therapists do "opened a whole new world to me."

The world of work that middle-class professionals, with their education and expectations, take for granted, was for Rebecca Lacey a revelation—work specifically defined by the word *autonomy*. "Once you have the knowledge and the techniques, you make the decisions. You're on your own."

"Parents' values for their children are values for themselves," social psychologist Melvin Kohn concluded from his study of social class, work, and child-rearing patterns.[21] For upwardly mobile black parents like Rebecca Lacey, translating these matching "middle class notions of the desirable" into actuality are goals with a high price tag. She realizes that the next step for her is going back to school "to get qualified for the kind of work I want to do." For the moment, though, Nelson's schooling is the only sacrifice she can afford. After she pays his $1,300 tuition, "I just can't do anything else on my tiny salary." There are no "extras" to be given up, such as new clothes or records. "Now," says Rebecca, "it's his education that counts for both of us."

Elyse Mayberry, forty-one, doesn't like the word *sacrifice*. Her son Clark's tuition at the Hughes School is measured against the "fantastic difference" it has made in his learning style and personality. "We really see his tuition like rent money," she explains. "A basic expense. Not an instead of. Like 'instead of' having a nice car or traveling." In the year since Henry Mayberry, a van driver for a moving company, lost his job, a lot of small "instead ofs" have had to go; and with the job market so uncertain, her administrative secretary's salary may have to support them for a while yet.

Elyse Mayberry grew up in a small town in West Virginia. "I'm a coal miner's daughter, too—just a black one."

It's hard to imagine Elyse Mayberry in a gritty mining town. At the end of a working day, the cuffs of her white shirt are still immaculate. Her mother, Elyse recalls, applauded every kind of effort, from tree climbing to reading the newspaper every day. "She was very much into her three girls being individuals, encouraging us to be very opinionated, even as children." Elyse thinks this influenced her ambitions for Clark and why his school is so important to them.

"Hughes has high expectations for the individual pupil," she says, "but at the same time the teachers are guided by the learning style of each child." And initially Clark needed that "comfortable black setting."

Elyse left her own comfortable small world at seventeen, just after she graduated from high school in 1957. "Except for the mines, there were just no jobs for young blacks near home," she recalls. Westinghouse was the major employer, and at the time, it was "whites only" in white-collar jobs. Arriving in New York, Elyse lived with a friend at the "Y" ("the only place my parents would consider"), moving up from telephone operator to receptionist to secretary.

Between the certainty of inflation and the uncertainty of employment, Elyse worries that "even if the perfect job came along, with all the challenges and independence I'm ready for, it's probably the wrong time to change. There's just too much hanging on my paycheck."

Elyse doesn't have specific career hopes for Clark. "There isn't any one thing I would like to see him do." Although she does want him to "become the kind of man who can express himself—not just thoughts, but feelings; the kind of man who would confront situations and not walk away from them—and who will feel good about himself as a man."

We know that individuals change, exchange, refashion and refurbish their values over time. But just why this happens, how values—those "criteria for choice"—modify what people want for themselves and their children is a mysterious process, where cause and effect are reduced to the chicken-and-egg dilemma. Which comes first, the desire for change—adopting the values that will make change a likelihood—or the opportunity itself? Aspiration or reality?

Through the very process of moving up, both Rebecca Lacey and Elyse Mayberry aspire to more autonomy and responsibility in their own work, even as they insist on schools for their sons that reinforce their upper middle-class values as parents.

Dr. Alvin Poussaint and Dr. James Comer, two black psychiatrists on the faculty, respectively, of the Harvard and Yale medical schools, in their book *Black Child Care* deliver Melvin Kohn's message about conformity to upwardly mobile black parents (the ones who will be buying their book), but they pointedly avoid dealing with the "class" issue. "New child-rearing techniques," they point out to their readers, "are designed to teach children internal control, discipline and direction rather than dependence on others to direct their behavior."[22] The message of Comer and Poussaint's child-rearing manual for black parents is nothing less than class reconditioning.

Think middle class. Value creativity, not obedience.

How do parents like Elyse and Henry Mayberry or Rebecca Lacey come to choose the values and experiences which promise mobility for themselves and their sons without any assurance that these choices will make a difference? For both women, their "work career" predated their parental one. Each was exposed to a wide range of people and—even more important—to a variety of experiences. They also came to know themselves better, so that both were able to articulate the need for precisely the kind of self-directed, intellectually complex work that Melvin Kohn "pairs" with middle-class parental values.

Like most of us, Elyse Mayberry isn't sure "where a lot of ideas and thoughts of mine developed or when." Yet, she is certain that she is influenced by the media: from *Essence* and *Parents Magazine*, to the TV documentaries she adores, like *Gideon's Trumpet*, which dramatized legal issues. "Everyday," she is convinced, "you read something without realizing you are putting yourself into being that character. And when you look at TV," she insists, "you see part of you, or someone you would like to be you. And when you see how certain children act, you may want your child to be like that."

Rebecca Lacey and Elyse Mayberry both feel their decisions and actions to be consequential. But the source of this feeling is an imaginative projection of themselves and their children that leaps ahead of their actual class condition. Their choice of values has propelled them further than the actuality of their lives.

Nevertheless, like many Americans, the economy has placed them in a holding position. If inflation and poor employment prospects don't sabotage their efforts and aspirations, they will move up, taking their children (but not necessarily the men in their lives) with them.

Elyse Mayberry's work, her evening courses at a suburban college and her son's education have all intensified in importance, because that other central middle-class goal threatens to elude her: home ownership.

"A house is still the American Dream," Elyse says, "especially if that's where you grew up. You just can't forget the feeling of the porch. The yard. And you want to end your days there. I don't mind the apartment for myself, because I have someplace else to go." The job "downtown," especially its attractive professional setting, is an escape from "being locked into substandard Harlem housing." But Elyse mourns what her son will never know—the freedom of the house and yard of his mother's West Virginia childhood. "Where if he wanted to ride his bicycle I wouldn't have to stand and look out of the window, or go downstairs with him to the park, so it won't get ripped off.

"That's what I think of when I hear or read the word *class*," Elyse Mayberry says. "What you want for your children that you can do without for yourself."

It isn't easy to find defenders of the largest American cities—especially New York. Increasingly, New York, along with other, older major metropolitan areas, is home to the rich and the poor. The number of middle-class residents of all races drops with every census count. Yet these large urban centers, whose problems weigh most heavily on the most vulnerable of their population, continue to fulfill a historic social role. Big cities still deliver on the promise of upward mobility.

The values of an urban college-educated middle class have shaped the aspirations of Elyse and Rebecca. They have decided on secular modernism as the way to mobility—that dizzying pluralism which New Traditionalist Ray Billings considers a falling away from sturdier values.

Urban strivers like Rebecca Lacey and Elyse Mayberry would be foiled without the supermarket of city life. In Abilene, Texas, or Davenport, Iowa, Rebecca would have no opportunity to "shop around" for the kind of schooling she desires for Nelson, or the job experience for herself.

And that illuminates yet another dimension of city life that links aspiration and achievement: access to professionals and professionalism. In urban America, there are still choices and chances a subway ride away.

MOVING UP THE MIDDLE:
SPRUCE ISLAND

When Doug Mueller moved with his family to Spruce Island, it represented coming home and a dream of success come true, both at the same time.

Eighteen years ago, as a scholarship student working in the kitchen of the city university, Doug read about the island in the local newspapers. He would linger over the weekend supplement with pictures of families racing their sailboats, kids accepting tennis trophies, early fall cocktail parties where guests on teak decks were silhouetted against the sunset sky. A causeway away from Doug's steam tables and accounting textbooks, Spruce Island might have been Bora Bora.

While he was growing up on the wrong side of the tracks in a nearby city, college, much less Spruce Island, was not a realistic option, because Doug Mueller's family wasn't even stable working class. They were members of America's least studied, unofficial minority: the white urban poor.

Life for the Muellers, Doug, his mother and two brothers wouldn't have been a question of survival if—the big *if* behind so many poverty statistics—his father hadn't been "mostly incapacitated by alcohol." Sometimes home, mostly not, his presence didn't make much economic difference to the family. Doug's mother supported them all, with any job she could get and as many as she could hold at one time, "from saleslady to cleaning lady."

The day after college graduation, Doug went to work for a company as a sales trainee. A month later he married his high school sweetheart, June. Recruits like Doug Mueller were hardly aware of learning the right clothes and style by emulation. As a westerner, Doug thinks he had it easier; in his part of the country, there doesn't seem to be those big differences in speech and manner he has noticed in his stints "back East."

Rewards for apt learners were conferred with gratifying regularity: letters of commendation, merit raises, help in buying ever-larger houses in congenial communities that eased the strains of frequent moves. When Doug returned to his home state he was regional marketing manager.

Doug Mueller finds nothing pejorative in the term *organization man*. He does not regard gratitude or loyalty as the traits of a toady. Company emphasis on the "team," moreover, offers security. Doug Mueller would be surprised to hear that his peers in other companies suffered pounding hearts and clammy hands at a buzz from the vice-president's office, or from insomnia and impotence caused by fear of being fired.[23]

The company, where Doug Mueller has enjoyed the "orderly career" that fascinates social scientists, is famous for personnel policies which foster just such steady upward mobility. But it is far from unique.

In an update of a 1950 survey of the social origins of big business executives, *Scientific American* found that as of 1964, the American business elite was composed to a larger degree than ever before of men and women from lower-status groups. Only 10 percent of the current generation of big business executives, the study reported, were sons of wealthy families; in 1950, the corresponding figure was 36.1 percent, and at the turn of the century 45.6 percent. The proportion of those from poor backgrounds, like Doug Mueller, who entered the top echelons of American business rose from 12.1 percent in 1950 to 23.3 percent in 1962.[24]

Spruce Island mirrors many of these changes in corporate life—especially the expanded middle levels. Only one small estate, with its main house, its guest house and pool house in matching "tycoon Tudor," remains from the period when the island was home to a few of the city's lumber and shipping entrepreneurs. Then, as the young executives and middle managers poured into this Hi-Tech boom town in the 1960s, Spruce Island became an unofficial, unplanned corporate community. From the island's main highway sprout roads carefully laid out for maximum scenic enjoyment. On either side, fir-covered embankments have been divided into quarter-acre lots, each with approximately five spruce trees, and one "semi-custom" house, all built by the same developer in a style known locally as Pacific Northwest Japanese.

"To meet middle class aspirations," notes a recent report, "housing [must have] enough bathrooms so there are no early morning lineups as the family gets ready for work and school."[25] And indeed, the dazzling "his," "hers," and "theirs" bath suites, each with an adjoining dressing room and shower, are the first stop on island house tours.

The rest of the Mueller house seems strangely bare. Besides the basics: sectional sofa, easy chairs, glass coffee table, the only other furnishings are provided by the Muellers' sporting equipment: bikes, tennis rackets, and in winter, skis, poles and boots. These costly, finely crafted possessions are basic to Doug's dream of success.

The island is "just peerless for kids," Doug says. "The opportunities they have growing up here!" Douglas, Jr., eleven, has already placed in tournament tennis, and Helen, nine, "seems set on being the fastest swimmer out there," her father reports proudly.

Like Ray and Noreen Billings, Doug and June Mueller's pleasures are centered on family activities, which means sports. But there are crucial differences. The games the Muellers, their kids and neighbors play are lifetime sports, and the social skills they confer are as important as athletic prowess. Parents may referee, but they don't retire, like Ray Billings, to the grandstands after their championship season. In communities like Spruce Island, the development of athletic competence in kids eases the social integration of their parents—no small matter for families who will move many times before their children are in college.

The Muellers and many of their neighbors rarely go into the city after the working day, and never on weekends. But unlike Ray Billings, their preferences for family-centered activities is based on choice, not economic necessity. Doug feels they should take advantage of the city's cultural resources, but somehow they don't get to the symphony, the opera, or museums. He admits, though, that they "really prefer being with the kids and their friends"; they all enjoy tennis, backpacking, sailing and skiing. His own father was a troubling source of guilt, shame and anger in Doug's life. For his children, he is determined to be a positive presence, sharing the activities that engage them. "All the material advantages we've given them don't mean anything without our involvement."

Other residents, though, take a less benign view of Spruce

Island's involved parents. "Sports are everything here," notes real estate agent George MacGreevy. "And kids' sports are the most intensely emotional. The kids' ability to compete reflects the father's success. I've had former clients sell their houses and move because their kids were no good at tennis. The parents were the ones who felt like failures."

There are three things that everybody on Spruce Island tells you about Murray Speiser, and always in the same order.

He's Jewish, he's a great tennis player, and he's a hell of a guy.

The "helluva guy" disposes of a quality most of Murray's neighbors—men from small towns or modest suburban communities around the state, who worked their way through the local university and up the corporation—would have trouble articulating.

Murray Speiser is a man of immense and compelling charm. And he is not only "a helluva guy" as a neighbor, tennis partner and poker player, but, where it counts even more: in his line of business. "I'm a born retailer," he says. But not because it's in the blood. Great-grandson and grandson of rabbis, son of a synagogue organist and choirmaster, Murray says of his father, "He was a man who touched a lot of lives; he was involved with many people in this city and he was straight with all of them. And that's part of being a success in my business, too."

Like most of his neighbors and tennis partners, Murray Speiser went to the city university, where he majored in business, working his way through school by singing in dance bands. "I think I've seen more high school gyms in the region than any college basketball recruiter." After one semester of law school, followed by a brief stint with an accounting firm, Murray went into business with his father-in-law. "A real institution around here" is the way he describes the family store. But it always bothered Murray that no matter how successful he was, "it could always be said that I was there because I was the son-in-law."

So with a certain amount of "bad feeling from the family,"

Murray recently struck out on his own, with a store in the new shopping mall serving Spruce and Fairhaven islands. "It's the hottest residential area in the state with the highest density of upper-income people. The perfect place for a unique shop featuring designer clothes—especially European ski clothes, sports furs, maybe eventually a very select line of home furnishings for country living."

Murray started playing tennis when he was twenty-four, "just after I got out of the Navy." After Murray Speiser and his family moved to Spruce Island, his wife learned the game. As he says: "It's a very nice social thing to do. There are lots of casual evenings when four or eight couples will reserve some courts; then we'll all go and have dinner."

President of the Spruce Island Tennis Club, Murray recently declined an invitation to apply to the City Tennis Club, which he describes as "the most beautiful club in the country, just magnificent," and restricted until recently against "blacks, Jews or Orientals." That policy has changed but, Murray qualifies, smiling slightly, "with temperance."

There was nothing ideological, he insists, in not taking them up on their "very nice invitation." "I really wouldn't use a club," he says, "located on the other side of town." And it wouldn't help Murray's game—or his self-esteem, he says, "to play with the chairman of the number one corporation in town."

For Murray Speiser, the ideological is excess baggage. As past president and board member of his father's synagogue, as a Jew who can happily turn down temptations to tokenism, his dues are paid, his conscience is clear. And his clarity about who he is, the limits he has set on assimilation, play no small part in the respect he inspires in his neighbors and in the larger community. The "helluva guy," that American male bear hug of admiration and affection, embraces more substance than Murray Speiser's warmth, his tennis trophies, and his business success.

Still, one part of Murray's heritage is carried less gladly: political affiliation. For him, the condition of "liberal Democrat" is irrevocable, no more subject to choice or change than being Jewish—but somehow more troubling. "There's no self-definition for me in being a Democrat," he says, but no possibility of denial, either. Whatever case Murray could make for diminished ideological differences between his inherited politics and the progressive view of liberal Republicans, this crossover would still be an unthinkable betrayal. He will not revise his code of concern for those excluded from his pleasant and prosperous life.

It would be complicated, though, to share these distinctions between an inherited code and the political choices of the moment—especially with his neighbors. So Murray has also adopted another American convention: politics as a private affair. In a decade of playing poker and tennis, "socializing" with the senior vice-president of the city's leading bank, a managing partner in a national accounting firm, and a lawyer active in the state Republican Party, Murray has never, he insists, "ever had a discussion of political or social issues with any of them. Not once." Or, for that matter, with any of his "many other friends on the island." Opinions on these subjects, Murray Speiser feels, are either "very personal or very trite." And he compares those who talk about their political affiliation to men who "kiss and tell." If such subjects do come up (and he's hard put to recall an instance), they would—yes, even in a presidential election year—"be touched on lightly, with nobody taking sides."

"It's a corporate ghetto, Levittown with fir trees."

Tim Donohoe is the hot architect in town. But he is hardly typical of what one sociologist has called "the patrician profession." Son of a local policeman, Tim went to college and architecture school here in the city, and after the "usual Academy year in Rome," he came home—where he has lived and worked ever since.

Prematurely gray, with a military brush cut, Tim Donohoe wears the uniform of American architects—$400 custom-made English tweed sports jacket, tan twill slacks, and desert boots.

Above the restored nineteenth-century square, the offices of Donohoe Associates, A.I.A., are designed for maximum exposure of the fine brick and iron work of early industrial architecture. The setting of archaeology-in-progress makes a perfect backdrop for several important works of contemporary American sculpture. "Unfortunately," Donohoe apologizes, "my best pieces are on loan to a museum."

Tim Donohoe started his career with a firm that was trying to build some "interesting" houses on Spruce Island. "They were one-of-a-kind designs, a developer's experiment and 'not saleable,'" he notes drily, "to the kind of people buying there." The "kind of people" Tim Donohoe is describing are *very* unsophisticated; basically still lower-middle class in most of their values, tastes and life-style. It's only their incomes that have pushed them into the upper-middle class. I guess those guys all must earn," Tim calculates quickly, "between fifty and ninety thousand. They're a highly mobile population," he continues, "but they haven't chosen to change their tastes or values on the way up."

And he isn't just talking aesthetics.

"Politically they're even more conservative," he says frowning. "I'll bet you 98 percent of the Island was 1,000 percent behind Reagan. The other 2 percent probably found him too liberal and didn't vote.

"The reason you always hear how great the Spruce Island schools are," Tim says, "is because they're the only lily-white schools in the district, and these aren't the kind of people who would feel comfortable with private schools." The "kind of people" who are Tim Donohoe's clients are either "comfortable" with private schools or "ideologically committed" to public education. They are also the "kind of people" who want houses designed around their art collections or their own dry-dock facilities for several boats.

But Donohoe insists he knows many other young professionals like himself and his wife, Tina, a lawyer (they have three girls), who live in renovated warehouse space—like his office—in the city's waterfront area. "I'm doing more and more of these." Still other young families, Donohoe points out, "are using a thousand cans of paint to rehabilitate the

Victorian gingerbread houses in the city's rundown neighborhoods. These are people who want urban diversity," who don't view cheering their tots over the finish line in the pool as the most fulfilling way for an adult to spend time with a child. But to live that way, you have to be willing to live next door to poor black neighbors in a rooming house with peeling paint, or to accept Indian winos wrapped in filthy blankets, sleeping in the square below.

There's more than a causeway, a tax bracket, a graduate degree—even the color collar your father wore to work—between Spruce Island and "downtown." Islanders and downtowners are both middle class; more, they are both upwardly mobile, upper-middle class—but Tim Donohoe is convinced the description is meaningless. There's no real common denominator anymore. Architect Tim Donohoe, many of his clients, and most of his friends, helped erase that middle-class common denominator. Pace-setting professionals, their work, politics and pleasures—and more important—their numbers and influence, have defined them as a new phenomenon, a "new breed," and to some, a New Class.

CHAPTER
THREE

HIGH TECH AND LOW MANDARIN: A TOUCH OF (NEW) CLASS

They toil and spin, but never own or control the corporations, newspapers, television stations, and certainly not the universities, foundations or government agencies that employ them. Still, they are not merely cogs, drones or interchangeable parts; no pen-and-pencil proletariat, punching in and pushing off at the sound of the factory bell. They require (and usually obtain) "high job satisfaction," and often, equally high rewards. However, unless they are artists or writers, they are not self-employed. Indeed, they are characterized by their critics as antibusiness and anticapitalist—as ambitious and successful individuals who are *against* ambition, success and individualism operating in the marketplace. They comprise an "adversary culture,"[1] Jacobins in jeans or pinstripes.

THE NEW CLASS

They are a class trained to plan and administer. Or, they are not a class at all, but a social stratum, an ethos, a mind-set,[2] or a group of new occupations searching for people to fill them.[3] Those who qualified for these new jobs in the affluent 1950s were knowledge workers who formed a "technostructure."[4]

Whether a scientific and technical elite or a cultural and humanistic one, the New Class consists, first and foremost, of degree-bearing animals: numbers crunchers, word wielders and symbol jugglers, they function in a realm of process, ideas and concepts. When they give birth to a product, it is likely to be a package for the handy processing and distribution of words, ideas and numbers: books, newspapers, magazines, cassettes, floppy discs, printouts or performances. They traffic in consumer perishables, not durables. And the most characteristic of their products is the most perishable of all. Talk.

"We saw the Fellini film last week," trumpets the man standing in line for a new foreign movie, behind Alvy (Woody Allen) and Annie (Diane Keaton) in *Annie Hall*.

"It's not one of his best. Lacks the cohesive structure, you know. Granted *La Strada* was a great film. Great in its use of negative imagery...." (He continues to pontificate, completely oblivious as Alvy's irritation turns to rage.)

"I can't take this guy. I'm going to have a stroke," hisses Alvy to Annie. But his persecutor is unstoppable. The recent Fellini film lacked that "simple joy of spirit," he announces.

"I found it *incredibly* indulgent," crescendoes Alvy's neighbor, who, it turns out, teaches a course called "TV, Media and Culture."

"The key word here is *indulgent*," sneers Allen, stepping out of character to share his mocking rage with us, the audience. But revenge is at hand: Woody produces the "real" Marshall McLuhan to demolish the phony film expert.

The New Class is a speech community. Its native language, as satirized above by Woody Allen, New Classman Supreme,* is *Careful and Critical Discourse* (CCD),[5] a hybrid of the therapeutic/scientific and aesthetic vocabularies, a lingo frankly incomprehensible to the unschooled or unscreened. Expert

*The subject of Allen's films, as well as the source of their humor and poignance, is the paralyzing effect of learned New Class attitudes and behavior (from self-analysis to speech) upon instinctual emotions and needs.

use of CCD, according to its discoverer, sociologist Alvin Gouldner, serves two functions.

The first enables New Class men and women, like mating Chinese geese, to recognize one another as peers (should dress, social context and other early warning systems fail). But the second, more important function of CCD is to maintain New Class influence through its persuasive verbal skills, namely, the power of members to formulate, express and disseminate opinion (their own) in a form that suggests Scientific or Revealed Truth.

Careful and Critical Discourse is a "linguistic variant" (a phrase that is a perfect example of CCD) enabling the speaker to distance him/herself from the speech. Unlike ordinary parlance, which reveals bias, ego, subjectivity, emotionalism and partial knowledge (or total ignorance), CCD in its dispassionate, neutral, impersonal style builds its case through self-evident logic, purged of value judgments. And finally, because CCD persuades through general principles or evidence, not the authority or status of the speaker, it is also a democratic (or at least meritocratic) form of expression available to all those with the endurance to stay in school—or blessed with an ear for languages.

Much of the humor of "All in the Family," Norman Lear's artful expression of middle-class status anxiety discharged as blue-collar bigotry, resided in the disparity between aspiring New Class son-in-law Michael's ("Meathead") use of CCD, countered by Archie's earthy, personalized response. "The Bible is full of magic," says the earnest young sociologist, refuting his father-in-law's claim that he "don't believe in no such thing." "What would an atheist like you know about the Bible?" demands Archie truculently, immediately shifting the ground from questions of general principle (are the miracles in the Bible magic?) to a personal attack.

A new Establishment is in the making. Who its members will be is, as yet, unclear. What mix, as one writer asks, of "industrial and financial leaders, of defense experts or policy intellectuals from Harvard or Rand, of cosmopolitans and provincials"? A "chastened new class or just the old Establishment refurbished"?[6]

Whatever the look, the sound will be CCD.

So they talk funny. Does that make them a class? Yes, insisted Gouldner, who had christened CCD.

They are a class in the classic Marxist definition: they stand in the same relation to the means of production (pretty far away). But they also behave like a class in other ways. Like the expensive accents of the Old Upper Class, a common New Class education, culture and language code facilitate the development of coteries, social circles, professional ties and political projects among themselves, reinforcing the tendency shared by all classes to "reside and vacation in the same neighborhoods and ecological areas, as well as intermarrying frequently with one another."[7]

However, Daniel Bell of Harvard disagrees, preferring to regard this amorphous group of "intellectual workers" as merely a social stratum with new matching cultural luggage and carry-on life-styles.

If nothing else is new about them, many of the jobs they fill never existed before. Philip Roth's Alex Portnoy, Assistant Commissioner of Human Rights, is a New Class antihero, with a title on the door that didn't exist before the 1960s. These new occupations—planners and programmers, urbanists and suburbanists, welfare organizers, population controllers and energy administrators—are the by-product of a postindustrial society in which the shrinkage of the manufacturing sector of the economy was accompanied by an explosion of the service sector—especially the public service sector. Big government created a big piece of the New Class.

PROLES
IN THE IVY

"Why go to Podunk College," *Time* magazine asked in 1946, "when the government will send you to Yale?"[8]

Why indeed!

But Henry Luce (Yale, class of 1920) was really asking after the fact. Returning vets headed for the most selective institutions which would admit them, and the Ivy League broke all application records.*

Thus, the G.I. Bill created another kind of mobility of particular interest to our scrutiny of the New Class. Young men appeared at elite schools with accents rarely heard in these halls. Through the new legislation, New Class met Old Money, influential teachers and future associates.

Common sense tells us that many G.I. Bill "first-generation" college graduates returned to Hometown, U.S.A., and the offer of a Chevy dealership. Others, like Homer MacFarlane (Yale, 1948), one of eight children of a single alcoholic mother ("I started as the poorest goddamn WASP you'll ever meet"), sincerely wanted to become very rich as soon as possible—a goal that he handily achieved, building the largest chain of supermarkets in a southwestern state. Untainted by any New Class antibusiness, pro-poor bias which may have been floating around postwar New Haven, Homer maintains that "anyone who can't make it in this great country of ours deserves to starve."

Self-made tycoons and used-car salesmen notwithstanding, almost one-half of G.I. Bill graduates chose those organizational, salaried careers designated as New Class occupations.**[9] The Veterans Administration counted among its

---

*But the force of numbers and the accompanying dollars upgraded many proto-Podunk campuses—including some of the Negro colleges. From this perspective, the G.I. Bill provided upward mobility to many institutions as well as individuals. Neither Podunk nor teachers' colleges benefited from the explosion of demand. They stayed undersubscribed.

**V.A. tabulations did not count either "public managers" (federal, state or local) or their corporate counterparts. But before the days of M.B.A.s running the world, management was most often drawn from the engineering and accounting departments of factories and corporations (243,000 accountants learned their bookkeeping on the G.I. Bill). So we can reasonably assume that many in the top ranks of International Anodyne had left their T-squares and eyeshades for the move into the executive suites. Had government workers (in other than engineering and science) been counted, New Class graduates would probably amount to three-quarters of those veterans educated on the G.I. Bill.

"alumni": 450,000 engineers, 360,000 schoolteachers, 150,000 scientists, 107,000 lawyers, and 36,000 clergymen. And in 1956 the President's Report on Veterans Pensions attested to the fact that returning soldiers had not only been most likely to succeed—they *had* succeeded. "World War II veterans occupy," the report noted, "in greater proportion than non-veterans of comparable age, the highest paid professional, technical... and managerial positions."[10]

Thanks to the G.I. Bill, the march of the nonpropertied New Class was in full stride.

TURNAROUND TIME

The summer of 1948, when Joe Nash received his Ph.D., he traveled south for a family reunion. It had been a while since Joe and his two brothers had been home together. For, despite the Depression, the sons of an unemployed shoe salesman were now a physician, an astrophysicist and, with Joe's new doctorate in hand, a political scientist.

"My mother was so proud of all three of us," Joe Nash recalls. She understood what Junior did, because there were stars up there, and one looked at the stars. And Dillon had his black doctor's bag. But she couldn't figure out what political scientists did.

"One day the phone rang, and the caller asked for 'Dr. Nash.' I heard Mama say: 'Y'all mean the 'sho-nuff doctor or the one what don't do nobody no good?'"

Joe Nash went on to become speech writer, budget analyst, author, urban specialist, policy advisor to three presidents, holder of two cabinet posts. He has been out of Washington for ten years, to other New Class jobs: head of a regional "Authority," then back to teaching and university administration, and lastly but briefly, occupant of a local agency hot seat. ("It was the one thing I hadn't done before, so it was an intriguing challenge.")

"We were the 'inner-outers,'" Joe Nash explains, of himself and the legions who followed in the career track set by the New Deal lawyers and economists.

In the fifties and sixties, a New Class of New Men "moved easily back and forth on the Washington-Boston axis. That became," he says, speaking of his wife (daughter of a prominent Philadelphia lawyer) and their four sons, "the pattern of our lives. TV was getting serious; polling was getting serious; parties were beginning to lose their relevance," Nash recalls. "By the 1960 election, television became the critical part; candidates had to say something plausible. They just couldn't do the old Mechanics Hall-Fish Market speech."

That was where the inner-outers came in. Elevated from the back rooms of budget and speech writing, they became part of an increasingly intense interaction of academe and government. For people like Joe Nash, this interaction occurred at a particularly welcome moment in their careers. They had written the books, the articles, the papers; their theories had been aired, criticized, applauded at seminars, symposia, conferences.

Suddenly, there was the possibility, no, the *plea* for those "ideas and concepts to become program and policy." And just as suddenly, "you weren't just scribbling for other academics." The "systematic courtship" of experts and intellectuals begun by John F. Kennedy and continued by Lyndon Johnson was on! He grins and there is a whiff of those heady days.

(*These guys were used, they were "had"—right down the line, notes a colleague, but one who was always an "outer".*)

Joe Nash isn't naive about who got what from whom and why. "You had to have a stockpile of concepts. The politicians needed the ideas and respectability, and we wanted to see our theories turned into reality. So it was an irresistible combination. If you were not a complete egomaniac, or just loving the prestige, or wanting Georgetown, you could hold your own. You could still maintain the best of two worlds." That "vast need" of the politicians created the perfect mechanism for an inner-outer to function.

So after the advisory committees, the task forces, the best idea from the stockpile of concepts, took off. The president challenged, "If you're so goddamned smart, why don't you come down and get it through the Congress."

"That's how I joined the Cabinet," Joe says.

In the 1970s and into the 1980s, the scene changed from Washington to state and local politics. The strategies stayed the same, the "capers, scrambles and no-wins," but the actors changed. "The further you got down there, the more it was all local power brokers." Joe Nash is suddenly a seedy "mole," a George Smiley in the statehouse corridors.

To the local power brokers, the old pols and even the young ones, the New Class creature was an outsider, a cipher. "People in this city have always been puzzled about me," he says with a certain relish. "I've never been a Yankee, I've never been Irish or Italian. I'm not minority. On the other hand, this has been my great asset, because nobody can peg me. But when it gets down to the class business," he admits, "even though I say I'm poor, that I come from poor, powerless parents, I still had all those degrees, from these Ivy League schools... and that didn't go down too well in the wards and neighborhoods."

Now, the inner-outer "pattern" is broken, leaving Joe Nash to reflect on how much time he has these days—for reflection. "For years," he observes, "there was no appointment on my calender longer than twelve minutes. Except with the president." He smiles an impish smile. He is not a pompous man.

Where are they now, he intones jokingly, the Wilber Cohens, the Orville Freemans? Does anybody know? In a sunny faculty office somewhere, like Joe Nash? Still, being an "outer" means a joint appointment at two prestigious universities; no commitments at either, an office in each. A long way from Joe Nash's first view of academic life in the East: "I arrived at the Junction in a double-breasted blue serge suit, with a switchblade in my pocket." Joe Nash swivels in his chair, glancing down at the students in blue jeans thronging through the square below. In those days, he recalls, "all southern boys carried a switchblade." At that time there was a quota: Jews, Catholics and high school graduates. "I was the high school quota from my state. I thought St. Mark's and St. Paul's were books of the Bible... and that the Main Line was just Main Street in Philadelphia." The culture shock was "extreme." "And between waiting tables, running errands, taking every job I could get—there wasn't much time to absorb it. The scholarship really wasn't enough. I was trying to send money home, where things were," he pauses, "very hard." So he concentrated on academics and boxing. "The new friends I had were so-called scholarship types. There were only fifty of us on full stipend. It was a subcaste system."

War came as liberation. The three years in the army were "very good years for restoring balance after the trying experience of three years served as an undergraduate." At the army university in Biarritz he found mentors, encouraging him in the direction of an academic career.

A decorated veteran, he came back to the university "full of confidence, even...," he smiles sourly, "to the point of thinking I could democratize the place." With another ex-soldier and subcaste member, a "poor Jewish boy from Minneapolis" headed for fame in atomic physics, Joe Nash stormed the financial aid office. "Besides our new G.I. Bill, we persuaded them that we should get our old scholarship back *plus accrued interest!*" He still whoops with triumph thirty-five years later. Restitution money.

"I inherited a family aversion to lawyers," says Joe Nash. "My father had good reason to dislike them, too, along with bankers and big business."

A week before the 1929 Crash, the shoe company where Al Nash worked required "all salesmen like my father to buy five thousand bucks' worth of stock." That was a lot of money in those days. "It was at eighty-three; then ten days later it was at thirteen. Then they took away their expense account and the drawing account and they collected on the commissions."

Money was a weapon, wielded always by others, by "them." There was only one possible defense.

"Power was always my strongest drive." Part of that drive, Joe Nash thinks, would have been obvious anyway, whatever the family circumstances, in his "classic narcissistic personality." The other part of his driving need for power came from "seeing the helplessness of my father and mother in the hands of *those* institutions. In the South, of course, there was a populist context for those experiences, those feelings. Since the Civil War, the economy had been depressed. The way to security was politics and power."

Populism, though, is hard to sustain once the power is achieved. In the back alleys of Camelot, horse trading in the Great Society corral, during the scrambles and capers, the "client" is never mentioned. The poor: always "invisible," absent—even to their advocates. Battle fatigue, maybe, after the speeches and testimonies, the facts, the figures, the "pilot," the "model," the "demonstration" programs.

Why are you surprised? demand New Class critics. Big government is comprised of arrogant men, remote not only from their professed constituency, the poor, but from the concerns of ordinary Americans. They know what's good for everybody, because the consequences of their planning will never affect *them*—or their children. They will never have to live with busing, urban renewal, halfway houses. Their kids will not be overlooked because of the quotas or goals they would set for others. "Whatever benefits the poor may have gained from the 'War on Poverty,'" writes sociologist Peter Berger, "there is little doubt about the benefits garnished by New Class professionals and bureaucrats administering the . . . programs."[11]

One of his "last tours of duty" ended for Joe Nash when the composition of his collective boss changed. "I couldn't let a board of trustees composed of neighborhood and local people dictate policy to me." Populism now would be as ill-fitting as the double-breasted blue serge suit, as inappropriate as a switchblade.

"It's always been part of my career plan not to know where my pension was coming from." Now, at fifty-five, he might like to know. He might even, for the first time, like to make some money. "A new adventure," he says. He is doubtful, though, about his "market value." The skills of public and private management are not really interchangeable. "If you have a budget, you don't have a profit and loss statement; if you have constituencies, you don't have markets. And then there is the all-important matter of executive style: the public sector is negotiation, not CEO."

Maybe, he proposes bleakly, New Class means a set of skills without a safety net. Professionals without professions. No engineering firm or law partnership to go back to—where you can get even writing your memoirs while earning five hundred Big Ones Per. "There have always been Rasputins," Joe Nash concludes, "left or right. But it's not a role you can institutionalize. When those in power don't want your knowledge, your information, your expertise, you're out of a job."

How is it possible, he wonders, to maintain a presence, keeping the liberal alternatives alive (and himself, too) "constraining the Neo-Conservatives, those who jumped ship in the seventies," he says without rancor. "Some of my best friends still...," he grins, motioning down the hall. Not by political journalism, the "semi-literary life," he adds with a tinge of disparagement, or by doing the "semi-beautiful people circuit—Aspen, the corporate think tanks. You can't go back into the ranks of faculty either; not after you've been riding herd over them. Individually, they're fine, but as a group they're just too silly." The emperor can't retire as foot soldier.

What's left, then? He doesn't know. But that's what this year is for..."not to have to decide what I want to do when I grow up." Turnaround time.

"I often ask myself why I didn't choose to *make* a lot of money," reflects Eliot Fein, at forty-four, "instead of writing about it or regulating the way other people can make it."

Eliot Fein is commissioner of a Western state regulatory agency. But he can also look back to possibly a record-breaking number of New Class careers—as financial and foreign trade correspondent for a national news magazine, two newspapers, a TV station, research director of a foundation, press secretary and economics advisor to a presidential candidate, owner/writer of a political newsletter (his one entrepreneurial activity so far), college teacher and author of four books on different corners of American private enterprise.

A big reason for not making a lot of money, Eliot Fein now thinks, was his father's blocked career working for an insurance company. "I knew that my father was the victim of discrimination. As a Jew, they let him go so far and no further. So there he was, a terrific salesman, breaking all kinds of records, always seeing guys he had hired promoted over him.

"I got the message early, I think: for a Jew, there was no chance to succeed in big business."

In his Long Island community, a mix of lower-middle and working class, Eliot Fein never met any self-employed professional Jews, "except for my dentist," he jokes, "and I never had the slightest desire to look into people's molars." His mother was very active in community organizations, so he always had a "positive feeling about helping people in that way."

As a scholarship student in the mid-1950s at a small New England men's college, Eliot Fein discovered that his class-mates all came from well-to-do Republican families in business or law, and "they were all going to follow in their father's footsteps.

"Since I never felt socially very much at ease, I certainly didn't aspire to the same things they were going to do." So like many another good student with unclear career goals, he found himself in graduate school in international relations, scanning the bulletin board for fellowships abroad.

"Becoming a foreign trade correspondent covering world organizations was a way of staying in Europe," Eliot Fein admits, "living the good life."

What brought him back was the political turmoil of the late 1960s. For someone who came of age in the Eisenhower years, he observes, this was an exciting time to be in politics. But despite the New Left role of his candidate, including a social issues platform that Eliot Fein helped draft, he is far from radical.

"I hated the war, and I couldn't stand the antiwar people. The Movement," he quips, paraphrasing Churchill's remark about de Gaulle, "was my Cross of Lorraine."

Unlike many New Politics New Class professionals, as

judged by their critics, he doesn't romanticize the poor, the consumer, the environment. Phrases like "a fair shake," a "simpler way of doing things," "not ripping off the public," are threaded through his remarks. "Besides," Eliot Fein says, "I've mellowed." When he was younger he had this "black and white view that things like teaching or public service were helping people, whereas business types were only in it for the money. Wrong," he notes. Now he has come to understand that what they do besides making money—like creating jobs—is useful and important. And perhaps more to the point, that business is no more monolithic than any other institution in its ratio of Neanderthals to enlightened citizens. "I may not share the same values as people in business, but I no longer see theirs as somehow 'lesser.' After all," he adds, quoting Max Weber, "Greed was here before Capitalism."

Only when he speaks of the oil companies does Eliot Fein's "mellow" feeling disappear. "Those guys lie all the time and they deserve no quarter. Absolutely none. Ever." You can't leave a New Classman without a single adversary.

Among the values Eliot Fein probably wouldn't share with those "on the other side of the table" is the conviction that Making the Most Money is the Highest Good. But from his new down-with-self-righteousness perspective, he views his own rural life, his choice of lower income, as "self-indulgence.

"I'm just about earning a living up here—instead of making a pile as a lobbyist in Washington—or doing corporate consulting in New York. Unlike Joe Nash, Eliot Fein doesn't feel "marginal" when he's "scribbling"—whether for academics or "real people." In fact, he is apt to describe his political stints as the "soft" jobs. The power—if such there be—is in the title, not the man. The man happily describes himself as a "writer" who, he admits, "tends to get drawn away from his study by those regular paychecks. But more and more, I'm able to say no," he declares.

Those who contend there is a New Class usually cite its subversive influence on American middle-class values. "Common to all elements of the New Class," writes sociologist Nathan Glazer, "is the rejection of the market as a means of allocating wealth...whether on grounds of justice or efficiency."[12]

New Class people, asserts Midge Decter, ex-New Class-person, are characterized by antivalues, defined more by what they are against than by what they are for. And what they are against, primarily, is the traditional bourgeoisie, the business community.[13]

WHY DON'T THEY
DO IT FOR MONEY?
(AND WHAT HAVE THEY GOT
AGAINST PEOPLE WHO DO?)

If you're so smart, why ain't you rich? goes a joke whose origins are lost in the mists of popular humor. It's a question that could only be asked in America. And one particularly applicable to the New Class.

Some of the answers have been provided by Joe Nash and Eliot Fein (and conveniently forgotten by New Class critics). The social origins and early experiences of many Americans convinced them, well before they chose careers, or class, that big business and its handmaidens, "bankers and lawyers," as Joe Nash noted, "were 'them,' not 'us.'"

The boardrooms and executive suites of corporate America were no meritocracy.* Those with the wrong accent, from the wrong schools—those lacking what David Bazelon called "a shrewd birth certificate" (meaning, in this case, Jews, Catholics, blacks and women)—had reason to consider institutions as alien, if not adversarial. And "small business" or local politics were not for these valedictorians, young men, often from Old World backgrounds seeking new worlds to conquer.

Son of a longshoreman, Daniel Connell was a partner in a medium-sized New York law firm. Fifteen years ago, he

---

*What "opened the doors" of corporations, banks, blue-chip law firms to "merit" in the late 1960s was not "affirmative action," but the need, in a cutthroat economy, to become more competitive.

took almost a 50 percent salary cut to accept a professorship at a distinguished law school. Now, with inflation way ahead of faculty salaries, he notes that his income is only one-third of what it would be had he remained in law. But, on the eve of a trip to London, where he will be honored at a dinner given by former students, Connell has no regrets: "I'm only a generation away from the bogs, so for me the psychic income—the honor, the prestige—is a much bigger thing than the dollars. . . . After all, lots of Irish have made money, but there aren't many of 'us' in the learned professions."*

Even when New Class members are not "professionally" engaged in reforming, regulating, protecting or advocating, "dispensing," as Daniel P. Moynihan describes, "services to those populations who are in various ways wards of the state," their "ethos" requires the passionate partisanship of these groups whatever the cost, consequences or even effectiveness of the program at issue. The peculiar nature of this partisanship, according to Midge Decter, is that it costs New Class people nothing. "Most of the people I know who publically identify with the poor and the blacks don't identify with them at all: they never go near a black. They not only don't know any poor people, they haven't possibly imagined what the experience of being poor is like." And, insists Decter, these are the people who advocate busing, who lobby against tuition tax credits, but whose children go to private school.**[14]

If hypocrisy, in its two-cents plain form, is the tribute that Vice pays to Virtue, New Class hypocrisy, Decter qualifies, adds another dimension, the Aesthetic. "Their stance on social issues is made up entirely on the basis of what looks

*A disparity documented by another Irish American, Daniel P. Moynihan, in *Beyond the Melting Pot.*

**In fact, as a number of opinion surveys have revealed, those "predictable attitudes" mentioned by Decter are more characteristic of the urban intelligentsia or cultural bourgeoisie wing of the New Class. University faculty, scientists, corporate managers barely differ on most social issues from the population at large. Only journalists on national newspapers, a group with preponderantly Ivy League educational credentials, were found by *Fortune* magazine to be to the left of their readers on most issues.[13]

nice, without any danger that the consequences of their positions will work themselves out on their own flesh, or even touch their own lives."

To maintain their aesthetic posture, New Class people get most exercised over issues as remote as possible from their own concerns, e.g., breast-feeding in the Third World. Look again, warns political scientist Aaron Wildavsky. Some of those concerns which seem remote, appearing to be attitudes struck in the hopes of looking good, are really a fan dance to disguise naked self-interest. Like environmentalism. Since New Class salaries, though comfortable, do not permit anything like the affluent life-style to which these salaried professionals aspire, they contrive to get the public to pay for the protection of beaches and forests accessible only to them and their "class" (and which function as a substitute for the private goods that only the super-rich can now command). Not content to rest with facile generalizations, Professor Wildavsky conducted field work to demonstrate conclusively both the hypocrisy *and* self-interest of New Class social attitudes.

In what appears to have been a series of surprise daytime visits to the houses of New Class friends,[15] Wildavsky found "household help"! But not just some scruffy *au pair*. *Maids*! Black and Hispanic. And although he does not mention whether he asked for their "green card," these maids (carefully hidden from view just when you might think they would be needed— at dinner parties) are assumed to be "illegal aliens." Wildavsky's daring Maid Raids thus conclusively demonstrate the functional convenience to the New Class of liberal immigration policies.

Maids as a measure of New Class hypocrisy raise a fascinating historical question: When did "authentic" radicalism and even liberalism require living like the proles? Rosa Luxemburg, for example, while organizing the German factory workers, used to complain in letters to friends about the servant problem in Berlin. Once upon a time, the work of revolution deserved a good hot meal (served by someone else) on returning from the barricades.

But revolution, or even radical reform, is the last thing the New Class desires, as they have much more to lose in a restructuring of society than their maids. As heavily mortgaged to "the good life" as are their business or professional peers, the New Class is unlikely to rock the boat for another reason: making it through "credentialed knowledge" themselves, they suffer from just "the right amount of insecurity," admits defender Peter Steinfels, "about passing this form of privilege on to their children, to prevent them from challenging 'the system.'"[16]

In a small makeshift office, one of many carved from a gracious eighteenth-century house in a New England college town, sits Gabe Licht, a tall sociologist of towering distinction. Internationally renowned for studies in occupational mobility, he is equally distinguished for his writings on poverty in the 1960s and 1970s, allied with activist efforts on behalf of the poor—especially minority youth. "The burden," he says, "can't be on the individual to succeed—especially when that individual starts out handicapped. Because then we really are requiring those with least to be most 'exceptional.'"

Society, moreover, rewards work unjustly—and not only in terms of dollars. Conditions of work are even more unfairly distributed. The worst jobs—those which are disproportionately held by young people—are debilitating; and too many kids never get away from them.

Rewarding the smartest at the top—or even helping the most able on the bottom, those "most likely to succeed"—are both wrong. The first perpetuates an unjust inequality, an unmerited meritocracy, so to speak, while the second smacks of the sinister process of *triage*, helping only those who are sure to survive. How can this kind of society be anybody's idea of a just social order? The interview over, we relax into a few moments of "personal conversation." Does he, I ask, have children?

Does he have children! He beams. Two sons at Harvard. And not just bright, like everybody's kids. "Brilliant." Whatever they do, these gifted young men will be rewarded. But not on "merit" alone; not just for their intelligence, their appetite for hard work. They will also be rewarded for that "shrewd birth certificate," for their father, the brilliant social scientist, and their mother, the noted pediatrician. For all of these attributes and more, Gabe Licht's sons, Jay and Donald, will be "disproportionately rewarded"—with high incomes and even higher job satisfaction, as well as greater access to society's goods and services. Gabe Licht, the father, spared no expense or connection to improve his sons' "life chances," while Gabe Licht, "committed" social scientist, refuses to accept as the natural order of things that other people's kids get stuck behind a counter at McDonald's.

Are these impulses, each praiseworthy in its separate domain, compatible? Class and status, after all, are "ranked order," with "positional scarcity," what the scramble is all about. Can you work to insure that your own children, unimpeded by any obstacle, go straight to the top, without assuring that the other people's kids remain on the bottom?

That is the classic New Class dilemma.

IS NEW CLASS OLD HAT?

Is the New Class, like the Hegelian state, in danger of withering away?

If, as political scientist Andrew Hacker suggests, it is not a class at all, but occupations looking for people to fill them,[17] then indeed significant segments of the New Class labor market are shutting up shop. Planned shrinkage of the public sector, especially those areas of the federal government once congenial to New Class "planners," are drying up. As a *New York Times* article noted, the march on Washington by young public-interest lawyers is all but over.[18] And foundations have joined in cutting back staff and programs.

Demography, too, has made a dent in New Class careers. The aging of America, and the shrinking of the traditional student population, has made academic life an unpromising choice. Inflation, and specifically the inflation which pushes the salaried "knowledge worker" into higher tax brackets, threatens to transform those in the "nobler and needier professions" into the poor and dangerous classes. Those who dispensed services to wards of the state are sliding into the "eligible clients" category.

MAKING MONEY IS IN

Getting the message, young people in record numbers have been flooding professional schools with applications. Business schools are enjoying a huge enrollment boom. With an M.B.A., the current wisdom goes, you can opt for old New Class favorites like journalism and publishing. But you do not arrive as the literate *lumpenproletariat*; you are the "young moneyman or woman on the move," hired to keep the intelligentsia from messing up.

This New Class career, moreover, is particularly congenial to the New Woman—at least, as a transition phase. In the foreseeable future, the women law graduates or M.B.A.s will be more welcome in the business or legal departments of the media or government, for example, than in the paneled boardrooms of corporate law firms (where salaries, unsurprisingly, are also higher). These kinds of jobs are where the seven thousand young women who have recently replaced that number of young men in our nation's law schools will mostly be headed.*

Finally, those who, like New Class son Jay Licht, have entrepreneurial hustle and who sincerely want to be rich, will not choose New Class occupations at all—not even private sector management. Working for a corporation is not the way to make millions, which is one of the reasons why, according

---

*There is an interesting parallel between the young women lawyers in government and another New Class vanguard: the Jewish law school graduates who came to Washington to work for New Deal agencies when Wall Street firms would not hire them.

to the U.S. Bureau of Labor Statistics, the ranks of the self-employed continue to enjoy unprecedented growth.[19]

IT'S PROBABLY TOO LATE

It is almost impossible to escape New Class values.*

Once contaminated by higher education, young people become "carriers." Even that minority of the college educated, the 40 percent who opt for business careers,[20] will have absorbed anticapitalist values from: (1) tainted sociologists; (2) New Class-controlled media; and (3) the culture-at-large.

Younger people will change the corporations and businesses more than they will be changed by them. Business schools are hotbeds of adversarial accounting professors. Besides, as Daniel Bell points out, among the inescapable contradictions of capitalism is its dependency upon the New Class impulse to costly—if understated—self-gratification. "Without the hedonism stimulated by mass consumption," Bell notes, "the very structure of the business enterprise would collapse."[21]

Who is flying those friendly skies? Buying the Betamax and Cuisinart? Drinking the vodka—or passing it up for Perrier?

We are them. They are us.

---

*Only by migrating to Texas—as yet completely uncorrupted by the New Class ethos.

CHAPTER
FOUR

I FOUND IT
IN THE MEDIA

MIDDLE-CLASS MAKEOVER:
THAT COSMO GIRL

"Wealthy people's children," she tells us, "sometimes have a hard time becoming who they're supposed to become. They don't have to work, you see, so their incentive is destroyed. That hasn't been a problem of mine."

Moist lips part to reveal small, shining, even teeth. Beneath fashionably luxuriant eyebrows, the large, ever-so-slightly slanted eyes, kohl-rimmed, shimmer seductively behind wisps of streaked bangs.

"My folks were poor," she continues, "and 'doing it yourself' was the only way to get on with your life."

Who is she?

From a full-page ad in the nation's leading newspapers, that *COSMO* GIRL beams her langorous, hungry gaze on hungrier advertisers—the object of her "high-on-mobility" message. Because she is also avid for things. And experiences she's never had before. The Cosmo Girl is Super Consumer.

Getting on with her life means the diamond studs that twinkle in each earlobe; the choker of diamonds-on-a-chain, each one the size of an M&M, that circles her neck; the fox shrug tossed over one shoulder—but not so as to keep any drafts from the deep cleavage.

It's not what you think, though. The message of this Delectable Person with Parted Lips isn't that Nice Girls Do—and Get Rewarded for Doing it Right. No, indeed! She's earned it all herself.

"They say working for what you want is the second (but just barely second!) best thing in the world to having people love you and loving them back," she purrs. And because *Cosmopolitan* makes sure there is never any unresolvable conflict between the goals of mobility and affiliation, "That magazine is my *bible*," says the sultry, self-made woman.

Cosmo takes little for granted about its 2.7 million readers. The magazine assumes that "if your folks were poor" you probably did not go beyond high school and may have missed out on certain social skills—especially middle-class rituals like entertaining.

"Always put the garbage out *before* the guests arrive," advises one article of advice to the neophyte hostess. And just in case her poor folks also lived in the Bible Belt, her new bible cites "more liquor than you think you'll need"[1] as the most important ingredient for a successful party.

Looming large as the afterwork acid test of new middle-class status is—the Dinner Party!

Readers are plied with advice on every detail, problem, obstacle that could possibly arise in connection with this event, starting with the tip: "be sure to clean up as you go,"[2] thereby avoiding an unsightly kitchen full of dirty pots and bowls, before moving to table settings, shopping hints, and meal preparation.

Cosmo urges its working readers to keep a larder "well-stocked with basics," making "spur-of-the-moment invitations a snap." The improvised, informal meal is clearly favored over carefully planned, candle-lit dinner parties. Come-to-my-place-for-chili is far less anxiety producing and more affordable than the dinner involving Beef Wellington and three kinds of wine.

Of course, the right setting is essential to this carefully planned spontaneity. An article on "How to Be House Proud"[3] advises the working girl to chart a careful course between the transient mentality which leads to living like "squatters or a family of mice," and bandbox perfection (which the reader can't afford). *Find* an apartment you can learn to love. Unless you're an heiress or very lucky, some compromises may be necessary, but *don't* sacrifice any of your important requirements (sunlight, a "*real*" kitchen). Of course, you will move on (and up) eventually, but why wait? Enjoy, live, *spend now*.

If anything signals the downward slide of the thrift-and-self-denial values of traditional middle-class America, it's *Cosmo's* message that mobility is money spent, not salted away. "Deferred gratification"—that old litmus test of middle-class values—will keep you tapping away in the typing pool forever.

Consumerism is always encouraged and is never regarded as *mere* self-indulgence. *Cosmo* urges fresh flowers, coffee-grinders, Cuisinarts, even an expensive Persian carpet, "whatever you crave; remember that the truly vital things are not indulgences, but smart *investments*. What you're buying is your own—and guests'—continued enjoyment of the place in which you live...now, what could be more important?"[4]

Possessions are experience, part of an ongoing process of self-development essential to middle-class status. But *Cosmo* wisely covers its bets on the degree of mobility. Another reason to live now is that moving up later just may not happen. However, if your goals elude you, as one article notes soothingly, maybe it's because you really don't want them. If you're single, suggests an article on "Managing Your Expectations," maybe "you don't really want marriage, children, warm family evenings in front of the fire, long afternoons with the whole tribe tracking along on a cross-country ski trip."[5]

Too high expectations—fame, fortune or the belief that any married man is going to leave his wife*—are discouraged as unrealistic. Aspirations, readers are cautioned, should be

---

*This warning is worked into as many features in *Cosmo's* contents as possible. Someone high up in the editorial hierarchy must have been badly burned by this particular "unrealistic" expectation.

scaled down to the possible, the easily—and painlessly—attainable. No major overhaul of psyches, but small changes, comfortable reorientations of habit and attitude.

Strangely enough, though, the examples offered in these modest suggestions of self-help, like "The Subtle Art of Timing," always involve fairly high-powered women: "Of course, Cynthia doesn't drive a cab, she's a fashion editor who got her last raise by asking for it." Nonetheless, Cynthia's mastery of the art of timing does not involve when to make the crucial bid on cocoa futures. "She is more attuned to the moods, needs and tolerances of the people around her than anyone I've ever known."[6]

With the most efficient functionalism, moreover, *Cosmo* self-help pieces almost always do double and even triple duty in getting you where you want to go. The same tips on timing stress that: "Knowing when the moment is opportune can get you career and salary advances, a happier social life, even more passionate experiences in bed."[7]

For the Cosmo Girl, there is never any "conflict" between display of cleavage, desire to advance on the job, a better sex life and more frequent dinner invitations. No trade-offs are ever required. Nor is it ever suggested that career advancement might be difficult, involving going to school while working (ugh!) or keeping punishing hours (as do young law associates). Job mobility means never having to say "I'm sorry, but I can't do it tonight."

"A Handbook for the New Executive Woman" sternly advises readers to search themselves for symptoms of "incipient workaholism." "Do you, for example, get over a fight with your man by working extra hard? If so, beware."[8] And since *The Cosmo Report* tells us that 55 percent of their readers have sexual encounters during lunch hour,[9] the sandwich-at-the-desk would not seem to be overwhelmingly favored as a way to catch up on work.

Unlike most upwardly mobile Americans, that Cosmo Girl is not going to reach her career goals through education. A little leisure-time self-improvement at home is about *it*.

Whether she is a housewife, single secretary or divorced working mother, credentials are gained on the job, and largely through enhancing personal characteristics. The Cosmo Girl's "human capital" never consists of skills or knowledge.

Indeed, like many self-made Americans, exalting the school of hard knocks and disdaining formal education, that Cosmo Girl's bible suggests that, far from being a disadvantage, lack of education is a plus. Don't listen to anybody who preaches that schooling is the key to success. "Money is an egalitarian force," a guest columnist assures us, "because everyone is eligible to own it."[10] (Unlike education, for instance, which the Cosmo Girl's family background may have rendered inaccessible.)

Columnist Junius Adams's view of money as an egalitarian force, more "available" somehow than education, is only about half a century out of date.* Today, the likelihood of an entry-level secretarial job or an entrepreneurial career without a college requirement decreases dramatically with every passing year. In the absence of college degrees or even compensatory overwork, just how *do* Cosmo Girls enjoy the career mobility their magazine insists is within reach?

"Congratulations," trills one quiz to test readers' "Boss Woman style." "After years of plugging away in lower echelons, you are now the staff manager, head buyer, sales director." *Cosmo*'s "new woman executive" has "finally made it out of her secretarial niche or junior-assistant slot to be an executive in charge of people."[11]

But how did she make the big leap?

The newly promoted occupant of the office with the title-on-the-door and the Bigelow-on-the-floor seems to have won her job in a state lottery.

"As a neophyte executive, you probably won't know how

---

*As is editor Helen Gurley Brown's message in *Having It All* (New York: Simon and Schuster, 1982) that a "mouseburger," whom she defines as the young woman she once was, with neither looks, intelligence, education or connections, can still go straight to the top.

to find your way around a financial statement, budget sheet, or any of a thousand computer printouts,"[12] the editors surmise. This highly mobile young woman must be a delectable person indeed, because she has risen with no form of apprenticeship. She's never served as assistant to an executive, never been a management trainee, nor, apparently, has she ever taken a business course that might have familiarized her with these basic tools of office life. Education is a "last resort," a desperation measure: "If you get the shaky feeling that now-is-the-time-they're-going-to-find-me-stupid, take a course," the author advises offhandedly. The *arcane* vocabulary of business is compared to a foreign language. "If you can interpret this arcane lingo, great. If you can't, get a copy of *The Language of Business*."

The Cosmo Girl may have some grammar problems, but in an article, "How Good Is Your English?" this revelation is softened by a "don't-we-all" approach. "Naturally, you think you speak beautiful, accurate English. Do you, though? Flawed language is much more common than you may realize; even professionals—journalists, commentators, politicians, scholars—use words, phrases, and sentences that are pompous, redundant, and plain *wrong*." A very low score, the author scolds, means "better polish your speaking and writing styles because you, my dear, are a language assassin." Her advice on how to "speak more elegantly and correctly" is "buy a copy of the classic *Elements of Style* by William Strunk and E. B. White. Spend an evening reading it, then *practice*."[13] (How? with a tape recorder? memorizing passages for recitation at spur-of-the-moment dinner parties?) Pity the poor young woman who imagines that slogging through Strunk and White late into the night will assure her of speaking "more elegantly."

Here *Cosmo* has backed into a corner. Liza Doolittle (and Henry Higgins) notwithstanding, lower-class diction, speech and accents are the touchiest subject in self-improvement, the one area nobody wants to talk about.

But the magazine isn't alone in backing away from the really tough question: Should people change the way they speak?

To acknowledge distinctly lower-class patterns of speech, and to admit these constitute an obstacle to mobility, is to assent to a definable class system that marks and stigmatizes those individuals at the lower end of the scale. More importantly, though, these differences cannot be erased by quick-fix consumerism—a reason that speech is avoided by self-help magazines and books.

John T. Molloy, whose syndicated column appeared in *Cosmo*, is the messenger allowed to deliver some bad news about class that *Cosmo* and all other purveyors of painless mobility usually prefer to avoid. The author of the best-selling live, dress, etc., for success books really sticks it to readers. Where editors of *Cosmo* (along with *Essence* and *Black Enterprise*) tiptoe around the class issue, Molloy plunges right in.

In a column on the "Executive Spouse" (reminding us that not all Cosmo Girls are single career women or even a member of two-career households), Molloy notes that, in a survey of why young men *and* women in the corporation failed to get ahead, "lack of formal education led the list." Nevertheless, according to Molloy, corporate chieftains were prompt to cite social failures of wives (still!) as the reason why their junior subordinates failed to win that promotion. "In many cases," Molloy states squarely, "the wife was guilty of a sin that theoretically does not exist in our democracy: she was obviously lower class—in dress, clothing, and speech"—a sin "effectively barring her husband from a shot at the executive suite."[14]

Just after winning the True Grit Award for dragging class out of the self-improvement closet, even intrepid John T. Molloy momentarily panics, disassociating himself from his own bad tidings: "I will be the first to admit that this is unfair," he concedes, but "it is nonetheless a fact."

The first question in Molloy's "Executive Spouse Quiz" (*Cosmo* is heavy on this form of self-diagnosis) is "Do I have upper-middle class speech patterns?" If you don't, though, Molloy doesn't provide any quick-and-dirty answers about how to acquire them. He knows this is a different category from never wearing a sweater in the office. (Sweaters spell secretary or "lower socioeconomic origins.") Unlike the "wrong" way of dressing, the way we talk is a complex legacy, an "advantage or disadvantage" inherited from family, reinforced by school and neighborhood. To urge a complete overhaul of this far-from-superficial class characteristic is very loaded advice. A makeover of this kind also means a repudiation of parents and community—the painful, ugly and, in some cases, grotesque side of social mobility.*

The role of advisor (whether magazine or mentor) in this enterprise becomes very sensitive. Especially since the 1960s, when many of us relearned that black, Jewish, Hispanic, Italian, Irish, Serbo-Croatian were all "beautiful," and a rightful cause of "pride," or at least not a legitimate source of shame. Consequently, removing traces of lower-class origins such as accents was treated as collusion with, and indeed perpetuation of, all that was bad about a newly discovered class system— even as its existence was strenuously denied.

The sober and conservative 1970s and 1980s reintroduced the rude realities: individual mobility was back (not that it had ever gone very far); and Looking Out for Number One, Winning through Intimidation, Power: How to Get It, Keep It, Use It and Abuse It, were O.K. ways of securing it.

As with many changes that seem cataclysmic at the time, but which prove to be only cyclical, there are still vestiges, shifts, small permanent changes remaining from the last cycle.

Since the brief egalitarian vision of the 1960s, it has been less easy for anyone to advocate—without choking slightly— surgical removal of the warts of lower-class origins. Not even for the good of the patient.

A friend who is also professor of history in a New York City college agonized over this problem. His most brilliant student is a young woman headed for law school and destined by her dazzling intelligence for a career "where every choice

---

*John Brooks, in Showing Off in America (Boston: Little, Brown, 1981) insists that speech makeover is also futile, leaving lower-class origins apparent to all upper-class listeners. There are many people, however, who would dispute this argument.

should be hers to make." Except that her accent and speech immediately identify her as Queens, Jewish, and lower-middle class. No matter that she will rank among the highest in her law school class and assuredly make *Law Review*. Someone else, with almost equal credentials, her teacher fumed, but with an accent that could never offend any client or colleague, will win the job that should be hers.

What should he do? Suggest that she listen to her voice on tape? Would a speech-and-diction "makeover," e.g., standard WASP American speech, necessarily be "in her best interests"? Should she even work for a firm—or other organization—that would not have hired her with her "native" speech pattern? Not necessarily, argued my friend. But she should have the *choice*. She shouldn't be restricted from "going as far as she can" by a "dumb thing" like the way she talks. What's fine for Barbra Streisand or Roseanne Scamardella will set limits on Shelley Stein's legal career.

"Each stage in the class history of the individual," note sociologists Arthur J. Vidich and Joseph Bensman, "presents a problem of learning new class patterns. The greater the individual's mobility, the greater the amount of 'flexibility' and learning necessary at each stage. And the greater the mobility," they add, "the greater will be the consciousness of adopting new patterns of conduct demanded by each change of status."[15]

It may be that Shelley Stein hasn't listened to herself; or, if she has, isn't displeased with what she hears. Possibly her teacher's ambitions for Shelley are in excess of her own notions of the desirable. Should she want to go "as far as she possibly can"?

Try dropping this "class dilemma" into a group of friends and notice decibels and temperatures rise, as heated argument ensues. Should individuals sterilize their speech of all traces of lower-class or ethnic group membership? Should teachers or other mentors endorse and aid this process?

Recognizing this issue for the moral, ideological and political minefield that it is, *Cosmo* wisely punts. Read your Strunk and White, but don't expect *us* to tell you whether or how to get rid of that Brooklyn, black English, cracker or "other" deviation from standard American speech.

The Cosmo Girl may rely on her magazine, but not for answers to the thornier questions of class choice.

Occasionally, *Cosmo* takes a quick peek at those pink-collar jobs held by most American women in the labor force—and whose "occupational mobility" is *zip*!

In an article, "Checking out Waitresses," author Andrew Feinberg and his editors have decided that an "image problem" is the biggest difficulty faced by the approximately one and one-quarter million American women who wait on tables. (In films, they're often depicted as wisecracking toughies, loose women, impossible dummies or malevolent tormentors, sympathizes the writer.)

Or, like Debbie Schwartz, happily slapping together the pastrami-on-rye-to-go in a Miami delicatessen, they have to contend with a snobbish boyfriend who keeps urging her to become a secretary: "He was ashamed of me," reported Debbie, "but I like my job." Obviously, Debbie should find a new boyfriend, suggests *Cosmo*, and she has!

Obstacles to advancement or even fair treatment are never "structural," located in the way society organizes and rewards such jobs. They are always personal—as in the "problem" of dealing with ill-tempered and capricious cooks. (Ingratiating yourself with these power-mad tyrants is the first order of business for any successful waitress.) Or fending off the unwelcome advances of drunken customers. Other problems, like the exploitation of a nonunionized work force, are never mentioned.

Moreover, waitresses' earnings as quoted here should certainly send every secretary scurrying from her Selectric, ready to grab the first tray in sight. Because the "kicker," of course, is that most of the income is unreported and hence "tax-free"—like the $320–$400 a week in tips earned by Denise Rose for four nights of work in an Italian restaurant in New York. Denise, as a result of unreported earnings, has the disposable income of someone earning $35,000 a year. Her friends, all "lawyers, accountants and teachers," actually envy her, she reports happily. Especially when they go to the theater, where "I like to get the best seats and they usually settle for the balcony." In fancier establishments, like the Brazilian nightclub where one young woman earned $125–$150 a night, tips can even "propel one into the upper-middle class," the writer assures us.

The earnings—tips and base salary—of the diner waitress whose friends are not lawyers, accountants and teachers, and whose night out is a once-in-a-while movie at the local drive-in, are not itemized. Because, as the delectable Cosmo Girl Who Did It All Herself reminds us: "poor folks" are not an excuse, they're an incentive, helping her choose to move up.

Instead of being incapacitated by "inherited advantages," like rich parents and higher education, the Cosmo Girl only gains from early privation, after which hard work and her magazine help her climb the socioeconomic ladder.

If she is a waitress, it is probably by choice, for "positive reasons" like "good money," "a great way to meet a lot of men," the "freedom from a nine-to-five treadmill." Sandy, twenty-six, has worked nights as a waitress since she graduated from college four years ago. Her job allows her "to take advantage of the sun and to forestall the inevitable, dreaded decisions about a career."

Cosmo's waitress population is heavily middle class;* aspiring actresses, whose hours give them the chance to audition, dominate *Cosmo*'s sample, which also includes a Princeton Ph.D. earning better money than her classmate, an assistant professor. The immobile "career waitress" is not an occupational category *Cosmo* cares to contemplate at length. A longer look might reveal how few choices women with meager education and skills have. Or that having poor folks isn't always a hidden advantage.

But the few quotations from "lifers" still manage to be upbeat. Mobility has simply been deferred. Their kids will

*See Chapter Five on the Savvy Skidders.

make it, even if they didn't. After losing a five-year lawsuit to admit women to the more lucrative floor jobs in four-star restaurants, tall, elegant Cathryn Smith, maître-d' at Windows on the World, plans "to keep moving up. I never wanted to be a forty-year-old waitress. I want the big stuff—money and power. And that's what I'm going for."[16]

Essence: "The Magazine for Today's Black Woman" is, in some ways, a black *Cosmo*, but with a difference. Similarities center on those basic social skills needed to negotiate middle-class life: as a parent, professional, tourist, hostess and black woman; a life for which *Essence*, like *Cosmo*, assumes little or no preparation.

Features in both publications provide help with table setting, dressing for success,* developing the self-confidence that gets the job or promotion, along with detailed how-to advice on "foreplay and good sex."[17] But interviews with successful women—a staple of both magazines—reveal in the choice of "role models" different perceptions of the mobility market "out there."

Like *Cosmo*, *Essence* is generous with glamour figures from show business or fashion: dancer Judith Jamison, model Princess Elizabeth of Togo; and for behind-the-scenes glitter jobs, a steady population of TV producers. Equal time, though is given to black women who have made it in "real life" careers—and here, *Essence* hits hard on education as the only way to go: Earlene Armstrong,[18] thirty-four, professor of entomology at the University of Maryland; Marian Wright Edelman, forty-four (Morehouse A.B., Yale LL.D.), director of the Children's Defense Fund.[19]

Wherever possible, the magazine hypes degrees. Even a feature on jewelry designer André Leon Talley stresses her educational qualifications. After dropping out of Columbia University and into an apprenticeship with a jeweler in New York, her studies at the Fashion Institute of Technology and

---

*Interestingly, the clothes in *Essence* are far more "high fashion" and expensive than are the styles chosen for the Cosmo Girl.

the Gemological Institute of America were all "priceless experiences" in furthering her career.[20]

Essence never skirts the political, either. An article on abortion sounds the warning loud and clear that poor black women are the group most adversely affected by obstacles to abortion, and the author takes a gutsy position of assailing black silence on this issue.

Dr. Michael Jackson, medical director of a Washington, D.C., abortion facility, reminds readers of his days as an intern at a predominantly black hospital: "Entire wards used to be filled with women who had undergone botched illegal abortions. They'd tried everything—Lysol douches, knitting needles. Some came in with coat hangers dangling between their legs. . . . There was so much hemorrhaging that the blood banks were drained . . . and many women died." Not a passage you'd be likely to find in *Cosmo*. "Now is no time for Black women to be uncertain. Or silent." And the piece concludes by advising readers where to write their legislators, to make the "voters' difference."[21]

"Our mothers and grandmothers and neighbors do not talk much about their illegal abortions. But we have only to look at their lives to see that the number of unwanted children a Black woman has, controls her life and health, more than any 'white only' sign ever did."

Passing another statistical reality on to its readers, *Essence* urges education—courses, skills, training. For black women, especially, that's the big edge.

Advice to "Build on Your Success" counsels that "if you've thought about going back to school, start by taking one course the first semester, two the next"[22] —advice that Elyse Mayberry, a devoted *Essence* reader, has followed.

In "Self-Confidence: How to Build Yours," Elaine Meryl Brown directly tackles the greater mobility of black women and the conflicts it causes. Many capable and gifted black women restrict themselves to "safe" jobs, or those traditionally held by black women, because setting high goals "may create conflicts in our relationship with men." The author notes acidly: "We're not supposed to exhibit self-confidence because it's threatening to our males." Even "some women with no men in their lives fear they'll never have one if they aspire to move beyond their present job."[23]

"Dealing with the Cheap Man" also deals, albeit humorously, with the class gap between black men and women: the problem of the woman moving up faster than "her man" and trying to drag, push or pull him along with her. What to do about the guy (earning good money, we are to assume) who "squeezes the dollar so hard the eagle can't fly? Persuade him to spend money on himself—but *you* have to show him how. Once inside the fitting room of that smart men's store, coax your man into that perfect jacket."[24]

Our most influential middle-class cues do not come from magazines, but from movies and TV.

"'Cause you're kickin' in for food, don't mean you don't gotta eat," Frank Manero shouts at son Tony in the opening scene of *Saturday Night Fever*. Dressing for the big disco night, Tony hadn't planned to eat dinner at home. Suddenly, he relents. At the table, tension and tempers run high. But the match that finally ignites the family's smouldering rage is kid sister Linda's contribution. As mother Flo praises her son the priest, Linda taunts Tony: "You're so jealous of Frank, Jr." At that remark, Tony gives Linda a push, Frank slaps Tony, Flo pushes Frank. Frank looks at Flo in astonishment and slaps her. Flo reaches across the table and slaps Linda. Frank hits Tony again. "Basta," says Grandma, calmly (but only when the action stops).

This is no Progresso Spaghetti Sauce commercial, and, note the stage directions: "this incident is evidently routine because it is forgotten in a moment and the family continues eating."*

---

*A scene like this could never be shown in a television series. The Italian-American Anti-Defamation League would be on the hotline to the station—and sponsors—for "negative stereotypes." Movies are still not "mass entertainment" in the sense of being, as one network executive explained, "invited into your home." Which is why they are allowed to show class differences—far more offensive than "explicit sexual content."

What isn't routine, though, is Mama Flo's part in the melee—and the way this "landmark event," as the script writer describes it, is viewed by her husband, Frank.

To settle the duel, Flo soothingly announces, "I got more pork chops. More spaghetti." At the offer of more food, Frank threatens to explode once more. Unemployed, he angrily challenges his wife's extravagance. "Whaddya doin'? More pork chops! I'm outta work!"

But Flo's pride in her own role of nurturer and cook won't countenance cutting back on the family meals—not yet! "Long as we got a dollar left, we eat good in this house," she asserts. And if that last dollar seems in danger, Flo hazards that she "might even get a job." Then, about to quote her TV heroine on that subject, she continues, "Maude says. . . ."

That's when Frank really lets fly! The red cape!

"Like hell you will," he howls.

With the erosion of his provider role, Frank's authority is threatened on every side. By his son's lurking contempt, and more shocking still, by Flo's reactions—hitting him for the first time, confirming his failure a breadwinner by announcing her intention to get a job.

Who has been the inspiration for this final betrayal?

In a media hall of mirrors, one of the most popular movies of the last decade, *Saturday Night Fever*, pays tribute to the influence of a television sitcom in changing class values. The role of mentor in Flo's "right to work" is none other than "Maude," the sassy (but kind), independent (but loving) wife and mother, liberated (but deeply conventional), obviously Jewish (but ethnically unspecified) suburban matron. And more important, the quintessential middle-class, middle-aged American woman.

Described as a cross between Bella Abzug and Lucille Ball (but with more than a touch of Molly Goldberg), Maude, as brilliantly played by Bea Arthur, is an approachably heroic heroine who speaks to Everywoman. Her theme cues us: "Joan of Arc, Lady Godiva, Betsy Ross. . . and then there's Maude."

The genius of "Maude"—like that of Lear's other, still

more mythic creation, Archie Bunker—lies precisely in the contradictions of class, gender and character she manages to hold in balance.

She may be sassy, even shrewish, but Maude's earthy mother-hen quality signals her acceptance that she is responsible for the well-being of her *schlemiel* husband, Walter, their daughter, maid and everyone else who comes under her wing. Even in her choice of work—selling real estate—Maude remains a "nest-builder" or provider for others. She has not really "left home" for the man's world. In any case, most of her token activity occurs on the telephone.

Despite a lot of lip and liberated jabber, Maude's solutions, like a more prosperous Lucy, are those of the sheltered matron—"unschooled" in the ways of the world.

In one episode, Walter's hardware business goes bankrupt. Desperately, he is casting about for a job. All hopes are pinned on a golf date with a manufacturer acquaintance rumored to be looking for a new sales manager. Inspired by a *Cosmo*-styled article, "Make a Loser in the Office a Winner in the Bedroom," Maude's solution to her husband's unemployment and depression is the Total Woman treatment. When Walter happens to notice a copy of the magazine, he becomes enraged. He rushes out of the house and tries to commit suicide with a massive dose of sleeping pills.

For a tough, savvy realist (herself a businesswoman), Maude never makes a single "practical" suggestion toward solving her husband's employment dilemma: people they know who might help or where he could borrow money to start over. There is no effort to encourage Walter on any level other than the (risky) one of sexual performance. But her creators aren't dumb. Maude's naïveté and ineptness at dealing with real-world problems will strike a chord in a blue-collar housewife, like Flo of *Saturday Night Fever*. Despite Maude's flossier life-style, there are more similarities than differences. If Maude can get a job (only out of necessity), then so can Flo.

"Maude is the character on TV I really identify with," said Janeal Pickens, thirty-four-year old black mother in a New York City job program for welfare recipients. "She cares about the people she loves," Janeal explained, but "she holds on to her own. That's the way I see myself. She's my ideal."

In her tough talk, her victories of wit and will over inept hubby Walter, Maude has a modern flavor. Yet she never gives up the nurturing role of middle-class wife, mother, and householder—still deeply dependent on the institutions of marriage and family.

Lower-class American women can identify with utterly middle-class Maude, who expresses both the actuality and aspiration of their lives. Yet, working-class and minority men and women on the tube are portrayed as equally middle class. Whether they are called Archie, Florida, Rhoda, Laverne, Sanford, Chico; whether they live in ghettoes, work in bottling plants or as maids, or drive a hack, they are—to a man, woman and child—middle-class Americans all.

The Class Convergence theory may have been discredited when examined against the reality of American life. On prime time television, it has, since the 1970s, been alive and well. Lovable, working-class "hood" Arthur Fonzarelli of "Happy Days" is the embodiment of upper-middle-class WASP values. His supercool style, with its occasional whiff of sexuality and violence, makes him a superpreppie. The Fonz is Holden Caulfield in a black leather jacket. A punk persona is required to protect the Fonz's sensibilities from the plastic "unreal people" on whom he must depend for survival.

In a middle-class suburban teen culture based upon peer groups and "in crowds," the rugged individualism of the Fonz is portrayed as lower class. In fact, his lack of conformity is the giveaway of his upper-middle-class—even aristocratic— sense of self. An "authentic" working-class Fonz would be more conforming, more needful of peer approval, more concerned with the group than his middle-class All-American counterparts Richie and Joanie. Never submitting to authority—*except* when *he* judges it to be legitimate—the Fonz embodies that first law of middle-class values: self-direction. But equally, he avoids the mindless "rebel without a cause" impulses of kids with few options. In fact, he is no rebel *with* a cause either!

Without any vulgar agenda of his own for "getting ahead," the Fonz's aristocratic autonomy exists for its own sake. Indeed, the hero of "Happy Days" could be viewed as the vanguard of the "me generation." An upper-middle-class narcissist ahead of his time, his glorification of the self is what arouses the envy and inspires the emulation of his peers, all of whom are in the process of being molded by middle-class expectations.

The Fonz is never made to suffer from his lack of "earlier advantages." His frequent displays of ignorance never threaten his leadership role. If anything, his innocence of both "book learning" and middle-class social skills cements his transcendental, self-created elitism. In supersquare suburbia, the Fonz is in a class by himself. He is no threat to the Cunninghams. They know he isn't going to seduce Joanie or lure Richie into downward mobility via dope dealing or even dropping out of school. If anything, his adopted family, like the teen culture that he dominates, constantly pays tribute to the Fonz's superior status. For his part, Arthur Fonzarelli is secure enough in his "class standing" to help reinforce the Cunningham's middle-class values—helping them keep *their* kids in line. "It's cool to stay in school," Fonzie will mouth obligingly—not only on the program, but even in "public service announcements." For those who need it, that is. Not for those who choose their own class—like the Fonz.

"Shirl," says Laverne, "we work in a brewery, we date guys from the Pizza Bowl. Face it, we've found our niche."

Thus the premiere of "Laverne and Shirley" "establishes" the "class identity" of its two heroines, friends, co-workers and roommates, as blue-collar young women of unspecified "ethnic" origins. Yet the "niche" neatly established by the story "concept" is immediately called into question.

In the 1950s, the only working-class girls who would have lived together, unsupervised, in their own apartment in a city like Milwaukee would have been working the streets—an unthinkable choice for two "decent, respectable young women." Laverne and Shirley are shown enjoying the freedom of a couple of Vassar graduates of the period.

Their way of life is already so much at odds with their work and the values of their "community" (or what these would be if there were any authentic social context) that boyfriends become even more problematic. Because of their liberated life-style, young men from the Pizza Bowl or assembly line are a comedown; the blue-collar family life they promise, a dramatic mobility drop.

A real-life Laverne or Shirley would probably consider marriage to the guy on the day shift as a liberation from a more oppressive home life. Laverne and Shirley's freewheeling, zany, fun-filled existence after they "punch out" could only be curtailed by marriage to a member of their own class. Laverne and Shirley are smart enough to realize that on the job nine to five and on your own afterwards is a lot better than 6 A.M. to 11 P.M.—the hours of any working-class housewife.

Upward mobility for Laverne and Shirley could only occur by ending the "status discrepancy" in their lives; a life-style of young professionals uneasily combined with blue-collar job, neighborhood and associates. The only solution to their split-level class membership is the shop girl's fantasy, marrying up. By the way they live they are halfway there.

Laverne and Shirley are two middle-class characters in search of a new script—and setting. And what do the poor girls get? Anomie in Los Angeles.

Moved out—but not up—a new season finds Laverne and Shirley resettled in L.A., part of a classless, middle class, jobless world of comic scenes and gags, appropriately severed from any recognizable context of class or status.

The contrast between two other working women on television beamed an even stronger message about why middle class is best—and how to get there.

Mary Richards, of "Mary Tyler Moore Show" fame, travels so light that her only baggage from the past is a blighted romance with a medical student. With the cultural neutrality her name implies, she has only her tact, grace, social skills, easy self-confidence, (unthreatening) humor and "girlish charm" to identify her as a daughter of the amorphous middle class. These qualities—not her credentials or professional qualifications—enable Mary to wander into a TV newsroom, apply for a secretarial job, and be hired on the spot as an associate producer.

But not Rhoda Morgenstern. Despite her superior intelligence, Rhoda is doomed—by her Jewish, lower-middle-class Bronx background and accent—by the nagging voice of her mother asking why she isn't married, by her brash, aggressive manner (masking the deep inadequacy within), by her plainness and her need for love. She is doomed to a boring job that she hates, and marriage to a man unworthy of her. Rhoda, unable to choose the social surgery needed to secure for her the goodies that flow, effortlessly, to her friend, returns to the Bronx to get married under her mother's grateful gaze. Mary Richards gets total mobility—social, geographical, occupational.

Roots are all right, but wings are better.

And now for that antihero and arch-enemy of middle-class liberal values, still the most famous blue collar in America: Archie Bunker. But just how working class is this superhard-hat? Is he really the ignorant, loutish loudmouth, knocking back beers, putting down women, culture, kids, blacks, gays, drowning out the sense of his own inadequacies and the injustices of the system? In fact, Archie is a middle-class Conservative, a Bill Buckley from Queens, who didn't go to Yale or inherit an oil company.

His knowledge is more encyclopedic than his prejudices. Archie is prodigiously well informed. He knows enough to despise that Cosmo Girl, the left-leaning strain of many sociology departments, liberals' self-proclaimed superior sensitivity to suffering, and the difference between atheists and agnostics, magic and miracles, and a host of other fine distinctions. Archie is a member of the closet *cognoscenti*, who has every upper-middle-New Class value "taped." He can choose to play some straight and run others in reverse.

Dr. Alan Wurtzel, director of audience demographics for the American Broadcasting Company, explained the genius of Norman Lear's creation by his broad appeal. As a "high authoritarian"[25] personality, Archie tapped into all those boardroom Archie Bunkers, upscale, but equally bullying, sexist, antipoor, antiblack, antiyouth; acting out for them values which, suddenly in the 1960s, became less publically acceptable for the educated upper middle class.

If anything, the end of the 1970s richly illustrated that Archie Bunker was no mere mouthpiece for the blue-collar backbone of America. The message of the 1980s, its move to the right, is that Archie Bunker spoke for the middle-class majority (including the New Rich, New Right), ready and waiting to return to the days when, as the program's theme song announces, "we didn't need no welfare state," a middle class evermore concerned not with getting but with keeping.

At one point liberal sociologist son-in-law Michael accuses Archie of overvaluing material things like TVs and toasters. "That's all you care about, Archie, is what you got and how you can keep it," says the Meathead, self-righteously. Archie's reply: "You'd care about it, too, Sonny Boy, if you had anything." Many of Archie's fans, as it turned out, had plenty; more than TVs or toasters, diet books or self-development courses, and they would prove less inclined than their hero to give anyone else a "free ride."

No program would survive, moreover, let alone command the popularity of "All in the Family," with a one-class, one-value-system appeal. As a network researcher told sociologist Paul M. Hirsch, "Any program whose demographic profile was distinctive would mean it is attracting some segments at the expense of others we don't want to lose; it would be canceled."[26] Other researchers have determined this trade-off to be unnecessary. As a mass audience, we come closest to a classless society. "Engineers, executives, middle mass and the underdog on relief," sociologist Harold Wilensky found, "are quite similar in their TV viewing habits—a group that includes men making more than $100,000 a year and others who have been unemployed for years."[27]

Archie "cares" about considerably more than his consumer durables. His "immaterial" concerns are quintessentially middle class: getting fat and getting old. In one episode, he bans discussion of old age from the table, refusing to admit that he looks any older, or that he is concerned about it. And while he stops short of springing for the Scarsdale Diet or enrolling in a "Y" workshop on "Creative Aging," Archie's anxieties about both middle-aged spread and mortality seem far more typical of the show's creator than its hero.

The "diffuse anger" that *New Yorker* critic Michael J. Arlen nailed as characteristic of Norman Lear's creations needed only igniting by more financial, social or mental instability to explode.

It's not hard to see Archie Bunker, like the *Network* newscaster gone berserk who arouses his upper-middle-class neighbors by yelling from the window, "I'm mad as hell and I won't take it anymore." Instead of ending it all, of course, Archie had a new beginning—with a new season. Born again, as his real "middle class" self, "Archie Bunker's Place" showed us a piece of the American Dream in action.

Upwardly mobile Archie moved from factory worker to small businessman—losing his class enemies in the process.*

It's no accident, as they say, that the first of the family sitcoms to deal with blacks, "Sanford and Son," was borrowed from a British TV series about a white working-class family.

A lower-class, middle-aged black man, Fred Sanford is slightly lying, slightly corrupt and slightly inebriated most of the time. And his junk business totters along only because of his partnership with straight-arrow son, Lamont. Indeed, the humor of "Sanford and Son" derives from conflicting class choices within one family. Father Fred Sanford embodies all

---

*Archie *redux* never really captured viewers. Falling ratings caused the show to be cancelled for the 1983–1984 season.

the negative attitudes ascribed to lower-class blacks—attitudes fostered (although we are never told this) by an "older" culture of poverty: lazy (though lovable), shiftless, fatalistic, spinning get-rich-quick schemes doomed to keep him poor. He is a con artist without artistry, skills or ambition. Allusions to a "checkered past," however, hint that Fred Sanford can congratulate himself on some bootstrap mobility. At least he's not in jail! Whatever his character flaws, he has managed to become a small, if marginal, capitalist.

Son Lamont embodies a middle-class moral guardianism that knows its place: which is staying in the ghetto (whether out of filial loyalty, or for other reasons, is unclear). Lamont gives "Sanford and Son" the opportunity to show the stable, respectable, disciplined side of those young people who aren't bent on escape—either through hustling or Harvard Law School. The friends of the two Sanford generations also underline the difference, not just between father and son, but between what the ghetto is and what it could become—thoroughly middle class. Lamont's associates are cops and prosperous dudes (though never, we are to assume, through shady activities). Fred, predictably, relaxes, deals a few hands, has a few drinks with those further down the scale, such as drifters and assorted low-life types—or the occasional "fine-lookin' gal" whom he tries unsuccessfully to woo.

Like all programs purporting to depict ghetto life, the setting of "Sanford and Son" resembles college-student clutter more than the culture of poverty. Fred Sanford may be "poorer than a junkyard dog," but as owner of the junkyard in question, he has first dibs on his own wares. Taxed with the discrepancy, one of the show's producers stoutly denied any disparity between real-life poverty and its TV equivalent: "Our researchers checked every detail for accuracy," he said. Pressed further, he conceded that "we're dealing with color TV, and you really can't show anything ugly—it looks terrible."[28]

The Evans family of "Good Times"—James, the hardworking father, his wife, Florida, and their three children—constitute a fortress of bourgeois values in the midst of the ghetto. Its problems—social or economic—never cross the threshold of their spacious, tastefully furnished apartment. As parents, the Evans's aspirations for their children leapfrog the merely middle class. James is determined that Thelma is going to make the big class jump. "I want her to get out of the ghetto, marry a professional man." The younger son aspires to be a lawyer. Son J.J. is an artist.

Despite providing such impeccable role models of black upper-middle-class values, a conference sponsored by the National Urban League[29] focused on "Good Times" as an example of everything that was wrong with the "black image" on TV. The auto-da-fé began with the basic grievance: Norman Lear had gotten "awfully rich," producer Tony Brown noted ominously, by projecting a "certain version of the black image on television." But just what kind of image is it? There were displeased comments about the character of J.J. Under the impression that it was J.J.'s comic antics to which the panelists objected, Norman Lear noted that "we took great pains to make him an artist with great talent."

His fellow panelists were not appeased. Lear moved from J.J.'s talents to his other qualities. "The show has made every single effort to make Jimmy responsible." And Lear unwisely pointed to the fact that when Florida (Esther Rolle) had to leave the show for a year, "J.J. was in control of the family. He was the man. That was the way it was envisioned and that was the way a lot of people responded to it."

But not the National Urban League panel on "The Black Image in Motion Pictures and Television."

A nineteen-year-old man-child "in control" was precisely the problem. Lear had simply illustrated that most hated "negative image" of the fatherless black family, whose substitute "head," in this case, was a "teenager of dubious distinction," as moderator Tony Brown called him.

An orgy of breast-beating followed. Despite the exemplary image of Florida as a supportive, loving, hardworking wife and mother, actress Esther Rolle plunged in to shoulder her share of the guilt: "At the risk of great economic loss, at the risk of emotional stress, I can't blame "Good Times" for making me present a bad image to your child," confessed the actress. "I can only blame me, because I am the one who did it." (Ms. Rolle never makes clear what she decided is "bad" about the image of Florida Evans; perhaps it was her acquiescence in playing "a single, female head of family.") Then, returning with a little defensive ammunition, Norman Lear puts his foot in it once again. J.J.'s "man of the family" role, he explains, was an interim solution to the departure from the show of actor John Amos (James Evans), and to Ms. Rolle's one-year leave of absence. As soon as Esther returned, the "parental image," Lear promised, would be strengthened. "We will be looking at a family."

Oops!

There are shouts of "Father, father" from the audience.

At this point, Lear meekly reminds his listeners that "It can't escape anybody's notice that fathers don't exist in every family." But this bit of bad demographic news isn't going to get *him* off the hook. After all, we're talking about "image" here, not reality—demographic or other.

Cleansed by contrition, Lear promises to do better. After James's death, Florida has taken off for the Sun Belt to re-marry. (He had been saving the good news for last.) And . . . she is back this season. Her new spouse is not mentioned, though.

The meeting concludes on a friendly note.

A class "Catch 22" is at the heart of this dilemma. It is not the powerful "mind managers"—advertisers, studio executives—who are most insistent upon homogenized, "positive images" of middle-class life. Watchdog groups representing oppressed minorities (gays and blacks) or ethnics (Italian-American Anti-Defamation League) appraise program content to insure that characters and situations suggest no social deviance or "negative stereotypes" on the part of their constituents. And that includes "victims" of the System. Minority children, who watch television far more than any other group, it is argued, must see powerful, assured, competent men and women, as well as hardworking, ambitious, achieving peers. Yet other writers point to the disparity between these middle-class characters, their attractive, comfortable surroundings and the world of many of their viewers as a source of shame and guilt.

Sociologist Herbert J. Gans notes the strange neglect of "differential effects of the overwhelmingly middle-class settings and populations of most entertainment fare on poor people. By emphasizing middle-class culture and attitudes," Gans notes, "the media have aided in the diffusion of these values; but by the same token, this dominance has also increased middle-class cultural and political power."[30]

And what about the rest of America watching all these coping, achieving, successful black men, women and children? If problems such as unemployment, welfare, illiteracy, teenage pregnancy, drugs or alcoholism do sometimes arise, they are solved within the family, and by necessity within the time constraints of the segment. No failure, or even immobility, is caught on television.

So what's the problem?

"The Jeffersons" emphatically do not have a problem.

As a "new rich" black family no one, not even the National Urban League, will defend them from "negative stereotyping." Because on television, the rich—any rich—are there to be pilloried.

George Jefferson has made it from the ghetto to an opulent apartment on New York's Upper East Side. Wealth, in the form of a chain of dry cleaning stores, has earned him the right to behave as arrogantly as all nouveau riche.

This is true equality of opportunity leading to equality of result.

On television, the old rich (rarely shown) or new, as in "Dallas" and its anemic imitator, "Dynasty," come off as a swinish lot. Their women are spoiled, petulant or retarded, as well as rudely imperious or ruttishly promiscuous. The men are gross, grasping, with manners apparently learned in *Animal House*, not at nanny's knee. Advantages, like elite schools, only produce psychotic villains. Adam Carrington of "Dynasty" wears his Yale sweatshirt while plotting with his evil mother against "good" Jeff Colby (alma mater unknown).

Is the negative image of wealth and privilege the result of an egalitarian impulse on the part of the media providers? Showing us that we should envy the rich only for what they have—never for what they are. If the Haves were shown, not only as having more than the rest of us, but *also* as better behaved, the guillotines and gibbets would be readied.

If "they" were also gracious, generous, civil, courteous, cultured, "real" ladies, "true" gentlemen—as in Cardinal Newman's famous definition—then we would recognize the full injustice of the class system at work. To the barricades!

...LEAVING

CHAPTER
FIVE

DROPPING DOWN
BUT NOT OUT:
THE SAVVY SKIDDERS

Their fathers are self-made men—New Rich or New Class: managers, technocrats, academics. For some, there is nothing new about the family fortunes. Grandpa did it all.

They grew up in the newly affluent suburbs of the 1950s, or the most desirable older neighborhoods of big cities. Many never finished high school. Others are graduate school dropouts, with a clutch of awards and fellowships to prove their promise. Large numbers were part of the "last wave" of privileged youth to serve the less privileged, working briefly as counselors, teachers, social workers to the poor, the young, the troubled. Still others broke away early from the once-predictable future of young people from places like Highland Park, Hillsborough, Winnetka, Short Hills, Shawnee Mission, Chagrin Falls, dropping directly into a life of pick-up jobs, or steadier work as farmers, carpenters, plumbers, shopkeepers or small restauranteurs.

Children of superachieving, successful, competitive and sometimes just privileged parents, they have chosen, despite all the options in the world, "a gently cushioned, downward mobility."[1]

Sociologists (usually upwardly mobile types themselves) label the downwardly mobile "skidders," a word that speaks volumes.

"Skidding," to "slip or slide," as the dictionary defines the term, must always be involuntary. Skidding is an accident; motion, human or mechanical, gone out of control. After all, who wants to skid?

A new New Class. The savvy skidders.

Unlike their counterparts of the 1960s, the savvy skidders did not drop out—into drugs, radical ideologies or communal living. They dropped down. Into the kind of self-supporting, self-respecting work that most Americans do, only less gladly. Unlike their predecessors, those "radical children of liberal parents,"[2] they display none of the signs of slumming: no torn jeans, body dirt, squalid surroundings, cultivated lower-class speech—all that constituted the rules of the game for middle-class children playing house in urban slums or rural shacks.

Unselfconscious and guiltless, the savvy skidders carry the visible attributes of their advantages: from the perfectly straight teeth to the personable self-confidence of the well-schooled, well-nurtured upper-middle-class child. Far from searching for new sexual configurations or noncapitalist forms of child rearing, many of these downwardly mobile young people are fervent believers in and builders of the most nuclear of families. The seriousness with which these young men take the role of husband and father is so conservative—in the sense of preindustrial—as to be the most radical element of their philosophy. Often, their belief in the primacy of the personal explains most about their choice of work.

SON OF NEW CLASS

"The most important thing in my life is my family," declares Zeff Randall—thirty-four, ex-premed student, ex-counselor of troubled children and for the past six years "journeyman worker" in an upstate New York auto body shop. "As soon as I realized that work would always have to come second to personal relationships, it became clear to me the kind of work I should be doing." Son of a geologist and federal science administrator, Zeff's family had moved from Baltimore to an exclusive Chicago suburb, when his father left the government to set up a private consulting firm. When Zeff analyzes his education, a first-class high school followed by a distinguished liberal arts college, he reflects on the irony of his present work. "I wasn't even interested in cars. And I never took macho courses like shop."

Zeff Randall had planned to study medicine, mainly because of a particular doctor, a friend of the family. Zeff describes him as a "wandering pediatrician, who traveled from one Indian reservation to the other, treating sick children in exchange for room and board." To Zeff this remarkable man offered a compelling model of disinterested service and complete freedom—an example, he would learn, that was hardly typical of medicine or indeed of any other profession.

It took a summer premed program at Stanford, an experiment in acceleration that selected the most outstanding undergraduates, nationwide, to change his mind about medicine. That summer, Zeff recalls, "really opened my eyes as to what people were doing to themselves and to others to become doctors." It was really frightening, he remembers. "Guys were flipping out, threatening suicide, if they didn't get an A." Being a doctor, Zeff decided, wasn't something he wanted "badly enough," so he returned to college and his interest in psychology. But after three years of behavioral research, he concluded that the "answers were so limited as to how people worked. All I could see were lab animals being sacrificed for arbitrary and equivocal results."

He was in search of work that offered "relatedness, not alienation." "That was the sixties ethos," he recalls, with a note of irony. Zeff, his girlfriend and his sister moved to New York, where he became a counselor in a psychiatric facility for severely disturbed children. Working all day with troubled youngsters was "an incredibly intense experience," but also frustrating and often depressing, with few positive results. And his need to be alone, to get over the "bends," was causing relations with his lover to deteriorate. Work wasn't working and neither was the part of his life marked "personal." Zeff realized that a choice had to be made between them. "That was when I decided to look for a job that would leave me free for what was most important in my life: the people I cared about."

This decision, he knew, would mean "very different work" from any he had been educated, or expected, to do. Zeff applied for three jobs he found in the "Help Wanted" section: elevator repair man, fire extinguisher maintenance, and painter's helper in a body shop. The last place hired him. But not without some questions "loaded in the direction of whether I was slumming." More than any other aspect of the job, Zeff loves the "craftsmanship" of his work. "It's so satisfyingly concrete. You can see and feel the results. Body work, unlike an engine job, has a number of degrees of acceptability. When it comes out beautifully, there's an aesthetic appeal to the work that really makes me feel good." Then there is the pleasure of "taking a job from start to finish";* so that a car "is all yours, whether it's a total wreck or a little dinger." Body work fulfills his need for "honest, useful labor—as opposed to selling people something they don't need. I sure sleep well at night." The body shop vindicated his choice completely. "I don't obsess about this kind of work. When I leave, I'm finished for the day."

When the body shop went out of business, Zeff moved upstate. One of five workers in "a really well-run, family-style shop," he lives with his wife, her eight-year-old daughter and their eight-week-old son, Roderick, in an old farmhouse "with our own beautiful stream, way out in the woods." To buy the house, Zeff and Meg Randall, a school teacher, "scrimped and saved every penny for two years." In contrast to what a lot of people think, nonunionized body work is not well paid. "We really need Meg's paycheck to make it." Money, Zeff says, has never interested him, but he worries that continued inflation and the rising costs of two children may force him to search for more lucrative work. If he were to make any changes in his life, they would be in the direction of "moving work and family even closer." He would like to take a more active

*The absence of such satisfaction, many researchers agree, is the greatest cause of discontent, boredom and low self-esteem among assembly line workers.

part in raising the children. "It seems absurd to be away from home all day when my family is my whole life."

"Sometimes I'm horrified by how easy it is to make a buck," confesses Nick Coulouris. Grandson of a Greek immigrant cook in a mill-town boardinghouse, son of a historian, what Nick finds so easy to do well is carpentry and "general contracting," as his business card reads.

Carpentry is the "skilled trade" of choice of the new New Class—whether high school, college or graduate school dropout. A "carpenter count" would probably reveal that over half of the "sizeable numbers"* of these young men are earning their living saw in hand.

Nick insists that he could hardly hammer a nail into a piece of wood, but he concedes that an engineering course in his freshman year, where he designed and patented a wood-burning stove, convinced him he was good at the "conceptual part." The hands-on work he just "learned by doing." What he also learned that first year was that he "hated college— even more than I had hated high school." Yet he felt he owed it to his parents to finish, while laying his plans for the non-professional afterlife.

The summer of his sophomore year, Nick called up the second nonunion contractor in the telephone book ("I had read that the first one in the book was always getting bombed by union thugs"), and announced: "I'm out of work and I'm hungry." To his astonishment, he was told to "come on over." In terror of being "found out," Nick got along by doing exactly what everybody else was doing. By the time they discovered what Nick, grinning, calls his "beginner's status," he was already part of the shop.

For two years, hoboing around the country, he supported himself by carpentry and odd jobs. Since moving to New York

---

*Riesman's phrase for a group whose membership no one is able to calculate. But it is easier to correlate the mortgage and housing squeeze of the late 1970s into the 1980s with the upsurge in carpenter demand: renovation is the answer to that unaffordable new house.

four years ago, Nick has been doing every kind of work, from apartment rehab, to building an additional room on weekend houses. "I'm an excellent carpenter." However, unlike Zeff Randall and others who choose hands over head, he preaches no crafts mystique or ideology of protest. "All work is boring, I don't care what it is," he states matter-of-factly. But for himself, "nine to five is out." What he likes about carpentry is that "as soon as I finish a job, I can split."

Self-employment is essential for Nick—as it is for many of his peers. Anything else he calls "giving your freedom." It doesn't matter whether you're giving it to the executive vice-president of a bank or the foreman on a construction site. Status, as translated into a prestige occupation, has no meaning for him. "The title on the door is a scam." But because both his parents came from working-class "ethnic" families, he is sensitive to the complex interplay of choice, chance and "inherited advantages." When Nick told a buddy on the construction site that he was quitting to strike out on his own, the young Puerto Rican electrician was horrified: "Man, you gotta be crazy. Eight bucks an hour? You got it made." Nick Coulouris is rueful about the shaping forces that persuaded his friend that "sticking a wire where the foreman tells you to stick it—even at eight dollars an hour—was the best life could offer." But he feels little can change what he calls the "prophecy"—where we are all likely to end up—except "personal risk taking and the will to defy the order of things."

Like most of the skidders, resistance to his own prophecy is individual. He is not looking to change "the system"—economic or social—just to make sure he doesn't get caught in its gears.

"My father is like a god in our family," Nick says. "He is the only one of eight brothers to have gone to college—let alone get a Ph.D. and become a professor." But what Nick admires most about his father is how unimpressed he is by status and prestige, his own or others'. "Maybe it's his peasant origins, but Pops has never been hung up on professional or business success."

When his parents have visitors, his father likes to show off Nick's bookcases. "Look at that work," his father points out proudly. "You don't see that kind of craftsmanship anymore."

"I always hated growing up in suburbia," announces Jon MacAndrew, twenty-seven, now a tenant farmer in California, "and I never wanted to raise my own kids there." Not because Jon's childhood was unhappy. "Not at all," he insists. Home was fine, his parents "super people." But even among the nicely tended lawns and large Victorian houses of the college-and-commuter town where he grew up, Jon found "too many people, cars and smoke." And although Swansea doesn't say "rich" to you right away, like Main Line or North Shore, it is still, Jon maintains, a "pretty snotty place" where kids were "obsessed with status."

When he was ten, Jon read his first book by Euell Gibbon—"the discovery of my life"—and began "gardening and growing things every spare minute."

Alan MacAndrew, Jon's father, was trained as an engineer, but was soon promoted to management, becoming regional marketing director for a large drug company. But because Alan's roots are in the soil of Kansas, where his parents were wheat farmers, Jon thinks his own early interest in agriculture was in the blood—"like a recessive gene."

Jon concedes that his father seemed "pretty satisfied with his work and with its rewards." His parents' income placed them "in the 60 percent tax bracket," where "they managed to keep up with inflation." But what Jon values more is the MacAndrews's honesty about their comfortable circumstances. There was no pushing Jon or his brothers to work* so

*The extraordinary number of daily newspapers in America that survived until the 1950s attests to the requirement that every able-bodied boy living in a neighborhood of single-family houses have a newspaper route. Not even the sons of millionaires were exempt from this rite of passage into the work ethic; see Anthony Bailey, *America, Lost and Found* (New York: Random House, 1980), for a bemused young English visitor's reaction to this curious institution.[3]

"they'll learn the value of money." No paper route—by which generations of middle-class sons assuaged the conscience of self-made fathers who feared the corruption of success.

Still, no oldest son of a corporate middle manager can fail to sense the strain—particularly when so much care was taken to keep it locked in the office. Jon suspects that his father was often "unhappy" when he couldn't make particular changes at work and disliked himself when he was "too scared" to press superiors who shied away from something "just because it was new."

What he guesses about this part of his father's career confirms Jon's own experience during summer vacations when he was an agricultural student, working on harvest crews: If you're an employee, it seems, you're always treated with "a certain lack of respect" which also makes it very hard, he feels, to sustain real self-esteem. "I'd rather make the mistake myself, complain about it myself, and penalize myself." Tenant farming, the first step toward independence, involves "learning to raise fruit and vegetables on a five-acre farm." In exchange for his labor, Jon gets 40 percent of the gross. The absentee owner, who also provides the fertilizer and equipment, keeps 60 percent. Eventually, he hopes to farm in a self-employed partnership arrangement: growing and selling goods locally at lower prices. What Jon envisions is a "very professionally run farmer's market."

Jon considers himself a "limited entrepreneur or agribusinessman," fine tuning his personal economy to satisfy both his needs and principles. "I consider my time is worth, at the maximum, twenty dollars an hour, or net, twenty thousand a year. Anything more is stealing from someone else!"

But, with his solid "aggie training" combined with "just loving the work," Jon says that "if I didn't watch things carefully, I'd get caught up in it...end up being *wealthy, God forbid!*" "It"...the expansionist spiral, the *challenges* that all bright, middle-class male children are taught, is manliness, if not godliness itself.

Resisting growth is a major problem for those determined to stay small. Dr. C. Hess Haagen of Wesleyan University in

Connecticut, author of a follow-up study[4] of his school's drop-outs, concluded that "with many of these young people, their own intelligence trips them up. They slide into becoming managers because their little service business is just so good." One of his former students, who left school to become a gardener, suddenly found himself an "operations chief with two helpers in the field, a secretary, accountant and lawyer, the whole thing. It's hard for middle-class Americans to say 'no' to success,"[5] according to Dr. Haagen.

SON OF NEW MONEY

Not everyone wants to be a Texas oil man.

Not even in a state where, according to Chris McQuade, "if that's what your daddy does, chances are you'll end up doing the same thing."

Almost all of Chris's friends are now working for their fathers, or for their fathers' friends. And eight times out of ten, Chris says, they're still living at home—"guys twenty-four or -five," like Chris's older brother! Home for Chris was "a nice $500,000 house on the nicest street in Houston's nicest neighborhood" where "they're prouder of having their own private police force than just about anything else."

Chris and his young wife, Diana, who is expecting their first child "any day now," live in an older, mostly Hispanic, working-class part of the city, in a house identical to their neighbors' on both sides of the street. "People used to just about pass out, when we gave them our address."

Chris had wanted to leave home since he was twelve, but he managed to wait until he finished high school. Then, with $4,000 saved from two years of after-school and summer jobs with a construction company, "making more money than anybody I knew," he moved out. Along with thousands of other young people, Chris "hung out" in Austin, like many university communities, a mecca for nonstudents, scraping by with carpentry jobs at five to six dollars an hour.

Returning to Houston two years later, he worked as a part-time clerk for a small real estate firm. When his employer went bankrupt, he offered Chris a truck in lieu of the salary he was owed. Now that he had a truck, it seemed as though he should do something with it, so Chris and a friend "started an outfit" for light moving. Two ads in the local paper brought them more jobs than they could handle, and Prime Movers was off to a rolling start. Two additional trucks later, Chris McQuade now presides over what he admits is a "pretty good-sized operation."

"I really enjoy the business," says the new entrepreneur. What he particularly likes, though, "is the thought of being able to sit here, taking calls and earning twenty-five dollars an hour. Actually it's just a way of making money without working," he says, with his easy laugh.

What makes his operation possible and modestly profitable is the changeable cast of "between one and three" part-time workers whom Chris hires as drivers and packers. Mostly friends, or friends of friends, these are young men looking for just the kind of pick-up work that Chris himself used to do. "Sometimes I psych myself up and work a lot. But unlike most Texans, I'm not really into the work ethic. I'm constantly trying to work less—not more." His ideal of success, he describes as a "situation where I can actually leave and do what I want, water ski, fish and play tennis, improve the house." The choice of leisure over the work ethic, Chris insists, is what will keep him trucking when his workers have moved on, or possibly back up to the white-collar world.

His philosophy of work that doesn't interfere with pleasure, Chris has decided, demands a plan of "no growth." What will keep him small, he claims, are those "too many other things" he likes to do. "I know that if this business gets any bigger, it will consume me, like it does my dad and stepfather. Then I'll need that private police force to guard my home," he jokes, "because I'll never be there either!" Unlike many New Class skidders who need to escape the "head work," the constricting definition of "merit" as a mental activity, Chris McQuade had no particular attachment to "hands-on" manual work, or any distaste for profits, as long as the business doesn't proscribe his freedom.

Where he is egalitarian, it is because he prefers the company of self-reliant, down-to-earth young people—like himself. For reasons of practicality, not politics. He lives in a Chicano neighborhood because "that was where I could afford to buy a house." But while poking fun at his parents' "enclave" and its private police force, he declares without apology that he wouldn't hire a black. Most of his customers, he claims, "just don't trust them, so it wouldn't help my business at all."

SON OF OLD MONEY

"I'm a multiple case of downward mobility," comments twenty-four-year-old Peter Wray, in the expensive accent and tentative smile of a not-so-long-ago preppie.

Peter Wray's grandfather was ambassador to a Latin American country. His father is a lawyer, and his mother has a "really important job" with a national public relations firm.

Four mornings a week, Peter works two Xerox machines at Letter-perfect, a Manhattan copying service, with his co-workers Mat and Evan, both black and part-time students. Together the trio manage to take orders for later pick-ups, expedite rush jobs for the waiting customers who jam the tiny store, and keep up a running banter among themselves, which occasionally includes neighborhood regulars.

Peter has not been a student since he left—or was asked to leave—"four prep schools and one public high school." Yet from the day he walked out of his last classroom, at the age of seventeen, he has been completely self-supporting. He got married at nineteen, then he and his wife separated. He supported them both, first by working in a factory on Cape Cod that made votive candles and "all kinds of rinky-dink brass accessories." It was tough, "assembly line type work" where Peter lost part of a finger. Transferred to the office after the accident, he became assistant to the director of operations, in charge of the ordering and inventory, which included a half-million dollars' worth of wicks and other supplies. When the factory folded, Peter Wray became an electrician's apprentice, working with his boss on contract jobs from 7 A.M. until 5 P.M., then taking over the bookkeeping chores until late in the evening. On weekends, he "went around selling our electrical installations," for which he received a 10 percent commission on the estimate, bringing his earnings to $20,000, "not *pre*-tax, *no*-tax," which in 1976 "wasn't bad for a high school dropout."*

Since leaving the Cape and separating from his wife, Peter has taken all kinds of part-time jobs—from "dismantling Santa Land at Macy's to work as a part-time paralegal for two Wall Street law firms. At both firms, his supervisors tried to persuade him to go to college and law school. "They kept telling me how smart I was and that I had a real feeling for the work." But he had no feeling for the highly charged competitiveness (including the efforts of one associate to pry him from a colleague's project). "There was a lot of ugly stuff going down there." So, instead of being lured back on the professional track, Peter, with two roommates, bought an old school bus and sold continental breakfasts in the Wall Street area "eighteen hours a day for one year." Besides the selling, he calculates that "every week, I made two hundred muffins and ten carrot cakes."

Peter Wray disapproves of his father's inherited wealth— especially its source. "It's dirty money—there's no getting around it. While my grandfather was ambassador, he bought up the silver mines, built the slum housing, and owned the 'company store' where miners and their families had to shop." Without this independent income, and his mother's earnings, Peter notes contemptuously, his father, who has a heavy

---

*Young middle-class skidders are a big piece of the "underground economy," which, according to economist Peter M. Gutmann, represents at a conservative estimate 14 percent of America's income. Not only are these revenues the IRS never sees but, as Dr. Gutmann calculates it, this share of our national earnings is growing at twice the rate of reported income.[6]

Whether they are self-employed lone operatives, employers "skimming" small businesses, or workers paid "off the books" (thereby saving employers millions in social security contributions), young adults in nontraditional occupations are heavily represented among these moles of the GNP.

drinking problem, could never have supported the family—not even in working-class style.

With the exception of his present part-time work "in the Xerox field," he says, mimicking the self-important manner in which professional men discuss their "positions," Peter has always "worked two jobs—one of them usually in a kitchen." Besides his other "varied labor experience, I guess I must have washed a million dishes." Sometimes, Peter Wray would like "more creative work. Actually, I'm quite a good cook." But this couldn't involve wearing a shirt and tie or "being a boss. Hassling a bunch of poor Hispanics in some kitchen! I would be my grandfather all over again, wouldn't I?"

SKIDDERS, UNDEREMPLOYMENT AND UNEMPLOYMENT

Some researchers find a strong correlation between the growing numbers of upper-middle-class "skidders" and the poor employment prospects for recent graduates.[7] The oversupply of college-educated baby-boomers, combined with a persistently wan economy, makes the right "fit" between education and entry-level jobs a rarity. One labor analyst has predicted that by the late 1980s one in four college graduates will be forced to accept "nontraditional work."[8] Indeed, "devaluation of the B.A." as career currency, along with the rush to graduate school, has already created some overqualified stock clerks.

However, the work done by these skidders was done by choice—not because it was the only job available. And for the college graduates among them, the choice was also a choice of a way of life.

WHERE ARE THE DAUGHTERS?

Observers of skidder sons, whether New Class, New Money or Old, all point to the relatively small number of daughters found among them.

The most obvious reason for this "underrepresentation"

of young women is their absence, generally, in the "nontraditional" occupations favored by downwardly mobile young men. How many women carpenters, contractors or electricians are there in the labor force? Or women running small farms or cartage operations? A "mom" enterprise without "pop" is still hard to find.

WHICH WAY IS DOWN?

With much "women's work," moreover, it's not easy to differentiate the skidders from the upwardly mobile. Many entry-level "professional jobs" traditionally held by young women, like assistant kindergarten teacher or nurse,* are arguably as menial, exhausting, and inarguably less remunerative than being a waitress. In fact, the success of recent efforts to unionize the overwhelmingly female clerical workers is based upon the recognition that most secretaries have more in common with assembly line workers than with management trainees.

(STILL) WAITING
FOR MR. RIGHT

Women's work is still regarded by many as an interim occupation, something a young woman will do until she has a family—a view often popular with her own family. Historically, the minimal importance placed by middle-class parents on their daughters' choice of work was based on the reasonable assumption that when a young woman marries, her new "ascriptive status" derives from the occupational prestige of her spouse—who will preferably *not* be the local plumber.

---

*The nursing profession itself has "skidded" since its beginnings. Always badly paid, nursing, like social work, originally attracted upper-class and upper-middle-class young women (which in England is still the case). As more and more of this group went to college, nursing, which never required a B.S., dropped in desirability and prestige, becoming a favored career for young women of working-class background, then in the 1960s as a "new career" for minorities.

"We're happy because she's happy" is the way Ingrid Lingard's New Class parents describe their daughter's chosen profession—hairstylist and beautician. Dr. Frederick Lingard is an urbanist with a background in engineering. Dr. Erica Lingard is a family therapist. And both are professors at a southern California university. Ingrid's older sister, Suzanne, just received her M.B.A. from Stanford. Younger brother Fritz has gone east with a graduate fellowship in mathematics.

"I decided in high school," says Ingrid, "that there were too many educated people in our family." And although she enrolled in the local community college, it was more for lack of any better ideas. Ingrid admits to being influenced by her boyfriend at the time, who worked for a construction company but not as a skidder. "Duane was from a real blue-collar family," and he had strong views about women and education. "School never did shit for you," he insisted. "Why don't you do like other girls and get a real-life job?"

So Ingrid tried the local school of cosmetology, and she "just loved it—from day one—everything: the cutting, styling, coloring, makeup." With her beautician's license, she moved to a highly competitive job with a branch of an international salon. To be sure, most parents want their children to be happy, but for sons, more than daughters, success in a status occupation is still considered, rightly or wrongly, a requirement for personal satisfaction. Would the Lingards have been as happy if Frederick Jr. was wielding brush and blow dryer, instead of his sister?

One New Class father and journalist says yes. Because Ingrid's parents are Californians, not urban Easterners. Douglas Kneeland, *New York Times* reporter who, with his family, has lived "just about everywhere," mentions the greater pressure on kids in East Coast metropolitan areas than in other parts of the country. There is far less parental concern in California, he observes, even on the part of professional, upwardly mobile parents, about a thirty-four-year-old son, still working in a gas station after dropping out of college fourteen years ago! And in poorer regions of the country, like Maine and eastern Massachusetts, says Kneeland, a New Englander, "the person who has any job—even a modest one like supermarket checker, is seen as lucky to have work."

Maine, notes a local newspaper editor, herself an immigrant of the 1960s, is a hotbed of low aspiration. And the perfect place to escape from the All-American Dream of Success. After all, points out Jean Hays of the *Bangor News*, the natives have been doing it for two hundred years. Growing up in suburban, upper-middle-class New Jersey, it was "total culture shock," Jean recalls, "to find yourself in a place where identity doesn't derive from work." Nobody in Maine asks, What do you do? because most people you know don't "do" any one thing. They're likely to be carpenters in winter, potato planters in the spring, lobster catchers in August, and in the fall, if they're short of cash, school bus drivers. What makes it possible to survive without drive in places like Maine is a standard of living based in large part upon self-sufficiency: growing it, building it, fixing it yourself.

An assumption of self-sufficiency also means far less anxiety about the future, about a helpless and abandoned old age, about retirement security.

"I talk to ninety-year-olds every day," notes Jean Hays, "who are getting along just fine on their own. And then there is the patron saint for half a century of many of these pilgrims, Scott Nearing, still raising all his own food at ninety-seven!"[9]

In upper-middle-class Connecticut suburbs, there are parents sufficiently doubtful about the strivings and compromises in their own lives to cheer their children's different choices. On the eve of his retirement as executive vice-president of a *Fortune* 500 corporation, Frank Meyerhoff compares his generation's constraints with his children's freedom. "We were children of the Depression, young adults in wartime, molded early into a way of life none of us seemed to question." Frank Meyerhoff had wanted to be a psychiatrist, but on returning from military service, it had seemed "a long and awfully expensive haul." Instead, he "gladly accepted the offer of a job" from his father, an executive of the same corporation from which Frank is about to be retired. "I have to admit that my career benefited from some timely nepotism."

This is something that certainly can't be said for the Meyerhoff children. The oldest is a sailmaker; his brother is a cook at the local community college, and their sister is the wife of a part-time Maine carpenter/fisherman/school bus driver. None of them has gone beyond high school. Still, as their father notes proudly, not one of the three has ever received a cent from their parents after the age of sixteen. "They're leading honest lives," says Frank Meyerhoff, perhaps enviously, "to their specifications. Not somebody else's. Not their parents! Not society. They're free!"

HAVING IT ALL WAYS:
THE LOWER RUNG
IS THE UPPER HAND

Along the "strip" the sign is visible a block away: "Eve's Apples." The words in sparkly script, lit by neon, snake across pertly drawn buttocks. On the thighs, smaller silver letters proclaim: "All Coed Revue."

Inside, a moat of busy bartenders separates the customers from the collegians. One at a time, in styles ranging from early Martha Graham to late Sally Rand, they prance, bump, writhe, grind and shake down the runway, to the steady pulse of a disco beat. Against a wall in the middle of the long room, between the entrance and a private "backroom" bar, the Beaver Dam, owner Greg Silvani sits at a high desk. Peering up from his clipboard, he looks intently at each job applicant. Why do you want to be a waitress? dancer? bartender? What have you been doing since your last job, he asks a former pediatric nurse. The aspirants smile tentatively, answering each question slowly. They move closer to their interrogator, trying to hear and be heard over the music. With his closely cropped dark hair and square, rimless glasses, Gregory Silvani suggests a defrocked Jesuit-turned-leftwing French intellectual, circa 1952.

"*Esthétique du mal* and *Notes toward a Spring Fiction*," he explains patiently. "I chose them for my senior thesis because, of Wallace Stevens's entire *oeuvre*, those two poems seemed to . . . ," he breaks off. Another applicant for part-time bartender appears in the pool of lamplight.

"You understand, don't you?" Greg warns, "how serious it is to serve alcohol to a minor? Any failure to ask for an I.D. here means immediate dismissal." The Star Chamber. The young man nods vigorously. "Money," Greg's voice turns lyrical, "is the last stronghold of the Romantic. Is that Norman Mailer or Norman Mailer quoting Balzac? I'm never sure."

Money—as opposed to Balzac, Wallace Stevens, and Norman Mailer—is a recent discovery for Greg Silvani. "I did all this reading in college and it filled my head with a lot of smarm," he says contemptuously. Before he discovered the Romance of Money, Greg Silvani was Exhibit A in the Great Meritocratic Talent Hunt; second-generation New Class, by way of Chicago parochial schools, followed by a scholarship to a "little Ivy League" college. "I'm quite certain," Greg says in the precise manner that leaves no shadow of uncertainty, "that I was the only blue-collar ethnic in my class, if not in the entire school."

Greg's parents separated early in his childhood. But until they did, he describes his home life as a "crisis-laden domestic scene." His mother encouraged his literary interests; she wanted him to be a poet or novelist, this he now thinks was her way of repudiating his father, an army technician who later worked for a commuter rail line. After graduation, like thousands of other young people in 1969, Greg Silvani shelved his literary interests—but for social activisim, not profit. As a communitiy organizer in a ghetto poverty program, he learned about "the way bureaucracies operate," but also that poverty was definitely a condition to be avoided.

Federal funding disappeared along with his job in the early 1970s. But Greg's interest in communities remained. So, "not having any better ideas about what to do with my life," he went back to school, and graduate work in anthropology. Greg married an Italian-American woman of "almost identical background, even to the fact that both our maternal grandfathers owned small restaurants." To support his wife and infant son, he started bartending at night on the "strip."

"Through my wife's family, I met people down here. That was my entrée." It didn't take long for Greg to feel "very disenchanted" with the academic side of his life, and particularly unhappy about "how little control I exercised over my own professional direction," acknowledging that his independence meant "I had a hard time dealing with authority, taking orders from superiors." Without "bowing and scraping to the powers that be," Greg felt he just wasn't going to get the kind of encouragement that leads to the right job—no matter how good his work was.

Part of his resistance to the "hierarchical authority structure"* of academic life, Greg thinks, "was ethnic. Italian men are taught to be egotistical." And in his own case, the absence of a father meant that he needed to assume responsibility too early. "I was the man of the family when I was a young teenager. So it was hard for me to play 'junior' at twenty-five."

At this low point in his life, Eve's Apples came on the block, a good buy, because the "owner was in hock to everyone. He owed $15,000 in back rent alone." "Through my father-in-law," Greg says guardedly, "I received the option of buying the place. The minute the possibility was presented, I knew it was what I should be doing." At first, buying the bar meant the opportunity to be "around a lot of pretty girls. The All Coed Revue was my idea.

"Before I bought the place, it was your standard brand old strippers. With my unhappiness about my life and its prospects, the bar was my fantasy outlet." Fantasies, though, are never harmless. They are always dress rehearsals for real-life action; and the student/strippers caused a lot of trouble with his marriage, followed by a lot of "counseling" for Greg and his wife.

Whether because of the counseling or because he exhausted his fantasies by acting them out, Greg came to realize that the real need Eve's Apples filled was more than sex. "Now I had an enterprise, a business, something I could throw

---

*Despite Greg Silvani's shift from pedagogue to publican, he still speaks in Careful and Critical Discourse (CCD) or New Class.

myself into, where I was *the chief*. Beyond even the authority, the control, though, were the dollars. I knew that if I could make a bundle of money, I wouldn't ever be in the position of kowtowing to a superior again."

In three years he made it. Eve's Apples, according to owner Greg Silvani is now "very, very profitable. I've made enough money now so that I don't *ever* have to worry about money."

As a "participant-observer" in his own life, Gregory Silvani, ex-anthropologist, ex-employee, also claims that he knows himself a lot better after five years in business, "than I could ever have as an academic. It's the decisions of the moment, involving loss and gain, decisions affecting other people's lives, dealings with the police, the staff," that make the difference.

If mobility is measured by the envy we inspire, Greg Silvani has reason to be satisfied. "I see a lot of guys wishing they had my success and my freedom." Money is money in America, he reflects, and in his experience, "it matters very little where, or how, you get it. Money buys class. It matters more than education and it matters more than family."

Nonetheless, Greg is hedging his bets. Three years ago, he started taking premed courses "in my spare time." He has just finished the last requirement, organic chemistry, with an A. "When I picked up the exam yesterday, the professor offered—*offered without my even asking*—to write me a recommendation to medical school."

"Part of me," he confesses, "still craves the status that I can never have running a strip bar, the prestige in the community that would always be withheld because of what I've done to make money."

In his upper-middle-class professional suburb, the owner of Eve's Apples will not be nominated for the Town Council or to head the United Fund. Then there is the dream of Greg's grandfather, the day laborer who became a restaurant owner, "to see his children and grandchildren 'professionals.' There's something in me that wants to make good on that dream," Greg says. Besides, if he can live with a little more "hierarchical authority" until he graduates from medical school, he will be once again self-employed as a doctor. "Just another kind of entrepreneur."

SELF-EMPLOYMENT:
CLIMBING AND SKIDDING

If he joins the professionally self-employed, Dr. Gregory Silvani will represent only 5 percent of the work force, the one whose growth is highly controlled by gatekeeper institutions like medical schools. But as an anthropologist turned small entrepreneur, Greg Silvani is part of a growing segment of the labor market.

The rise of the New Class or "salariat," according to one theory, turned us into a nation of employees. Many of their children are part of a Great Leap Backward—a mushrooming movement back to a nation of shopkeepers, farmers, and small service providers.

Although many skidders-by-choice are obviously choosing the least possible involvement with work (meaning that someone else makes all the decisions), many more speak of "control," "freedom," "splitting after a job," "not bending the knee to anyone." Work requirements that all spell self-employment.

In 1980, the *Monthly Labor Review*, which keeps a steady finger on the pulse of how we earn our living, noted that between 1972 and 1979 the number of self-employed Americans rose by more than 1.1 million, "reversing decades of steady decreases." Most dramatic was the surge in the post-recession years of 1976–1979, when the increase in the number of self-employed workers surpassed the comparable increase for wage and salary workers: 12.4 versus 10.8 percent. When agricultural self-employment is subtracted (the only area that continued to decline), the nonfarmers had set up shop in the neighborhood of 1.3 million.[10] The statisticians at the U.S. Department of Labor remind us that these figures do not reflect the "moonlighters"—those self-employed at second jobs, or the moles of the "underground economy"—who work full time "off the books."

Robert Zager, vice-president of policy studies at the non-profit Work in America Institute, predicts that "we're going to see a proliferation of free-floating enterprises; some will coalesce into larger ones, then dissolve back into smaller operations."*[11]

According to Professor John Hornaby, director of the entrepreneurial studies program at Babson College in Wellesley, Massachusetts, the basic requirement for entrepreneurship is intelligence.[12] However, those that will succeed, according to many researchers, have benefited from "socialization" or "inherited advantages" enjoyed by the middle class, enabling them to survive and even prosper while skidding. Somehow, it is easier for the college-educated son of an archaeologist to find how "disappointingly" easy it is to make money as a carpenter than it is for the son of a carpenter.

Whether it is confidence, competence, previous experience of success, or security, born of affluence, that allows risk-taking, these attributes are precisely what middle-class kids seem likelier to possess—and what lower-class, minority youth frequently lack.

Sociologist Paul Lazarsfeld arrived in this country from Austria in 1937, where he had been studying unemployed youth, to examine a similar population in Depression-devastated Newark, New Jersey. He used the term "effective scope" to describe what lower-class jobless young people in both places didn't have. And what Savvy Skidders do.

"Should I address the phenomenon of voluntary skidders as a professional or a sibling?" jokes Janice Walsh, a Washington, D.C., labor economist.

The oldest of five children in a prosperous Irish Catholic family, she is also the only "professional" among her brothers and sisters, ranging in age from twenty-four to Janice, just turned forty. "Well, let's see, there's my sister the cleaning

*Rising white-collar unemployment has given this prediction the weight of fact; moreover, the "tertiary economy," consisting of small service providers, has suffered least.

lady, my brothers the tree surgeon, the carpenter and the ashram cook. Then I've got hordes of cousins who represent an even wider range of blue-collar and artisan trades."

Why? is a question that interests Janice Walsh personally and professionally.

In her immediate family, Janice thinks that their father's profound ambivalence about his work made a conventional business track very "unappealing," especially to his sons. Her father manufactured a household product that "really took off in New England" in the 1950s. Yet he insisted that his work was "just something I do to make money." She cannot recall ever catching a note of pleasure, pride or sense of achievement in her father's remarks about his business.

Also, in the case of her brothers, there is "still the anti-Vietnam residue." Even though the "movement" as such no longer exists, anti-authoritarian, anti-hierarchical values are its legacy. "That's why those self-employment figures keep on rising." But, she adds, from her own observations of favored areas for skidding, like Maine and Vermont, one of the reasons why so many "lone operatives" survive and prosper "is the way in which many of their crafts occupations, cottage industries like wooden toys and pottery, hook into national marketing channels." So before we assume that a particular region is supporting goods, services and people, we must examine whether their products are shipped out, or even, conversely, if the young people themselves may be commuting from their rural homes to urban "work centers."

Wearing her economist's hat, Janice reminds us of Say's law: "Supply definitely creates demand." The first Holistic Food Hangout on a dingy square in an unprepossessing part of town seems to create the need for six more—all with the same "spider fern and butcher block."

Several years ago Janice Walsh studied the economics of food service delivery for a major university, and she has a special interest in this area. These young people, with their easy sociability, are a "natural" for service enterprises like bars and restaurants, especially in mixed neighborhoods. They seem to have a knack for creating the kind of atmosphere in which different social classes and age groups feel at home. Far from the old stereotype of a privileged, sheltered youth producing adults "unfit for real labor," Janice argues that the middle-class background of these young people makes them even more likely to succeed at working-class jobs. "Being educated means you know how to learn; whom to watch, or when you have to go read a manual for six hours." Even more importantly, though, this group is "shrewd at psyching out the market. Take my brother the carpenter. Palo Alto has a lot of free-lance hammer and two-by-four guys. But it also has a significant population of 'experimental, avant garde' young architects." Janice's brother created a subspecialty. "Weird designs are his thing. He taught himself to do stuff that would send a union carpenter running."

Another "skill" this group has developed may be the most crucial of all to their survival: "They've become expert at living on nothing," and they're absolute pros at it. They're the super nonconsumers," says Janice, with a touch of envy, ticking off her mortgage, two cars, private kindergarten and sundry other forms of thralldom to upper-middle-class professional life. "My brother probably doesn't spend more than two dollars a year on clothes. They nose out the best secondhand stores, for the absolute necessities, and they recycle children's clothes endlessly among their friends."

Even though these young people are noncommunal in living arrangements, their economy is based upon cooperation. Time and labor are the substitute for money, so everything from home births to food co-ops become part of a return to a noncash economy. One prominent New York business-man—himself the father of several "skidders" now in their thirties—is sympathetic to their rejection of the gross aspects of consumerism. But he regards them as bad news for the economy. "What happens to the clothing industry—including Puerto Rican garment workers—when more and more people are spending two dollars a year on their wardrobe?"

Finally, Janice Walsh ponders whether her siblings won't

end up ahead of "knowledge workers" like her, her husband, and all their friends. "There just isn't the career mobility, especially in the public sector, that we were led to believe in when we were in graduate school. Frankly, most of us thought that by this point we would be way ahead of where we are." Now she is convinced that for "any of us who do move up that career ladder, luck—just luck" is the only explanation.

Lots of their friends, Janice says, are talking about "small neocapitalist ventures. That's a euphemism for one of those little restaurants with spider fern and butcher block."

The choice of downward mobility by these privileged young people illustrates the sharpest dispute about class in America.

Is it income, education or occupation that defines our place in the class structure? Or attitudes and "values"? If skidders take their middle-class values with them, have they in fact changed class? But again, how long do values last when they no longer apply to our way of life? Finally, how does the "psychological cushion" of being able to ascend as well as skid, affect class identity?

For the answers to these questions, we would have to "track" these young people "over time" to note where they are in ten or fifteen years.

The skidders, even more than the upwardly mobile among us, argue for a more dynamic, less static class structure. Cross-fertilization of classes is another way of understanding this process.

Rafe Englander, thirty-three, traded in neuropsychology at M.I.T. for peat and vegetable farming in Maine, the Academy of Science for the local growers association. Choosing downward mobility for the joys of independence and the rural life, he is helping other young people move up. During the winter months he teaches modern farm management to Maine natives, many of whom are the sons and daughters of failed local farmers.

A lot of seminal events can occur, Rafe says, when people choose to change class.

CHAPTER
SIX

DOWN WITH DIVORCE

In every way, divorce is a downer. The pain, caused by feelings of failure, defeat and guilt, loneliness and bitterness, loss of appetite, potency and self-esteem, concentration and sleep, is so well documented as to make divorce, after sex, the most studied phenomenon in our time.

Never mind "creative uncoupling" and no-fault divorce. Nobody wins and no one is all right when a marriage ends.

But while the psychic wounds of splitting—and how to heal them—continue to enrich armies of therapists, authors and publishers,* the class wounds of divorce, the damage of downward mobility to women and children, have been largely ignored. From loss of income and social standing of mothers, to diminished opportunities and "life chances" for children, every measure of class and status tells us that marital dissolution means a precipitous and often permanent slide down the socioeconomic scale.

THE RICH DON'T DO IT

Never mind the gossip columns. Their highly volatile mix from the world of sports, show biz, Seventh Avenue and the in-

---

*Not to mention divorce lawyers, who could certainly reverse the Spanish proverb, to affirm that revenge (other people's) is the best route to living well.

ternational jet set is not even a representative sample of those who hath. The Beautiful or Semi-Beautiful People are atypical in an important respect: their propensity to divorce. The really rich are different from the glitterati—and from you and me—in yet another way: they divorce far less frequently (thereby staying richer). In other words, divorce and separation *decrease* as income rises. The more money a husband earns, the more likely the marriage will survive.

Dr. Paul C. Glick, senior demographer in the U.S. Bureau of the Census, informs us that those least likely to be divorced in America are the highest-paid managers, followed by physicians.[1] Among the chief executives of the nation's fifty largest corporations, only three had been divorced—and one of them was Henry Ford II! The low divorce rate among high-earning corporate officers and the highest income category of self-employed professionals confirm the need of successful men for a well-tended nest—and of their wives' keen awareness of their status as bower birds.[2]

Yet while income may be the most reliable indicator, it is not the only reason why the wealthy weather marital stress better than those of lower socioeconomic status. Money has a "hidden multiplier" effect. Or in the language of sociologists: "the decision to terminate a marriage is the outcome of the level of satisfaction with the marriage and the level of constraints that inhibit marital dissolution. The higher the income, the higher the level of economic and social constraints that inhibit hasty marital breakups."[3] For "upscale households" the loss of social status and supports may be more of a brake on divorce than actual belt tightening.

This also explains the low divorce rate of physicians. We do not even have to know how highly they "place" in occupational prestige scales to be aware of the status enjoyed by doctors (and their wives) in any community. A doctor's neglect of his family may be forgiven—even admired as altruism. His wife's complaints may be treated as failure to understand the demands of her husband's profession. Similarly, the doctor's grueling schedule makes peaceful domesticity more attractive than the delights of born-again bachelorhood.

In a study of sexual and marriage patterns among the affluent, psychologist John F. Cuber lets a number of upper-middle-class Americans describe what he terms their "utilitarian marriages."[4] After briefly contemplating separation, one husband explains the decision-making process that persuaded him to stay put: "It's like making a major adjustment in the business. The choices aren't quite black and white, and so you try to work out the best course of action, on balance." Said another executive, whose marriage "understanding" included the right to privacy of each partner: "Neither of us has ever welched out on the bargain." These are cost-benefit couples with limited-liability partnerships. In most cases both spouses are clear as to why they married—and stayed that way. Managers or successful self-employed businessmen and professionals, they rationalize their marriages in market terms: "on balance"; "on one side of the ledger are the kids. . . ."

Dr. Cuber was more surprised to learn that wives' rationalizations differed little from their husbands'. To these wives, success is either a joint-stock venture or an offering: either way, a legitimate substitute for other, more intimate pleasures. "He's given me and the children everything we could want"; "he's worked so hard for us"; "I'm so proud of him"; and still more impersonal, "this community owes him a lot."

Some wives had "high satisfaction" careers of their own. Like their husbands, they derived professional as well as material advantages from marriage and a well-run (by others), attractive home.* The intense energy that they, too, invested in work allowed them to place the "male-female stuff" on the "fringe of importance" to their lives. "We have it worked out perfectly," said the principal of a suburban private school. "He travels—the whole Southwest now that he's been promoted—and only gets home alternate weekends. We've

---

*In many respects, these mergerlike unions, designed to maximize social and occupational mobility, simply harken back to an earlier Old World tradition of arranged marriages. The only difference is that here the spouses—not their parents—did the arranging.

moved to the country now and Joey can have his horses and Ellen has her sailing and swimming close by."

In these highly class-conscious, high-mobility marriages, much would be lost, in the partners' view, and little gained by seeking greater fulfillment through divorce. Less civilized and more crass are women who hang in, and hang on, just for the money and perks. "Half the women I know in Houston who are still married," observed the recently divorced wife of a high-ranking oil company executive, "are there because of the income and status. Only, they'd rather die than admit it." But one woman (northeast of Texas) not only admitted it, she even cited figures: "If that crazy bastard was earning $35,000 instead of $350,000 per," said the wife of a bank president, "I'd have taken the kids and been gone long ago." But it isn't the charge cards or the social status that finally allows her to stay married. "Just when I'm on the verge of killing him—or walking out," she noted, "he's off on a business trip to Korea for two weeks—and everybody cools down."

The advantages of staying married for Crazy Bastard are both obvious and not so obvious. His "lovely wife and children" are available for display at the required times. And if he is half as impulsive, irrational and nearly psychotic as his wife claims, these qualities are far likelier to become dominant as a born-again bachelor. A host of studies have shown that the rates of mental illness and suicide soar for single men, including the separated and divorced. As free-floating currency, Crazy Bastard could prove more of a liability than asset to his bank.

Then there are those wives of very rich men, determined not to experience downward mobility, especially if divorce is not their choice. (Their well-publicized settlements may encourage togetherness among the wealthy.) "I've had the benefit of the advice of a couple of dear old friends," one such woman ominously confided to a psychologist with a tape recorder: "They are the wives of men who have made it very big and they are treated royally. They're the 'buy me, take me, bring me, show me' ladies and they say: 'Don't be a nice girl for anything. Get everything that's coming to you. You deserve every goddamn penny and more!'"[5] One spouse who either took or did not need such advice was Harvard-trained economist Mrs. Ellen Samuels, former wife of John S. Samuels III, a self-made financier and chieftain of a mineral empire. Mrs. Samuels, whose divorce settlement was alleged to be "one of the largest in the history of New York State," was awarded eight million dollars *plus* the cost of living quarters equivalent, square foot for square foot, to the double-sized Upper East Side New York town house she had occupied when married.[6] Displaced but not downwardly mobile, Mrs. Samuels confounds the statistics in yet another important respect. Unlike most divorced wives, it would be difficult for her to improve upon her present economic circumstances through remarriage.

...BUT THE POOR DO

If high income buys space, social status (and social sanctions), the glue for sticking together, low income is an all-too-reliable predictor of divorce.

"Perhaps few sociological findings are better established," states one researcher, "than those indicating that marriages tend to be more stable among the well-educated, well-paid white-collar workers than among the poorly paid, less-educated blue-collar workers."[7] And even more overwhelming is the agreement that of all these other factors, income is the most important determinant of lasting marriage. Sadly enough, though, greater incidence of divorce among the lowest-income families means that those who can least afford it are most prone to dissolve unions.

For the working class or working poor, the breakup of the family can be the crucial factor leading women to seek public assistance. According to one welfare official in California, the state where one of every two marriages fails, families that were "just making it"[8] drop, with divorce, into that ominously expanding population of "single female heads of household," 34.6 percent of whom, along with their children, fall below the poverty level. [9]

One California study that followed divorced families of all classes for five years reported that, although three-fifths of the women and two-fifths of the men had experienced a "substantial decline" in their standard of living as a result of the divorce, "the decline was most serious, the financial picture most erratic and unsettling when both the father and mother were in the lower socioeconomic class." At this level of working poor, divorce triggered "household chaos and instability" on every front. From the children's perspective, everything seemed to have fallen apart.

Only the very poorest families in the study,* the very rich ones or those in which the divorced wives remarried men with high incomes, showed no economic ill effects from separation. [10]

WHO ELSE CHOOSES DIVORCE?

Women, overwhelmingly. In almost three-quarters of all divorce cases, by a conservative estimate, wives are the initiators of marital breakup. [11]

Writing on the future of marriage, University of Pennsylvania sociologist Jessie Bernard accepts this rather astonishing news as the altogether natural outcome of her well-documented case: that by every measure of well-being, marriage historically did little good and much harm to women. She interprets the exploding divorce rate as a reflection of "the fact that there are now better alternatives for women in expressing their dissatisfaction in being able to 'vote with their feet.'" [12] In other words, it is specifically the alternative of participation in the labor force that has made this "new choice" a realistic one for women.

*Those for whom welfare and unemployment were already a way of life as intact families.

A recent study might seem to confirm Bernard's perspective that for women, work versus marriage spells divorce. Social psychologist George Levinger had the opportunity to compare three hundred reconciled couples with three hundred couples who decided to proceed with divorce. Money, Levinger found, how much, who earned it and who didn't, explained most about reconciliation and divorce. Levinger's evidence suggested that wives, the plaintiffs in four-fifths of the six hundred cases, made economic comparisons between their husband's income and job security (internal attraction) and their own earnings and/or employment opportunities (external attraction).

High husband income, interpreted as "attraction" to staying together, led to reconciliation. An independent wife's earnings (or the imminent potential thereof, like a law degree in sight) proved a "barrier" to reconciliation and functioned as the "external attraction" encouraging divorce.*[13]

However, Bernard's happily emancipated wives, earning their way out of the house of bondage, and Levinger's prudent spouses, looking before they leap to freedom, would together appear to represent a tiny minority. Most women who "vote with their feet," whatever other benefits they may realize, vote for reduced economic circumstances, diminished social status, a precarious and uncertain future for themselves and their children.

The best source of what happens to husbands, wives and children after divorce comes from a representative sample survey of five thousand American families, first interviewed in 1968 and reinterviewed every year until 1977 on all issues affecting the social and economic aspects of their lives. The Michigan Panel Survey of Income Dynamics' subgroup of divorcing couples among its five thousand subject families is particularly important: first, because economist Robert Hampton and his staff interviewed both husbands and wives over

---

*This conclusion suggests that those traditionalist men who object to wives working are not expressing mindless macho notions, but fears grounded in reality.

the seven years of the survey; and second, because his sample of 133 families was limited to those couples who chose to terminate a marriage. The decision was mutual.

WHO MOVES UP—AND DOWN

By far the most startling evidence from Hampton's study is that "*after separation, the economic status of former husbands improves, while that of former wives deteriorates.*"[14]

One way of measuring overall economic well-being is by comparing the ratio of family income to family need. In a 1981 study of three thousand California divorces, Stanford University sociologist Leonore J. Weitzman found that men's standard of living increased by 42 percent in the first year after divorce, while living standards for women and children decreased by 73 percent.[15]

SAVING IT, SPENDING IT
AND WORRYING ABOUT IT

Although many men have attested to the difficulty and/or impossibility of their circumstances following divorce,[16] the spending versus economizing habits of the ex-husbands in the Michigan Panel Survey's sample suggest additional dimensions of how much better off divorced men are than their former wives and children. Husbands and wives were each asked about their "economizing measures" in 1968 and again in 1972, based on such questions as: How much do you spend on alcohol, cigarettes? On eating out? Do you own a late model car? With far less relative income, wives economized dramatically more than their former spouses.[17] And although we can interpret this to mean that they were both wiser spenders and better savers (thereby increasing their assets), the particular questions about consumer patterns also illustrate the fact that they spend much less on *themselves* than on children or household maintenance.

The relatively easy-come, easy-go attitude about spending that characterized the former husbands, emphasizes who *has* more discretionary income. It also points to the physical absence of children, making it easier for most fathers, most of the time, to spend most of what they earn on themselves. According to psychologist Angus Campbell, director of the University of Michigan's Institute for Social Research, 58 percent of ex-husbands claim they never worry about paying their bills, compared to 30 percent of divorced wives with so little anxiety about money.[18] So there is no doubt who suffers the social and economic consequences of divorce: women and children.

The reasons are simple. The first is that men earn more— so they are allowed to keep more. Even in "community property" states, like Idaho and California, where the assets of divorcing couples are equitably divided, the future earnings of the spouse may not be included in the settlement. Unless the wife is adroit at converting savings and property assets into "human capital," enabling her to become an earner as soon as possible (or the assets are so large as to yield "unearned income" when invested), she may shortly find herself not much better off than the wife who is awarded little or nothing in other states. Especially in states like California, where selling a large, expensive house means having to buy a much smaller, much more expensive one. Community property settlements have created a new species of downwardly mobile: the equity poor. Even when divorced wives are lucky enough to find jobs or continue working, their income—across all occupations—will be 40 percent less than their male counterparts.

In addition, many men pay nothing at all toward the maintenance of their families. In one study of nonsupporting fathers, three (male) researchers concluded that "while men complain about the economic strain of supporting two households, only one-third of husbands were found to be contributing to the financial support of their ex-wives and children."[19] Even more alarming, research has shown that the level of their support diminishes over time. A Wisconsin follow-up study found that within one year of divorce, 42 percent of fathers made no court-ordered child-support payments. After ten years, the proportion rose to 79 percent.[20] Of the Michigan Panel Survey families interviewed in the last of the seven years following separation, fewer than half of the divorced or separated women were receiving any alimony or child support.*[21] This refers *only to court-awarded alimony or child support*. A significant percentage of women never receive child-support awards in the first place.

In a 1975 survey of American women taken for International Women's Year (IWY), only 44 percent of the divorced or separated mothers reported that they had been awarded child support. Of these 44 percent, fewer than half of the IWY survey women with awards received support on a regular basis. One-third reported receiving payments irregularly or not at all.[22]

In most states, mothers with children must prove "destitution" in order for the courts to make a serious attempt to locate and try to compel compliance of nonsupporting fathers. Similarly, middle-class women are ineligible for the kind of legal aid that would help them file a suit against a husband able to pay, or to return to court for an adjustment of child support. Women who would not qualify for public assistance have to locate the agencies or lawyers who allow sliding-scale fees. The waiting list for this kind of legal service is not short.

Until very recently, moreover, there was a traditional "bias" among social workers and other "family helpers": don't make the man mad by suing for nonsupport. Such action, it was argued, might result in the severance of all paternal attention or worse—invite reprisals and harassment. With the exception of recent father-finding programs keyed to reducing public assistance, efforts made by the courts or other government agencies to locate derelict fathers and "encourage" them

---

*46.3 percent for whites, 36.7 percent for nonwhites. The most "puzzling" evidence about minority families to emerge from the Michigan Panel Survey's computers is why black fathers in professional/manager occupations proved far more derelict in child support than black blue-collar or sales/clerical workers.

to ante up, have been rare.* The burden of time and money falls entirely on the former wives.

One study by a Michigan county found that an average award of 35 percent of a father's gross income netted an average of 16 percent of that income in payments to his family.[24] In short, there is every incentive for a man simply to forget that he has a family. Especially if he starts another, and clearly, the burden of a man's fathering a second family falls squarely on the first.

In a study of child-support policies in seven states, only Iowa refuses to reduce the husband's payments to the original family, based upon subsequent children he may have.[25] The other six states implicitly believe that a man has no responsibility to limit his brood; the oldest will simply have to make do with less—if they get anything at all!

THE NEW POOR AND
THEIR CHILDREN

With divorce, poorer women and their children are locked into permanent poverty. But the shock troops of America's divorce statistics are those women who were well off and middle class—by virtue of marriage. These are the "displaced homemakers,"[26] the three million older women with empty nests and no marketable skills, or women who, employed or unemployed, find themselves with the entire responsibility for raising young children on less than half their former income.

"I feel," said a San Francisco divorced mother of two, "as though I were treading water in a tidal wave."[27] Seventy-seven percent of these divorced wives are working mothers.

---

*The problem threatens to worsen through cumulative force of numbers. In 1982 the divorce rate (just over the million mark) was double that of the early 1970s. At least half of these divorces involved at least one child under eighteen. As the chief of the New Jersey Bureau of Child Support noted: "A divorced woman today has only a 10 percent chance of being paid on time and in full," adding that 90 percent of all child-support payments in his state are in arrears.[23]

If there is a recurring image they use to describe their lives, it is the image of sinking, drowning or struggling to stay afloat. "You have to flog yourself every single day to do more, earn more," said a New York free-lance graphic artist, the divorced mother of two young daughters. "If I'd known how terrible it would be," she added, "I never could have done it." How "terrible" it is, refers to a double shock: the experience of "real" and "relative" deprivation. First, there is the drop in real income, often of one-half or more, of wives who, in 88 percent of all divorces, are also the custodial parent;* and second—even harder to bear—the bitter contrast between past and present circumstances.

"Divorced women," observes Callie Richards, with good-humored cynicism, "have a unique opportunity to move through different classes of society. From the top down." Outside her cubicle office, in a Phoenix pediatric clinic, Chicano women, accompanied by infants and toddlers, sit patiently, enjoying the Muzak and air-conditioning. Carolyn Selden Richards has worked here since her divorce six years ago, moving from typist to administrative secretary. The center's flexible shifts make it possible for her to be a part-time student. At thirty-five, she is finally finishing the three years of college she missed by marrying at nineteen. Besides her job and classes at the university, Callie is also the mother and—for all practical purposes, she adds ironically—the "sole surviving parent" of three boys, now eleven, fourteen and sixteen. Although she can't even count the times she has been tempted "to pack it in" from sheer exhaustion, Callie knows the degree is essential, both to her ambition to become a health administrator and because she "desperately needs to earn more money."

Callie was lucky to get that starting job. Her only previous work experience was as part-time receptionist for a Cincinnati radio station, lasting the six months between dropping out of college and getting married. "Mary Tyler Moore, I

---

*The rise in joint custody and child-support awards in some states is too recent for reliable data on social and economic consequences.

definitely was not." The Richardses moved to Phoenix from Pittsburgh because two of the three boys had chronic asthmatic bronchitis and sixteen sieges of pneumonia between them. Jim Richards accompanied his family, but the marriage didn't survive the move.

A marketing executive, Jim Richards at thirty-four was "at the top of the heap, and I was very much a part of taking him there; the right dinner parties, the right women's lunches, the right charities...well, me and a million others," she reflects. But Jim's career somehow ground to a halt after the move, and "he could never forgive me, even though the kids' problems with breathing Pittsburgh air weren't exactly my fault." Although he is now a highly paid executive, he never made "that leap into the Young Presidents Club that was the next step." His bitterness about his career, his anger at Callie for relocating, and finally, Jim Richards's rapid remarriage, followed by two more children, are the answer to why, until recently, "he was just giving us pennies. Now it's down to nothing.

"It's not really hard for him to forget the kids exist, since he almost never sees them. Things got too uncomfortable. The boys would go there for the weekend, and there would be the contemporary adobe-style ranch house, the fancy modern furniture and the free-form swimming pool. Then it would be back to the four of us crammed into a tacky garden apartment—only with no garden."

Downward mobility is not a figure of speech for divorced women and their children. Twenty percent of *all* moves made by the five thousand Michigan families were in response to changes in marital status.[28] And all other researchers note that for women who are also custodial parents, a change in neighborhood or housing is usually for the worse.

In a study of sixty San Francisco area families during the five years following divorce, social psychologists Judith S. Wallerstein and Joan Belin Kelley noted that "moving to less expensive housing became the focus and symbol of increased financial hardship for many families."[29] With its particular interest in children, their study found that within eighteen months of divorce, more than a quarter of the youngsters had moved to more suitable, e.g., cheaper, housing. A number of the children had moved twice during this same period. Other researchers have probed further—relating a change in housing and neighborhood to poorer schools, lower educational achievement and higher incidence of juvenile delinquency.[30]

"When I took the kids and left," Julia Donnelly recalls, "we moved from one slum to another. Or if they weren't slums, they were 'temporaries,' like the studio of a photographer friend." Julia Donnelly's present apartment is tiny and bare. A scrap of plant-filled terrace extends the living room a few feet further into the smoldering city afternoon. The children—eighteen, twenty and twenty-two—are gone now. At forty-three, age and youth are blurred in Julia Donnelly. With her red-gold bouffant and cord Bermuda shorts, she is still Sacred Heart, Junior League and a shelf full of golf trophies. Except that Julia has been a working journalist since she was fourteen—"when my mother got me my first job, after school, with a local newspaper."

Married right after graduation from a California Catholic woman's college, Julia moved East with her husband, Harold. He enrolled in graduate school, and Julia started as a cub reporter on a New York City newspaper. From a long career as a graduate student, Harold, a psychologist, who never managed to get any degree, had moved from one quasi-volunteer, citizen's-action job to another. So Julia kept on working, moving to a woman's magazine when she was pregnant with her first child. For the fourteen years and three children of their marriage, Harold's parents had helped out minimally. But when she left with the three kids, there was no further help.

"We were in and out of Family Court for years," Julia recalls. "Arrears, nonpayment. They always said Hal had to pay something. But child-support laws have no teeth in them."

"I've just never had the money or time to pursue him through the courts," Callie Richards says. Even her typist's salary of $9,500 a year made her "too rich" for legal aid. "And compared to the women out there," she says, motioning toward the waiting room, "I *was* rich."

Callie Richards was, in fact, fortunate to find a job—any job, especially one that pointed her toward an eventual career. But luck is the most unreliable factor in the chance of an unskilled, inexperienced, recently divorced mother finding work.

To determine how women like Callie do manage, one Boston study followed thirty divorced mothers with at least one child under eighteen for five years following their separation. Although it was the women overwhelmingly who had left the marriages, an astounding fifteen of the thirty respondents reported that at the time of the divorce, "they had no concrete plans for how to support themselves." Only 16 percent of the husbands provided any financial support at all, while only 9 percent provided as much as 50 percent of the family income at any period following the divorce. Thus, the researchers report, for all of the women in the sample, representing a range from lower- to upper-middle-class families, "women's own work or welfare had to provide *immediate* substitutes." Also, the "new" earnings represented a decrease in average income of just over one-half. The eight highest-income families dropped 60 percent. As the Boston study's authors make clear, "the overall average obscures an important class difference. The higher they start, the further they fall."[31]

When she left her husband, the house, the social life, and the church disappeared even more dramatically from Elizabeth Perry's world. And for Liz, images of sinking and drowning are not poetic license.

Water pours through a piece of missing roof in the abandoned farmhouse that the landlord rents to her for "almost nothing." When her son Robbie—the only one of her five children to visit her (the others are away at school most of the year)—first saw his mother's new home, he was shocked. "Mom, a sharecropper wouldn't live in a place like this," he said.

Divorcing her husband, Rob, two years ago also meant

leaving "one of the loveliest Federal period houses ever built." But like many "grace and favor perks" that come with lower-paying, high-status jobs, there were hidden costs. "It was a three-servant house, but I was the only servant." The husband Liz left in the elegant white-columned house is an Episcopal bishop. "Rob is a remarkable man, utterly devout, but also an intellectual and a scholar." It was through him, after all, she explains, that "I really got into the social gospel," where her lifelong involvement began: "working with people who couldn't make it at all, the trash of this society. Even with five children, Rob's missionary work was always the totality of our lives."

Yet, seeping through the praise of her husband emerges a sense of vocation betrayed. The urbane bishop was no longer the young idealistic missionary she had married when they were both students and she shared his work (unpaid, of course, like all ministers' wives). In the community (an eastern sea-board city) the Episcopal bishop, Liz notes, is automatically a member of the elite ruling class, and of course, there is a definite role carved out for his wife. "Unfortunately, it was not one I felt very comfortable in, and although I didn't show it, I think I was very angry inside because this was the headiest period of the civil rights and women's movements, both of which I was heavily involved in and neither of which meshed very well with my other 'job.'"

It shocked her, Liz admits, to realize how quickly "Rob took to the country-club part of the role right away. He had a natural bent for high life. He's tall, he's handsome and he's a snob. In the old days I was the 'people content' of his very austere, very devout ministry. I never imagined that the 'reward' for our collaboration would be debutante balls and country-club luncheons."

Her husband has "not given her a penny" since their separation. Not that he has much to give. But when her first paid job, as director of social services for a senior-citizen residence, dissolved, Liz found that she couldn't live on unemployment checks. "I learned what it was like to go in and ask for food stamps. That experience really changes you." It was a terrible period because of the double guilt: "leaving my family and jeopardizing their social position (it's that kind of city). And then being on public assistance. Both 'unthinkable' in the way I was brought up. Not when you were the winner of the D.A.R. Award in high school!"

With her new job, counseling parents with a record of child abuse, she can "just support herself with no frills or extras. I don't feel I have any social position now, and it's very liberating. I don't have to 'live up' to social peers, do any role playing, not talk about the 'wrong' subjects."

When you're suddenly poor but still have rich friends, you've just added to your problems, says Mimi Elias, reflecting on a long period of her life. "It's so awful. I still get anxiety attacks talking about it."

An alumna of an eastern women's college, with a graduate degree in psychology, Mimi married after "the usual one-year job." And for twelve years she and her husband George had an "ideal suburban marriage. We had a beautiful house, and a marvelously interesting group of friends—doctors, educators, museum curators as well as executives like George. The same ten couples," Mimi recalls, "saw each other every Saturday night. *Every Saturday night.*"

Mimi left her husband when his mental illness recurred, triggered, she thinks, by his having to take over the large family business when his brother died. "He would be institutionalized and start improving, then once back home he would become violent again." With two young children, the situation became "unmanageable." Because of her sense of guilt, it wasn't hard for her in-laws to persuade her against going to Reno in favor of a divorce in their state, which just happened not to have alimony or child-support requirements. "They" would take care of us, she says bitterly. They didn't.

Moving to New York City with her two daughters in the early 1950s, she found a job in a social-work agency at seventy-five dollars a week. "The first order of business was to support my family, so we could move out of my mother's apartment, where the three of us were living in one room. People were terribly nice to me. I never experienced that 'fifth wheel' attitude toward an extra woman." She does not deny that the beauty and style which helped her to "pick up the odd modeling job" made her a more than usually welcome guest.

While Mimi did the dreary rounds of "twenty-seven employment agencies," her affluent friends, lawyers and psychoanalysts, "who helped get the kids scholarships to private schools, advised, 'You're a social worker, a professional! You wouldn't be happy with just *any* job.' When you make lots of money in a high-status profession," says Mimi, "you can't understand that some people have to work *just* to earn a living." Being the "poor friend," like the "poor relation," becomes a role you adapt to, but there are new scripts and stage directions to be learned.

On a visit to a friend's weekend house in Connecticut, Mimi arrived in a 1940 Plymouth a cousin had sold to her for a dollar. Her hosts were horrified that the car had no rearview mirror. "I explained that I just couldn't afford that 'extra': it would have meant digging into food or rent money. It was an awkward moment... for them to have to confront the realities of my life." They insisted on giving her one "as a present." Gratitude and resentment still overlap at the edges of her voice.

Relations with her older daughter, then twelve, had "started to deteriorate badly"—a state Mimi describes as brought about "by my own tensions, the constant money worries, and less time for Katey, when she needed it most—the beginning of adolescence." All of which, Mimi insists, was exacerbated by Katey's father, now in a period of remission, who wanted his daughters back. "He played on her discontents and feelings of privation—all of which were real enough. We lived in a three-room apartment in a middle-income housing project meant for 'young families on their way up,' except that we were a family on the way down." The girls had the only bedroom, and Mimi slept in the living room; so it was never easy for Katey to have friends visit her. Then at her progressive school, she would be faced with questions by the other girls: "why do you always wear the same shoes every day? ... that kind of thing."

When Katey decided to live with her father it "seemed the best arrangement under the circumstances." By this time, Mimi had managed to "parlay all those psych courses" into market research, but "I kept changing jobs all the time for even a couple of dollars more a week. That was a lot of strain.

"There was no money at all for household help. Ten-year-old Janet did all the ironing, most of the cooking, and a lot of consoling." When Mimi came home one day, crushed at having been turned down for a job as research director of an advertising agency—one, because she was a woman; and two, because at forty-one, her spy told her, she was "too old"—Janet was in the kitchen making dinner. "I could see from her body movements that she was getting angrier and angrier as she heard the details of the day's miseries. Her movements became more and more abrupt as she moved from stove to refrigerator. Finally, she wheeled around angrily and burst out: 'Mom, what would I do with a ten-year-old male mother, anyway?'"

Janet always had feelings of great pressure. She "was always aware of a stack of unpaid bills, and that we lived completely from hand to mouth." At one point Mimi was out of work for six months and they were living on unemployment insurance. "We had seven dollars left... literally. I went out and bought a steak and wine, lit candles and I said: 'Janet, we're having a celebration tonight.'

"And Janet replied: 'Yes, Ma, I know. The end of the money!'"

Researchers Judith S. Wallerstein and Joan Belin Kelley noted that by the end of the fifth year of divorce the "downward slide of the wives seems to have stabilized."[32]

But the woman you read about in *Savvy*, the magazine for the executive woman, *Cosmopolitan* or *Working Woman*, forced or liberated into the work place by divorce, moving (under the goad of necessity) either from sandbox or secretarial pool drone to Executive Suite, is not even a statistical twitch. Her real-life counterpart will be slogging away, working by day, doing housework, or homework (to increase her earning power), after hours.

THE "BOUNCE-BACK" PHENOMENON?

The few exceptions among the women in the California Children of Divorce Project and in all other samples, are those wives who remarry.

Indeed, it is a measure of both the low-paying nature of most women's work—and the lack or dwindling of child support—that downward mobility for divorced women is only reversed by the income contribution of a new spouse.*

The "Cinderella Complex," the need for dependency and hope of rescue, as discovered by Colette Dowling,[34] may indeed prevent a few highly talented women from aiming for and attaining high rewards. But most middle-class divorced Cinderellas with children, unless rescued by Prince Affluent, can expect a drop in class and status for themselves and their families. Here, demographics—if not inescapable destiny— are a determining factor in who stays poorer and single, and who remarries and "bounces back."

The census confirms that age before beauty does not apply to remarriage. Of divorced women in their twenties, 76 percent will remarry. For those in their thirties, the figure has dropped to 56 percent. The remarriage rate of those in their forties shrinks to 32 percent. And at fifty and beyond, fewer than 12 percent will marry again.

Children are less of a barrier to remarriage than age. A childless divorced woman has a 72 percent chance of remarrying. With two children, the odds decrease to 63 percent. With three, they diminish to 56 percent. But a woman in her twenties with three children has a better chance (72 percent)

*Many of whom, notes child-support analyst Judith Cassetty, assume the support of their "new" family, and most of whom do so through lack of choice.[33]

of remarriage than a childless woman in her thirties (60 percent).[35]

In an essay that elicited powerful reader emotion and a flood of mail, *New York Times* columnist John Leonard described a dinner party he had given to honor a famous visiting writer, recently divorced and moaning about his loneliness. The idea of the dinner party, relates the disillusioned host, was to introduce the Lonely Literary Lion to "several intelligent and charming women who happen, at the moment, to be unattached." These "adult women," old enough to have voted for JFK and to also remember Adlai Stevenson, as Leonard lovingly describes them, have "callouses on their experience, and children whom they ring to say goodnight, removing an earring before cradling the receiver between their shoulder and chin."

But Formerly Lonely Famous Writer has already been consoled. He arrives with a sex kitten twenty-five years his junior clinging to his arm. What, John Leonard wonders, "will happen to my friends" sitting in his living room, "competent, complicated and lonely."[36] They will, he concludes, stay that way, or have affairs with married men. Still, if these women did not do credit to their host with their careers in "law and science and teaching and journalism," they would not only be lonely, they would also be POOR.

Movies about divorced women have managed to clothe a hard message about class in the soft wrapping of romance. Bouncing back requires a Prosperous Prince Charming.

It takes a rich rancher (Kris Kristofferson) or a hugely successful painter (whose Soho loft is only slightly smaller than the Astrodome and features Persian carpets!) to liberate Alice from her diner (*Alice Doesn't Live Here Anymore*) and Jill Clayburgh from a part-time job tapping the Selectric in an art gallery (*An Unmarried Woman*). (Since her husband-the-executive is the one who left, he is both guilty and prosperous enough to keep paying the maintenance on her glamorous digs.) Just to play it safe, both the waitress and the well-off matron have only one child. As does the out-of-work divorced actress (Marsha Mason) in *The Good-Bye Girl*, renting a room to Mr. Wrong (Richard Dreyfuss) in order to help make ends meet.

In *Starting Over*, Jill Clayburgh—childless this time—is a divorced kindergarten teacher (another "female ghetto" job) whose one-room apartment is furnished in Early Nursery School. When recently divorced boyfriend (Burt Reynolds) has an anxiety attack, it takes place in Bloomingdale's, where, despite a modest job teaching in an adult extension program, he is buying furniture for his spacious new digs. Still more revealing—and painful—is the brief vignette of a nervously ingratiating divorced mother who does *not* get Burt Reynolds and his new Bloomie furnishings. She is crammed into a tiny apartment with two unhappy and diabolical youngsters. Consummate in the art of sabotaging Mom's Big Date, they are unaware that they conspire against their own life chances.

Mobility—up and down—is a process, the economic and social history of an individual or a family. Some changes connected with this process can be measured almost as soon as they occur, such as a sudden shift in income, or housing. The day a woman walks into that first job necessitated by the last day of marriage is a specific calendar day. Other changes—values, attitudes, expectations for ourselves and our children—are like the growth of children themselves. They are the human analogy of geophysical shifts; like the erosion of dunes, "slip slidin' away," in the words of Paul Simon. Suddenly, we turn around and the kids have grown. We look middle aged to ourselves. Without our realizing it we have lost or relinquished certain values, certain "notions of the desirable" appropriate to another way of life and social class.

The "downward slide" of many women following divorce does eventually stabilize. Some, like Callie Richards, will triumph over punishing schedules—work, study, child care—and real privation, living on "beans and bottle returns" to emerge with modest "professional" jobs. But something has changed. "My middle-class aspirations for my kids have gone out the window," she declares. Along with the music lessons, the private school blazers, and their father's Princeton Phys. Ed. Dept. sweatshirts. All of "that" went in the face of an "unmovable reality, lack of money. I just can't provide for my kids anymore in the way I would like to, the way I was raised or the way they lived before.

"If they get to college at all," their mother insists, "it will be the state university, through their own efforts. But it sure won't be Princeton or Harvard!"*

Jim Richards's lack of interest in his sons' academic future—reinforced by his diminished contact with them and the competing demands of his new family—is far from exceptional. Researchers working with the Michigan Panel Survey's sample of divorced families noted that, regardless of economic circumstances, "many husbands would no longer express plans for their children's education."[37] Withdrawal of paternal interest, as family-services advocate Alvin Schorr has pointed out, means that children have access to fewer adults (including father's friends and colleagues), with the result that kids of divorced parents depend more on other kids—on "peer culture"—for their cues about goals and values.[39] It is the mother who lives with the competing demands of parent, provider, housekeeper, and the cruel irony that by her very efforts to improve her family's circumstances, she deprives them of irreplaceable attention and time.

"I feel uneasy," Julia Donnelly says, "and just plain guilty about the time I didn't have for the kids because I had to work to support them." Julia's son Brian, twenty, moves in and out a lot. After "lots of problems" he graduated from a local community college and is now an office worker at his mother's magazine. His dream is a job in the library of the Museum of Natural History. "It seems like a pretty low dream

---

*At least one study found evidence that college admissions discriminated against children of divorced parents. But as the divorce rate has climbed steadily in the twelve years since that research, incoming classes of even the most select schools could probably no longer be filled by children of intact families.[38]

to me, but I hope he gets it." Daughter Kathleen, now twenty-two, dropped out of an assortment of parochial schools. Finally, she was induced to stay until she got a diploma at a "progressive dropout academy," which never did manage to teach her to read or write too well. She lives with a man, and "every now and then she will string some beads together and take them around to a boutique." Julia often worries about Kathleen's inability to support herself.

"I think my working so hard was very bad for her, that she felt, seeing me—always needing the overtime or bringing home extra free-lance assignments—'Boy, I'm never going to do this.' So she made sure to find a guy to take care of her. So much for those professional-women-as-role-models that girls are supposed to need," Julia says drily. Only Ian, the oldest, seems to be "doing fine." Always focused, he knew from the time he saw his first cartoon that he wanted to be in film animation. "From his special high school for gifted kids, he just got himself into the best art school for what he wanted. I had nothing to do with it."

Her own diminished expectations, though, are the bitter core of Julia's self-reproach: the overwork, her lack of time for the kids, even the "terrible" schools were, she recognizes, beyond her control. "I wasn't working for fun, after all. Expensive private schools or a better neighborhood was just out of the question." By the time she had to support the four of them herself, Julia acknowledges, "my 'aspirations' for them—and me—were, I hope we get through the week! And when they were in high school, when they most needed some sense of future, it was the worst period for me, financially. So I just accepted their expectations for themselves, instead of giving them any, the way my parents had done for me. Because just getting through was the big thing."

Economists David Greenberg and Douglas Wolf of the Urban Institute have explored the effects of marital disruption upon the labor-market productivity of children.[40] Using the Michigan Panel Survey's families as well as other studies, they analyzed such readily available "numbers" as parental resources of time and money (how much of each mothers could "invest" in their children) along with subsequent earning levels of those children as young adults. Their conclusions confirmed every harried single working mother's fears: for white males, both labor-force participation and wage levels appear to be lower in one-parent families, with mother's income *and* "home time" together the "most statistically positive influence on future earnings."*

To further complicate matters, the California Children of Divorce Project found, among its sixty participant families, gender differences in terms of children's needs and mothers' conflicting obligations. Daughters' educational achievement was apparently more affected by their mothers' economic uncertainties. Young boys suffered more from diminished maternal presence.[41]

Mimi Elias doesn't need econometric models to compare the earnings and occupations of her two daughters. The oldest, Katey, who went to live with her father, benefited, her mother says, not just from a very expensive education, or even her own intense ambition and hard work, but also from her father's frustrated desire to be a doctor. Katey is a psychiatrist on the staff of a New England hospital and also has her own thriving practice. "The kind of life Janet is living now, she would never have led without a lot of early privation." A nursery schoolteacher in rural western Canada, she has always saved half of the tiny salary she earns—which never exceeds $10,000 a year. From the time she enrolled in a midwestern college on scholarship, Janet kept heading further west, to ever more remote rural settings. "I think she was always looking for a place," her mother reflects, "where money and success mattered least, and where you suffer least from not having them."

---

*As economists, not family therapists, Greenberg and Wolf can't counsel single working mothers about how to choose between these "inputs." Their policy recommendation, however, is in the direction of eliminating the "work less/earn less" bind: an income-maintenance program to compensate the custodial parent for the loss in family income after divorce, thereby insuring against less productive (male) adults.

Divorce is a classic case of conflict of interest.

Closest to home, there is the basic conflict between husband and wife that ends the marriage. But once we move to the larger social picture, marital breakup places two opposing values, two "notions of the desirable" in head-on collision.

On the one hand, there is the Moral Imperative to Personal Growth. For whether we submit to being called a "culture of narcissism" or a "me generation," the shape of our national character has changed in the direction of an enhanced sense of self, as in self-development and self-realization. Which means that personal growth, our perceived "right" to ample sex, sharing and even "space" has legitimized leaving marriages that fail to provide partners with most of the above.

Free to be you and me has placed impossible strains on the remaining us.

In a therapeutic society, improved health and well-being justifies most other choices. Where desertion, violence and flagrant adultery were once the only causes serious enough to warrant divorce, now healthy change, unhealthy failure to communicate, or simply outgrowing one another are justifications for splitting. Destructive marriages, child psychologists now tell us, are more harmful to the young than creative divorce. So "staying together for the sake of the children" is thrown into the junkheap of quaint phrases from a primitive past.

Even more solidly entrenched in our culture (because its been around longer) is the Moral Imperative to Upward Mobility. Every choice we make is supposed to find us at least a rung higher on the ladder of success, as defined by wealth, status or prestige.

It is not only the mayor of America's largest city who asks voters, "How am I doing?" We all measure ourselves against our "peers"—in office or playground, assembly line or dinner party—to gauge the distance we've traveled. Anything less than a long way, baby, is not far enough. Anyone who doubts this has never been to a high school or college reunion. As Americans, we judge ourselves and each other by how well we make use of opportunity.

Most Americans, including the record-breaking 1.18 million of us who divorced in 1980, probably believe that social supports—especially where children are concerned—should be blind to distinctions between choice and chance. But many other Americans—whether they constitute a moral majority or a highly vocal minority—emphatically do not. And they raise a valid philosophical point.

Dissolving a marriage, like getting married, is still a discretionary act. The question remains: Who should pay for its costs and consequences? At present it is clear who does.

Whether "she" throws the bastard out, or "he" decides to start over with his secretary, or the decision to split is mutual, the economic and social consequences spell downward mobility for ex-wives and children.

"My biggest fear," said one woman, "is that I might remarry out of financial need, because I just can't make it. Isn't that crazy? From choosing marriage, to choosing divorce, to having no choice at all?"

THE GREAT
FERTILITY
DIVIDE

CHAPTER
SEVEN

PARENTS
ARE POORER

"I was fifteen when I got pregnant, sixteen when I had my first baby, back in 1953. I guess that would be considered pretty mature now. But that just shows you how bad things have gotten."

Marian Sims lives in a ranch-style house in a small, mostly black suburb outside Washington, D.C. Grouped loosely in a large circle, all the homes in the hilly wooded area have ample, well-tended yards. But the Simses—Marian and her second husband, a retired Navy cook—enjoy the most picturesque location (because they were the first to buy there). From the picture window in the basement "family room" they look down to a stream below.

Marian and the seventeen-year-old boy who was the father of her child did what most kids, especially poor kids, used to do. They both dropped out of school in the 10th grade and got married. "My father was so upset." Pain still sounds in Marian's voice, twenty-five years later. "Dad was a steel-worker and he'd never had the chance to finish high school, because when he was coming up, it was the Depression. We were always very close. He was so proud of my getting good grades and being on the student council. When he found out I was pregnant, he said: 'You had so much promise.' That really killed me. When he put it in the past tense." He was right. Like the eight out of ten young women who bear children in their teenage years, Marian would never finish high school.[1] Her promise seemed to be fading fast.

GETTING PREGNANT:
STAYING POOR:
GETTING POORER

For all races, nearly six out of ten women who give birth at age sixteen or younger achieve eight or fewer years of formal education. One out of eight finish high school. Fewer than two in one hundred go on to further schooling. And of these girls many, if not most, qualify as functional illiterates.[2]

Moving the age up two years brightens the picture only slightly. Twenty percent of women who bear a child before the age of eighteen have completed high school, while those who wait two more years have a five times greater chance of obtaining that first crucial credential. Even during the Baby Boom, that frenzy of fertility among America's middle class, the reproduction among women with some college education during the 1950–1970 period was well below that of women who did not complete high school. Of all factors together (including family income, education and occupation of father), *age at first birth* is the strongest influence on educational attainment of women.[3]

Education has been steadily moving up, gaining on "inherited advantages" as a lever upward, especially for women.* Every year less of schooling diminishes the prospects for economic independence. So direct is the link between education and earnings that, as one researcher notes, "women who begin childbearing in their teens have (almost irreparably) disturbed

*A 1982 survey, *Does College Pay?*, found, in tracking the high school graduating classes of 1972, that the answer was "Yes" for young women, but "Not Yet" for their male classmates. Wage rates of women college graduates quickly catch up to and overtake those of their classmates who did not attend college. In contrast, it takes eight years for male college graduates to earn more than their peers with only a high school diploma.

the process by which one achieves success in the market place."[4]

EARLY MOTHERHOOD:
ROADBLOCK TO MOBILITY

By shutting off access to better jobs, early loss of schooling becomes a permanent liability. Young mothers never catch up with their later-child-bearing peers. If anything, their "relative position" (the basis of class) declines. As those childless young women in the 18–24 child-bearing cohort acquire more years of schooling (thereby adding to *their* "human capital"), the gap widens between them and their contemporaries. Through its effect on schooling, notes Urban Institute economist Kristin Moore, an early birth "reduces the occupational status, hourly wages and annual earnings of working women."[5] And no matter how many years she may work, the teenage mother, white and nonwhite, never catches up in earnings to her later-bearing peers.[6]

GIRLS WHO DO…
AND DON'T:
HOW DO THEY DIFFER?

Which comes first, a "predisposition" to drop out or getting pregnant? Some researchers have found that those less likely to succeed anyway, are probably more prone to get pregnant and to become mothers.[7] However, a more recent study of a New York City sample of girls with nearly identical socioeconomic backgrounds concluded that the aspirations—and more significantly, the abilities—of the pregnant dropouts scarcely differ from their more chaste, or careful, classmates.[8]

Less than a year after her son was born, Marian Sims found herself back in the same hospital giving birth to her second child, a daughter. She had just turned seventeen.

"I had two babies in ten months. I knew somewhere within me that this wasn't what I wanted—a house full of children. There was something more I wanted to do. I didn't

—161—

know exactly what it was. I knew one thing, though. I wasn't going anywhere with a houseful of kids. I tried to tell this to the white nurse. I begged her: What do I do not to have any more children? She just smiled and said: 'We'll see you next year, honey.'"

She did. For Marian's third and last child. That Alida was her mother's final pregnancy and birth was due only to chance. When the five of them could no longer squeeze into her in-laws' tiny apartment, Marian and her family finally qualified for public housing.

"I was desperate with the fear of getting pregnant again," she remembers. "The last time I had tried quinine, lifting heavy furniture—everything. All that happened was that I was sick as a dog—too sick to do the housework or take care of the kids. Now I was ready to try anything—a tubal— anything. But I couldn't even get information about it.

"Right after we moved into the project, a neighbor just casually asked me if I'd seen that lady who came around talking to people about not having children. 'Oh God,' I said, 'who is she?' They didn't take her name, they didn't do anything, and this is what I'd been waiting for."

SOONER MEANS MORE

A racist nurse withheld from Marian Sims the right to stop having children. Other barriers, however, seem to discourage early starters from stopping at one or two. Psychological obstacles to returning to school combine with circumstantial ones—like inadequate child-care facilities. In fatherless households, welfare benefits increase with each child. An unschooled, unskilled young woman will learn that it is nearly impossible to find work that represents an "improvement" over public assistance.

The Urban Institute combined two national surveys, one tracking the labor-market experience of young women, the other a study of five thousand households over a ten-year period. Their study found that among this large population of mothers aged thirty-five to fifty-two, those who were fifteen or younger at the birth of their first child had an average of three children *more* than women who were at least twenty-four when their first child was born. And those who had their first child at age seventeen or younger had an average of more than five![9]

A decade after Marian Sims was refused contraceptive information, a family-planning clinic in a black Baltimore neighborhood noted gloomily the results of a follow-up study of young mothers who had received contraceptive information and counseling after a first unintended birth at age eighteen or younger. Nearly one in four became pregnant again within twelve months of the birth of the first child. By three years, half of the women with two children had become pregnant a third time.[10]

Slender and boyish, with a luxuriant Afro, Renée Pinckney wears her urban guerrilla garb with just the right air of humor. Her camouflage jacket may suggest jungle warfare, but her machine-gun rapid speech is all New York. She is the first to tell you how old thirty-one can be.

"I have been . . . *through* . . . *it all*. Sometimes I feel more like *eighty*-one." Then she grins, looking suddenly closer to eleven, the age of her youngest and third child. "I didn't want to drop out of school. I didn't want to marry Robbie. I didn't want that first baby—and I sure didn't want two more. But somehow, I did all of those things." And interwoven with "all of those things," that started with getting pregnant and dropping out of school six months before graduation, is the obstacle course that described Renée's life for thirteen years: separation from her young husband, drugs, hustling, prison. The life, in brief, of a dealer/addict who also happens to be a woman.

Demographer Arthur Campbell could have been thinking of Renée when he described a sixteen-year-old mother, especially a black sixteen-year-old mother, as someone who "suddenly has 90 percent of her life script written for her. She will probably drop out of school. She will probably not be able to find a steady job that pays enough to provide for herself and her child. She may feel impelled to marry someone she might not otherwise have chosen. *Her life choices are few and most of them are bad.*"[11]

Seven months after the birth of her first child, Renée was pregnant again. She celebrated her eighteenth birthday by having her second baby. "I had really had it with those ridiculous jobs that paid fifty-five dollars a week." She had tried contraceptives, but somehow they weren't "effective." And even though she had certainly not intended to have a second child, or even to stay with Robbie, "it just wasn't about abortion. I don't know why. But it just wasn't." Renée was atypical in her efforts, however unsuccessful, to use contraceptives at all. Twenty-seven percent of the nation's estimated 12 million sexually active teenagers[12] and nearly two-thirds of unwed teenage women practice no contraception whatsoever; young black women are one and one-half times less likely than whites in this age group to use birth control.[13]* More characteristic is Renée's attitude about abortion. Although the abortion rate for black women over twenty-five and under fourteen is two-thirds higher than their white counterparts,[15] 94 percent of black teenagers elect to keep their babies.[16]

When her daughter, Andrea, was born, Renée moved out of her mother's house, into an apartment of her own, and onto the welfare rolls. "Did I tell you my mother was a college graduate? And here I am on welfare!"

For a while, Robbie lived with his young family. "Until he got busted," charged with assault with a deadly weapon. "That was nothing compared to what he could have gone up for. That boy was all potential. But he just couldn't seem to do anything with it. Lots of people tried to help him. He couldn't deal with responsibility. Not for himself. And not for us."

Even if Robbie hadn't spent most of his brief married

---

*A 1981 New York City study of young welfare mothers found that two-thirds of the black and Hispanic women interviewed reported "negative attitudes" concerning contraception. Only one out of ten used any form of birth control before a first child was born.[14]

life in jail, the prospects of the Pinckneys staying together as a family were, by every measure, dim. A teenage husband of any race has been described as the weakest link in the chance for an early marriage to become a stable union.[17]

The likelihood of a young father under eighteen dropping out of school is two-fifths greater, meaning that his "human capital"—education and "hands-on" job experience—will be smaller than his later marrying and fathering peers. In his efforts to act as provider for his family, he may be forced to stay with the least desirable, and lowest paying jobs *if* he wants to stay employed at all. Thus, he is likely to become still more "disadvantaged," more vulnerable to taking off or branching out into crime.

With her marriage ended, two young children (joined by a third child twenty months later), Renée's welfare status was all but guaranteed:[18] no high school diploma or job-related skills and a sporadic employment record. Because of their mother's drug addiction, Renée's three children spent six years with their grandfather, a worker in a New Jersey paper mill. "Pops wasn't much of a father, but he sure was some 'gran,'" his daughter notes gratefully. "While I was in and out of every detox program in the city, he kept the whole family together for me. Not one of my kids ever spent time in foster care." Nevertheless, Renée acknowledges that Andrea, Robin and Spence have "a lot of problems—especially with school." She worries even more about the girls. "They were into sex real early, earlier than I ever was. I keep trying to tell them: 'Don't get knocked up. Stay in school. Look how hard it's been for me—for all of us.'" But she isn't sure the message is getting through.

UNDERAGE MOTHERS: UNDERCLASS CHILDREN

Wanted or unwanted, children born to very young parents do worse, in every way.

A Johns Hopkins Child Development Study tracked 525 children born to girls who were sixteen years or under at the time of giving birth. Accidents and child abuse were "over-represented in the study population." At age four, 11 percent of the children scored 70 or below on I.Q. tests, compared to only 2.6 percent of the general population of four-year-olds. While approximately one-quarter of all four-year-olds will demonstrate an I.Q. of 110 and above, only 5 percent of children born of very young mothers will score that high. Dr. Janet Hardy, author of the study, underscored the greater prevalence of school failure and behavior problems among the group studied.[19] Renée Pinckney's worries about her kids are all too justified.

WEDLOCK (IN AND OUT), WELFARE (ON AND OFF), AND CLASS

In 1980, half the black infants in America were out-of-wedlock births, nearly one-third of them to mothers under eighteen.[20] These figures are usually cited in dismay. Yet the high mortality rate of teenage marriages generally, along with the greater likelihood of marital breakup among black families, suggests that for young black mothers, particularly, starting out married is no leg up the socioeconomic scale.

A young mother 14 to 25 who is also a "single head of household" is seven times as likely to be poor—whether she begins her maternal career wed or unwed. As a New York City study confirmed, teenage pregnancies are "the primary precipitating factor leading economically marginal women"[21] to seek public assistance.* The legitimate/illegitimate issue is more moral than material.

STAYING HOME AND MOVING UP

Much more startling is the dramatic improvement in life chances for the unmarried teenage mother *if* she continues

---

*72 percent of white and 89 percent of black teenage marriages dissolve.

to live with her own family.[22] Dr. Frank Furstenberg, University of Pennsylvania sociologist, and his co-researchers followed a group of mostly black, pregnant adolescent girls for five years, beginning with their first prenatal visit to a Baltimore clinic. The young mothers who continued to live with their parents were far likelier to return to school, graduate, land decent jobs and avoid welfare dependency than those young women who struck out on their own—with or without a mate.* *Parental* assistance—financial (where possible), psychological, and child care—is far more crucial than *public* assistance in overcoming the social and economic handicaps imposed by adolescent childbearing.

The results of the study contradict the present family planning/counseling emphasis on the young mother as an independent parent. Instead, argue the authors, aid should be channeled to "those families willing to help their young daughter to advance her educational and occupational prospects." Welfare policy, they conclude, has tended to push these very young women into premature independence and permanent poverty.

Due to the crippling arthritis that kept her from working regularly, Renée Pinckney's mother never managed to convert her college degree into an "inherited advantage" for her daughter.** But if Renée had stayed with her, she might not have had two more kids. "At least, I wouldn't have ended up in the East Village, alone, with the scuzz of the earth. I dream about my Momma all the time," Renée says. Her mother has been dead for eight years. In her dreams, they talk intimately about Renee's life and the "grans." "I wish she could see me in my digital computer class, showing off, talking about 'analogs.' It took half my life to get to where she wanted so bad for me to be."

Ellin MacKenzie, welfare rights activist and family-plan-

---

*This held true even though one out of four of the families was on public assistance.

**For the first time, in the late 1960s, note Blau and Duncan in the revised edition of their classic *The American Occupational Structure* (New York: John Wiley, 1967), blacks were able to pass on "inherited advantages" like education to their children.

ning administrator in a New England city, often feels "schiz-ophrenic. Last month I lobbied at the state capital for raising welfare benefits. Today, I'm confronted by one result of our efforts to help teenage girls become better parents of healthier babies. There are more babies and younger mothers every year."

Ellin charts the inexorable process, starting with "peer approval" of getting pregnant. Then the health services in her city see to it that the pregnant girl receives "the best of every-thing. We encourage these kids to have babies by providing them with more special attention than they've ever seen be-fore in their lives. Starting with a special school, special smaller classes, special counselors for health and nutrition teach her how to shop for the baby. For the first time in most of these kids' lives, they're treated as 'a unique person.'" But these girls are being cheated, Ellin believes, "because no effort is made to show them the long-range, negative effects of being a parent at this age. They don't realize that other choices— more schooling, decent jobs—will be closed off to them."

As soon as the mother turns eighteen, like Renée Pinck-ney, she becomes eligible for her own welfare grant and apart-ment. This is how the ghetto adolescent escapes the constraints of family. "It's the poor kid's equivalent of going away to college." A separate household is official recognition of ma-ternity as a rite of passage to adulthood. The young mother's own residence as the final reward, presents a dead-end life on welfare as an attractive choice. To Ellin MacKenzie's clients, "an apartment of your own where your boyfriend can visit anytime," feels less "impoverishing" than the hassles of home. "We're working against ourselves," Ellin says wearily. "We punish these kids for being born poor. Then because we're 'humane,' we reward them for staying that way."

WHAT ARE TEENAGE
PARENTS CHOOSING?

Sex, first of all. At first glance—or even second—it appears, paradoxically, that the availability of birth control information, and the legality of abortions, has paralleled an explosion of younger teenagers conceiving, having and keeping babies. The increase in these pregnancies is explained by the increase of sexual activity among teenagers—and consistently younger ones. By 1981, an estimated 50 percent, or 12 million, of the nation's thirteen-to-nineteen year olds were found to be sexually active—double the number in 1971.[23]

CHOOSING NOT TO CHOOSE

Estimates vary widely as to how many sexually active teenagers use contraceptives: always, sometimes or never. The Alan Guttmacher Institute maintains that only 27 percent use no form of birth control. Yet they also acknowledge that use of the "more effective methods" has actually declined by 8 percent in the past part of the decade.[24] Explanations given for nonuse varied, ranging from the sporadic nature of sexual encounters, to the reluctance on the part of many girls to confront themselves as someone "planning on sex," to teen folk wisdom that it "couldn't happen the first," second or tenth time.[25]

Researchers Kanter and Zelnick conclude they don't really know why so many adolescents continue to choose to do nothing to prevent unwanted children.

BUT ALSO CHOOSING
TO HAVE BABIES...

Despite the evidence that abortion and contraception have meant a *million fewer unwanted children* born to high risk sexually active teenagers, the 1.1 million live births to young women under nineteen—now less inclined, like the rest of America, to marry—indicates some choice.

One Massachusetts health educator noted that in 1977, 65 percent of her program's clients were keeping their babies, compared to the 95 percent who opted for adoption in the 1950s. Now she reports her sixteen-year-olds, mostly lower-income clients, are often "delighted" to discover that they are pregnant.[26] Nor is this relatively new phenomenon of "delight" confined to the nonwhite urban poor. One visitor to an upstate rural New York high school observed that halftime at football games is also the time for the ritual display of new babies, born to 9th, 10th and 11th grade mothers. Squeals of "Let *me* hold him" in the stands accompanied the more traditional "Do-I-Hear-a-B" from cheerleader classmates on the field.

A family planning speaker, invited to organize a "rap" session with high school students in a small Arizona town was more overwhelmed by the boredom than by the soaring birth rate among the local fifteen-year-olds. One hundred miles from everywhere but a nearby army base, he found it hard to make a case for contraception when the gamble "If-you-do-it-are-you-going-to-get-pregnant" is the only excitement in town.

"There's just nothing else for kids to do—or look ahead to doing. The boys all join the army. Girls can look forward to working in the five-and-ten, or the local diner." It takes an enormous and sustained effort of the imagination to envision a life beyond Vista Verde. Beyond Vista Verde, or southwest Washington, there's "something more" you have to want, in the absence of any available reality.

IT REALLY MEANT SOMETHING
TO GIVE TIME

Marian Sims spread the word about birth control through Washington's black neighborhoods. Alone at first, she begged for the use of recreation rooms in the 'projects' to demonstrate. "I would go anywhere in the District where there were young mothers. In those days you had to be married and already have children to attend birth control classes without breaking the law." A little later, she was joined by three neighbors, "all of us with a couple of kids, so it really meant something to us to give some time." By then, they had established a small community clinic. Evenings when one or two of them were on duty, the others baby sat.

It had to mean something to Marian to give up her time.

She was working a split shift in a dry cleaner—a single mother with three kids, "barely making it. The split shift meant I had to come all the way back home on the bus, check on the kids, turn right around and go back to work—at 4 in the afternoon! I got paid forty-five dollars a week. There were no food stamps then. Plenty of times when there wasn't enough to eat— neighbors fed the children. The grandest group of people, and we're all still close."

After five years as a volunteer, Marian was offered "a real job" with a family-planning organization. "God, was I proud! Then I remembered. I didn't have a dress to wear. Debbie's soles were flapping from her shoes. It was one of those agonizing decisions. She needed the shoes and I needed the dress. I decided the dress was essential for me to go to work and support the kids. So that's what I bought. But it was a terrible choice to have to make. I just don't think things are as hard today."

The kids Marian used to counsel have turned into street smart, savvy, self-assured young adults. They have all the answers and none. Poor and black, they are Marian at six-teen—and total strangers. She is mystified by the connections they don't make between where they are and where they want to be. She doesn't want to sound self-righteous. But, when she *was* their age, it seems to her now, there were fewer possibilities and prospects, less knowledge and heavier burdens. For one thing, "there isn't the racism—not like it used to be," Marian remembers.

Her daughter is a sales clerk in the home furnishings department of the city's most stylish department store. When she first moved here, Marian insists, you wouldn't have seen blacks buying or selling in that store. "And when I walk into government offices, I'm still surprised by who is at those desks!

"When I would talk to these girls at the clinic, I'd say: 'O.K. You're pregnant. What's going to happen tomorrow? What are you going to do when the baby gets here?'

"'Oh,' they'd tell me, 'Momma's going to help me,' or 'my boyfriend is going to help,' or 'I can get on welfare.' This is really all they know, especially if they live in a welfare family.

"I remember talking to a seventeen-year-old girl who was a high school senior. I reminded her that she would be graduating in June. 'Are you really going to drop out of school *now*?' I asked her. 'Think about it,' I begged her. 'At least finish school.'

"But she couldn't see it that way. She did not want an abortion. Her boyfriend had some little job after school, making fifty or sixty dollars a week. She figured they wouldn't need more than that. Then, of course, Momma would help. That really incensed me! 'Do you think that's what your Momma wants to do,' I asked her, 'after she raised you and your brothers and sisters? Is that what she should be doing? Are you looking at what *you're* going to do, what role you're going to play? The freedom you're not going to have any more?' But it just doesn't sink in, the sense of responsibility for another life."

Marian worries about the contradiction. "They don't live in the vacuum that we did. In one way, they know so much. They pick up a lot from TV. You'd think if a kid is observant, he or she couldn't help but be aware that there are other things than your own environment, than where you are right now." Today, they see black performers, politicians and newscasters, but they don't make the connection.

She is still angered by the mention of the genocide argument against birth control. "It didn't end with the 1960s. You still hear it today: Contraception and abortion are the white man's plot to destroy black power." She recalls the stormy meetings. "I would always ask: 'Why isn't it genocide to bring several children into the world that you can't possibly take care of? If you can't feed or clothe them decently, if the parents are alcoholics or drug addicts, if this isn't genocide, it's at least as cruel for the individual child.' But when you would get into mixed groups—men and women—Oh boy! Some guys would shout 'genocide' when I would be talking about contraception, and the women would yell at them, 'Are you gonna take care of these babies; are you gonna support your children?' It was always the guys yelling 'genocide' who would be perfectly happy to see their kids supported by welfare."

June Butts, a black educator, has also run into political hostility to birth control. "The black health care professional who advocates planning and spacing one's children, who informs the public about the availability of vasectomy and tubal ligation, who cautions adolescents against casual sex, who understands the need for some people to remain 'child free' in their marriages, who sponsors and supports adoption, such a person is deeply suspect in many quarters of the larger black community."[27]

Marian thinks kids are ready for a tougher message—sooner. "We used to avoid making the connection between poverty and fertility just because most of the people we were talking to were black and poor. We didn't want to offend what was seen—mistakenly, I think—as 'part of the culture.' So we kept it very neutral: This is birth control, here is how it works. We've changed that, though, just *because* we're dealing with younger and younger kids, trying to get there *before* they're sexually active. That's where we can really focus on *choice*: Where do you want to be? How are you going to get there? How contraception relates to your whole life."

In a Peer Counseling Program on sex education, six black girls and one white boy, sophomores and juniors, take turns rehearsing their show-and-tell versions of how babies happen and—with the use of contraceptives—don't happen. They will be delivering their talks to their homeroom classes. Then, armed with practice in answering questions, the students will operate a Teen Hot Line. Their teacher, a slender black woman in her late twenties, laughs good-humoredly at the inevitable giggling and obscene jokes that accompany the unpacking of the demonstration kits.

"How 'bout that!" shrieks sixteen-year-old Diane, as Carolyn lifts a remarkably lifelike plastic model of black male sexual organs from their molded case.

"O-ooo, do me, baby!" Rosalie moans in mock ecstasy. The female model, transparent and racially ambiguous, receives little attention.

Taking turns, they begin with short presentations of how contraception works. The bored, memorized deliveries are greeted with groans from the teacher, Nell Lowry. "C'mon, Rosalie, a little expression! If sex were that boring, none of us would be here."

More shrieks. These are sexually active kids. That much is taken for granted. But despite their savvy and high spirits, Nell Lowry is discouraged. Three-quarters of the class haven't shown up. The schools insist on scheduling this program at the same time as two extracurricular favorites: sports and choir.

More seriously, she faults the educational system for not providing alternatives to kids who aren't college bound. Unless there is strong motivation from home, those are the ones who will get pregnant, drop out, and be locked into poverty forever. "A girl who has watched her mother's welfare check increase with each child has to be shown there's something better for her out there. The schools aren't showing her. Nobody is."

Seventeen-year-old Cynthia waves her intricately beaded corn rows as she heads for the door. "Don't worry 'bout me," she calls to the teacher. "*No way* I'm going to get pregnant. My mother, she'd *kill* me! She's *expecting* me to be a lawyer."

WHO CHOOSES—
AND FOR WHOM

The role of choice in fertility is far from simple. Using or not using contraceptives; getting pregnant and staying pregnant; seeking or not seeking abortion; planning or not planning to be a parent—all these decisions involve the complex interplay of conscious and unconscious needs and desires, social and sexual identity, inherited and "learned" attitudes, values and perceptions.

Since no one is rational about sex, how could fertility be free of ambivalence and contradiction?

Behind those tidy categories on the left-hand side of demographers' charts and tables—"unintended births," intended births," "preferred, expected and actual" numbers of children—lie tangled knots of will, chance, power, revenge, hope and despair. Divorcing sexuality from procreation—as one family planner tidily described his goal—is no modest agenda. Until we are all sent back to the laboratory for new parts (and not just reproductive ones), the combined weight of instinct and culture seems destined to confound those enlightened rationalists (by day, at least), the planners among us. Failing brand-new psyches, with a new set of matching cultural luggage, there is nothing "simple" about any choice relating to reproduction.

If choices about children, about "controlling fertility" are never simple for men and women (and it is still women who are held responsible for these decisions and their consequences) of any age, class or race, they are harder to make for the young, poor and nonwhite.

Several decades ago in a classic study of lower-class white wives, *And the Poor Get Children*, Lee Rainwater produced poignant and plentiful evidence of a seemingly inevitable triad: low income, high alienation and high fertility. Both the experience and world view of the poor women Rainwater interviewed made planning anything seem futile; most things "just happened" to them, including having more children than they wanted. Many, like Renée Pinckney, had tried contraceptives, only to find that "nothing really worked for them." Family planning was an "ego function" determined by socioeconomic status.[28] Rainwater and others could not foresee how many millions of poor women, white and nonwhite, rural and urban, would avail themselves of contraceptives and abortion when these became legal, free and locally available.*

---

*Abortion has remained the preferred method of fertility control for nonwhite women, although its incidence among black women 20–34 has decreased slightly since 1977— suggesting improved use of contraception.

It is no coincidence that the four years between the Supreme Court decision legalizing abortion and the Hyde Amendment of 1977 restricting it to those women who could pay,* was the period in which the class and childbearing equation had just begun to change.

Free contraceptives and abortions, paid for by Medicaid, accompanied by a proliferation of local programs in family planning, were starting to reduce the fertility gap between rich and poor women. Women of "prime childbearing age," between twenty and thirty-four, white and nonwhite, were bearing fewer children. And as startling evidence of the diminishing factor of race in fertility, black women with one year of college were having fewer children than their white counterparts.

Sex and childbearing bring out the irrational beast in all of us. But when these "private" choices enter the public domain, doublethink—and triple thinkers—sound from every soap box and editorial page.

While generally deploring "welfare brood sows" and other examples of how the excess fertility of the poor drains the public coffers, political conservatives are also heavily represented in the ranks of abortion foes, especially of federally subsidized abortions for poor women.

A persistent belief in the innocence of childhood combined with the fear of government usurping the rights of the family, tends to enlist the Right in the cause of those who lobby against sex education and contraceptive information being provided to the young "outside the home."

That teenage parents currently cost billions of dollars in public assistance does not weigh heavily on conservative calculations. According to one estimate, one-half of all AFDC (Aid to Families with Dependent Children) and Food Stamp payments, or $4.65 billion out of a total of $9.4

---

*As one federal health official notes, the Hyde Amendment of 1977, restricting public funding for abortions, did not increase the number of illegal abortions; it simply "reduced the number of legal abortions obtained by poor women," increasing by the same number, we can assume, the birth of unwanted poor children.[29]

billion,* was disbursed to households of women who were teenage mothers. Overall, among women fourteen to thirty in AFDC households, 61 percent had borne their first child in early adolescence. Otherwise, those who favor scant spending on social programs would be elated to learn that it would cost only about $112 million to provide modern birth control services for every sexually active teenager at risk of an unintended pregnancy who is not currently receiving them.[30]

Ellin MacKenzie, pondering the "schizophrenic" nature of her dual advocacy roles, welfare rights and family planning, is describing a classic liberal dilemma. In many areas, a humane society has no choice but to reward the very attitude and behavior that it seeks to change. Making teenage pregnancy an acutely undesirable state ultimately means punishing another generation of poor children. Without the "special" treatment for young mothers, their infants can expect poor health and more social and developmental problems than their parents endured. "You can try to influence people, but you can't force them," concluded one sociologist on the Left. Nor, if you are a traditional liberal, can you justify "negative reinforcement," punishing those who refuse to be "influenced."

However, by the mid-1970s it became apparent that education, jobs and political participation—not making more babies—were the crucial goals for minority men and women. There was more opportunity for upwardly mobile black and Hispanic Americans, but a shrinking economy promised less—fewer jobs and social programs for the least employable. The genocide argument lost credibility, along with the "culture of poverty" view, which held that early and excess fertility were "adaptive" not "dysfunctional behavior" in the poor. As Marian Sims noted, though genocide theorists (and "culture of poverty" romantics) tend to be male, whatever their race or class, they are rarely responsible for the care of all those politically desirable, or culturally determined, kids.

*This figure is underestimated because administrative costs have not been figured in.

CHAPTER EIGHT

CHILDLESS IS RICHER

Children are useless, Fran Lebowitz observed, as they are "rarely in a position to lend one a truly interesting sum of money."[1] This childless chronicler of metropolitan life didn't go far enough. In most industrialized societies where child labor is outlawed, children are less than useless. Kids cost. How *much* they cost from birth to the day they liberate the line for "Dependents" on your tax form varies. And the answer really depends on who is counting.

According to the no-frills calculations of the U.S. Department of Agriculture, the direct costs of a child born to a young woman on public assistance in 1980 from birth to the age of eighteen are $2,000 a year, or $37,115. Moving from the "minimum cost" of a child—raised at or below the poverty level—there is the moderate cost model. The same USDA computers decided that a total of $134,414* will see the average child, born in 1979, to a family in the "urban North Central region of the country" to his/her eighteenth birthday.[2] As one economist and father was quick to notice, however, these figures take no account of such basics as diapers—making for a very bare bottom line indeed.

*Based on an inflation rate of 8 percent.

Writing for the upwardly mobile middle-class readers of *Parents* magazine, Thomas Tilling, author of an article titled "Your $250,000 Baby," soon leaves Pampers for the realm of values and aspirations—always the priciest items in every budget. No child of his or his readers, he assumes, will be deprived of private flute lessons. Nor will any teenager he knows tolerate a junk-food-free diet, or a family budget without a line for "record collection."[3] Middle-class values impose a heavy investment in what economists poetically term "child quality." And private flute lessons are the least of it.

Neither the USDA's austerity budget nor *Parents*' Pamper-padded one (both minus college) address "indirect costs"—like the high rent/high property tax neighborhood to which many middle-class Americans mortgage themselves, in the name of "quality schools" for their children.

"We live in a ghetto that's just starting to see a few middle-class blacks and whites move in, but we're no cutting edge of gentrification," says Ralph Gerosa. "We moved here to avoid spending most of our income or sinking all our savings into housing." For the cheapest rents in their midwestern city, and "a great group of neighbors," Ralph and his wife Donna, both thirty-four, describe themselves as "able to live with" the high crime rate and drugs on the street. But what is acceptable for two adults would be "impossible with kids." The local public school alone would "rule out this neighborhood," adds Donna, who teaches French and social studies in a parochial elementary school across town. "This is just one of the choices we could never make if we had children," Ralph says; it's one of the reasons the Gerosas give for choosing to be childless.

Who are the couples who are not families, those "childless by choice" whose numbers have increased dramatically since the 1960s? The Baby Boom children became Baby Bust nonparents. If we study Madison Avenue's market "profile," they are "upscale" young professionals and voracious consumers—especially of leisure products. They flash their plastic cards for cameras and Club Med packages, Perrier and running shoes, stereos and skis. Or, they are "dual career" couples, with a double determination to make partner or vice-president, bag the big account, the residency in neurosurgery, the chair in psycholinguistics.

For these young wives, with their experience and professional training, government figures on direct costs of children are of less significance than foregone "opportunity costs"— what a young mother is giving up in unearned salary by staying at home.*

No one is at home to bring up children. Yet, raised by Supermoms, they feel children shouldn't be brought up by "professionals," even if one could find "quality child care." So they defer, or postpone until she is "in a better position" to take time off, or demand a part-time arrangement, or they are both doing well enough to give in and give over their young to "significant other(s)."

Many young women said "later" and meant it. The number of first births to women in their thirties doubled from 4 percent in 1970, to 8 percent of all births in 1979, causing a startling increase in the number of first-time mothers who planned to stop at one—42.5 percent according to the 1980 census.[4]

Yet some researchers agree that many current deferrals will become "permanent postponers," sliding into unplanned childlessness, the way the poor slide into unplanned childbearing. Demographer Charles Westhoff hypothesizes that 25–26 percent of American women now twenty-five years old will remain childless,** with 25 percent more stopping at one.[5]

However else they are defined—consumers, careerists, narcissists or non-committed—the childless couples are invariably described as "upwardly mobile." And based on the high correlation between education and childlessness, their mobility assumes a "starting line" of middle class. These col-

---

*If, for example, she has a brand-new law degree from a prestigious school, she may be trying to choose among three firms offering the 1983 New York City "competitive starting salary" of $46,000.

**Thus breaking the 1908 cohort's record of 22 percent childless.

lege-educated couples, it is widely assumed, all began as children of privilege. Some did. Many, however, did not.

Ralph Gerosa grew up in a working-class Chicago neighborhood, the next oldest of six brothers. His father, a diesel mechanic, had never finished high school "because of the Depression." Like all the kids in their neighborhood, Ralph and his brothers attended the local parochial schools. But there were big differences between them and their friends. "No one else we knew slept four in a room. And unlike other families, none of us—parents *or* kids—ever went on vacation, not even for a week of Boy Scout camp."

Ralph was the first and only one of his family to go to college. (He is also the only brother who is not still living at home.) "I was always, deep down, aware of how stifled my mother was with all those kids. She was so smart," her son recalls. "She read everything. And more than anything else, she had wanted to go to college, to become an archaeologist." His mother was gifted. She could really have gone far, Ralph was convinced, "if it hadn't been for the combination of too many kids and too little money."

Ralph met Donna at a large urban university during their freshman year. Like Ralph, she was a product of parochial schools and a "first-generation" college student. Donna's father, a truck driver turned bookkeeper through years of night school, had already moved from blue collar to lower-middle class. Both her parents felt that a career of nurse or secretary was "enough" for a daughter. She is still resentful when she describes their opposition to a liberal arts education.

A pregnancy scare in college made Donna aware of how closely she identified children with "dropping back," blocking every possibility of escape, stifling all aspirations. She recalls, "I was terrified. Two of my friends had gotten stuck that way."*

---

*Donna Gerosa is right about premarital pregnancy blocking mobility. A Detroit study tracked a sample of over 1,000 white wives in the area. The effect of premarital pregnancy and length of child spacing on later economic achievement was dramatic. The premaritally pregnant couples never caught up with the others in assets or consumer durables.[6]

Both Donna and Ralph knew that they would never have children.

Ralph describes their life as "caught on the upward mobility spiral," but his measure of moving up is not primarily material. With a combined income of $36,000, the Gerosas' "wish list" is modest indeed: a "newer" car, a solar house in the woods "some day," a first trip abroad for Donna, a French teacher who has never been to France.

Ralph Gerosa's definition of mobility is lateral—horizontal rather than vertical. Children are powerful reminders of failure. For him, childlessness is the freedom *from* success—a freedom that doesn't entail penalizing kids. "Not having children made it possible for me not to work for fourteen months," he points out, "while I was rethinking what I wanted to do." When Ralph, a college administrator, discusses their "mobility spiral" he isn't describing the carrot that the success ethic holds out—always just out of reach. He speaks of "more interesting, rewarding work. Once I've done something, I'm looking for the next rung, but the next rung for me means more interesting, not necessarily better paying. Not having kids makes it possible for me to make those changes without feeling guilty."

Jean Veevers, a Canadian sociologist who has analyzed childless couples from many perspectives, notes a surprising difference in the meaning of remaining child-free to men and women. For wives, voluntary childlessness is associated with higher career involvement, competitiveness and a craving for success. For husbands, no children often spells the reverse: the freedom to be *less* engaged professionally or to choose other career satisfactions over money. "By implication," Veevers notes, "it is not enough for a father to be employed to support his family. It is also implicitly incumbent upon him to be as *well* employed as possible.... Conventionally, a responsible man takes the 'best' job, the one that pays most."[7]

The uniquely upper-middle-class American value that Talcott Parsons called "instrumental individualism"—doing good and doing well, demanding rewards from work beyond, or even instead of, the bonus, raises or "perks" associated with advancement—is considered by many childless men to be incompatible with parenthood.*

Mobility, for many of us, is more a matter of what we flee than what we seek.

For Ralph Gerosa, kids mean being mortgaged to the future. They mean possessions not possibilities; they mean striving for the title on the door, not fourteen months of leisure to contemplate his future. And, as Ralph has observed, even the expected gains of higher paid work are wiped out with children. "As soon as any of my friends gets a raise or a better job, one of the kids always needs an ear operation." His perception is certainly confirmed by the facts. To analyze the impact of children on a family's standard of living, demographers tracked four hypothetical families with zero to three children over time, beginning with the birth of the first child (the children are assumed to be spaced two years apart). The expected increase in real family income did not keep pace with the "growth rate" of expenses incurred by children from birth to eighteen. Their conclusions: *The family with no children is the only one of the four whose level of living goes up.* " The other three families' standard of living declines as the children grow older. (And the more children, the more rapid and steep is the drop!)[9]

Thomas Espenshade, a demographer with a special interest in the cost of children, and what kind of people "cost them out," notes a related phenomenon. It is not only that kids consume more as they get larger—and that this happens "faster" than parental income increases—but money expenditures on children rise as family earnings grow, because the standards of what should be provided for children climb with socioeconomic status.[10] Even having *fewer kids* doesn't mean

*Veevers also notes that childless couples, in dramatic contrast to the rest of the Canadian-American society, share a distaste for credit culture and a resistance to debts of any kind. Although she describes her "sample population" as middle class, in both origin and present socioeconomic status, this characteristic seems rather to confirm my own evidence; at least one spouse comes from a working-class or lower-middle-class background with little or no "net" of any kind and, consequently, acute money and status anxiety.[8]

more discretionary income or assets. Investment in "child quality" is somehow more seductive to parents than Lindblad tours to the Galápagos or salting it away in savings. As soon as Mom or Daddy gets a raise, or a tax cut, Debbie gets orthodontia *and* dancing lessons when, in fact, only one was indicated by the actual dollar improvement in family fortunes.*

In a large research project on the value and cost of children (including urban and rural parents of all classes in the continental United States, Taiwan and Hawaii), Espenshade and his colleagues found that middle-class urban Caucasians were the likeliest to give finances as their principal reason for restricting fertility. Yet even among this group the actual dollar costs of children were wildly underestimated. Urban middle-class white parents believed that child-related expenditures account for only 8.1 percent of yearly income; in fact, when broken down for individual children, estimates of actual costs show that 30.5 percent of annual income is typically spent on the first child and 14.7 percent on the second in middle-income families.[11]

A fourth-generation Californian, Wright Madden's grandfather was the president of the small, prestigious private college from which Wright and his father, an insurance executive, were both graduated. A state housing administrator specializing in energy problems, Wright, who has advanced degrees in economics and engineering, knew "from the day I entered college that I was, one, headed for graduate school and, second, for a career in public service."

Elaine Walsh's father has been a clerk for the same oil company since he graduated from high school forty years ago. Wright and Elaine met in college when she was a sophomore and he was a senior. Even with a full scholarship, Elaine found that "getting through school was very hard for me financially." As the second of four children, she is sympathetic to her

*An obvious argument against "supply-side" economics. Debbie's parents will spend, not save or invest more, thereby fueling inflation.

family's money squeeze ("It was murder supporting six people on a clerk's salary"), but not of their efforts to discourage her educational ambitions. She is the only one of the four to go beyond high school. Besides studies, college for Elaine required "so many jobs I can't even recall all of them. I was a clerk in Sears, waitress in the college cafeteria, 'cleaning lady' in town. If I wasn't in the library or writing a paper, I was working. There was really no choice."

She and Wright were married the same month Elaine started graduate school in educational administration.

"Two years later," Wright remembers, "we were watching a '60 Minutes' segment on child-free couples. We looked at each other and realized at that moment what neither of us had ever said: We never wanted children."

"Kids are expensive things to keep running," Wright explains. He is used to thinking in cost/benefit trade-offs. Having children would have precluded a lot of other choices. "When I chose to go into housing administration and remain in the public sector, I was choosing a non-money-making job. If we had kids, I would have felt the pressure to do something that earns more."

Like Ralph Gerosa, Wright Madden sees escape from the provider role as the only way to justify success on his own terms. "Without kids, I can maintain my standard of living *and* my moral self-esteem," he says, with a mock-seigneurial wave toward the spectacular view of the bay and distant mountain.

Elaine Madden fits the current model of the fast-track young professional woman. At twenty-eight, she is a bureau supervisor in the county school system. "It took a lot of effort and energy to get where I am now. I know I couldn't have done it if I had had children." In contrast to her husband, whose pleasure in his surroundings moves indoors to embrace every handsome piece of furniture, Elaine seems indifferent to appearances—whether of nature, home furnishings or her own. She plucks at the torn plastic daisy on her flip-flops as Wright turns over a bowl, the work of a local potter. The way here from a cinder-block tract house has not been scored by new interests in style, aesthetics or "the good life." For Elaine Madden, mobility means unencumbered movement, no roadblocks, *not* being thwarted by parents—or children. "What I like best about the house is my separate study—down there," she points to a shingled screened studio, almost hidden by trees. "I can work there weekends without any interruptions. When I was a kid, I don't think I was ever in a room alone for more than five minutes—well, maybe the bathroom."

For both Maddens, ambition is not a dirty word. They are frankly, openly, almost ingenuously ambitious. "Maybe because we're not in it for the money, it's easier for us to be upfront about expecting success in our work," Wright reflects. Both of them speak easily about moving to a "policymaking role" with larger, national organizations. Wright mentions moving from the state to the federal level.

The Maddens are characteristic of a "no children ever" marriage. University of Kansas researchers divided their childless sample of one hundred white middle-class couples into three groups: couples who eventually intended to have children; couples who were unsure of their intentions; and those who had firmly decided against being parents. The "intention never to have children," the study found, "was not related to employment aspiration, but instead to employment success." As a group, those who had firmly decided against having children were already experiencing (at early stages in their career) far greater rewards from their work "and they expected even greater ones in the future."

The authors predict that the growth rate of childlessness will depend on the state of the upper-level job market for women, since women make the final fertility decision.[12] If room at the top remains token, and professional opportunities fail to expand, the "might-as-well-have-a-baby" mentality takes over.*

---

*Veevers points to the high incidence of respondents who "changed their minds" about having a baby when they suffered a career setback, e.g., failing to get a promotion.[13]

"My father was a migrant worker, from Mexico, and my mother was Portuguese, so the hardest thing for me about being childless was fighting all that ethnic pressure to have kids." Jaime ("Jimmy, since I started school") Viveros, thirty-four, thinks this pressure was the reason that he and his wife Dale, thirty-six, were "permanent postponers" for five years. Jimmy Viveros is a psychotherapist—"the only one I know who also has a degree in library science." He is quick to point to the seasonal nature of his father's work and his own insecurity about "making it" as a self-employed professional, to explain his earlier need for a "fall-back career in case I didn't work out as a therapist." At the California university where he was an undergraduate, the "smart Chicanos were headed for law school or Stanford M.B.A.s; it was either big bucks or politics, *la raza.*'" His fellow students in psychology were, without exception, middle class, "Anglo" or Jewish. He was the only one who had to keep dropping out for financial reasons.

He recalls feeling "relieved" when he won a fellowship to a midwestern university, as much for the location as for the money. And when he met his future wife, a fourth generation Ohioan, it was assumed they would remain in the Midwest.

"I see kids as 'privative'—is there such a word? Even though there were only four of us (practically *no* kids by Mexican standards), my father usually had two jobs, picking any fruit or vegetable that was being harvested. Finally, when he did leave agricultural work, it was for a job in a limestone quarry: better paying and steadier, but very, very dangerous." His father used to joke that "Thank God, he was too young and dumb to realize just how dangerous the work was, or he would have been too scared to do it." Actually, Jim thinks that his father realized only too well, but he was desperate "to keep us fed, and together, and above all, to see that we all stayed in school." As much as Jim's father regretted that his early education ended in the 6th grade of a Mexican village school, his son recalls, he was even more disappointed that his two jobs, and later overtime in the quarry, kept him from taking advantage of free night classes in the local community college in the 1950s. "If he wasn't working, he was just too exhausted. That's what I mean by kids being 'privative.' We deprived my father of the chance to be all he could have been. Five people depended on him to be the breadwinner."

Jim was attracted to Dale Allen because she "seemed so independent, someone who would naturally expect to pull her own weight." And he still marvels that with her comfortable "All-American" childhood, his wife is "not at all spoiled."

Dale Allen Viveros, business manager for a regional chain of women's apparel stores, echoes her husband in describing her own childhood as "Saturday Evening Post—braces, ballet lessons and the back porch glider for dates." Her father, a lawyer, and her mother, who went back to work as a real estate broker when Dale and her sister were in school, encouraged both girls "to go as far as we could." It was always understood that parental help was over after college.

By the time they were married at the end of graduate school, Dale remembers, "we were ready for a better cash flow—not kids and worse poverty—because when you're not a student anymore, there seems no real excuse for being poor."

The contrast between "scrimping as a student couple" and making money as two professionals was "such a nice change for us." Dale, an economics major, spends two evenings a week taking art and music history courses at the local university. "I'm really an illiterate in the humanities." But it's expensive, at $300 a semester. "I just know that with kids, I'd feel that kind of enrichment should be for them."* And when the Viveroses contemplated two incomes for two people versus one income for three or four, "the equation didn't work for us." Jimmy and Dale spend almost three hours a day commuting from a turn-of-the-century farmhouse to their city jobs. It had been Jim's dream to live in the country—never mind the gas and getting up at 5:30. "We even have a goat. I tell her, if she isn't better tempered, she's going to end up as *cabrito*. I'm still a peasant," he grins, "but not a poor one."

*She is typical, researchers claim, of the self-improving bent of childless couples. They are less likely to be turning well-oiled bodies on sandy beaches than signing up for adult education courses.

FERTILITY GAP AS CLASS CHASM

While the "haves," especially those who aspire to have more, are bearing fewer, later or no children in ever-larger numbers, the youngest and poorest Americans are doing the reverse.

As black and white women of prime childbearing age, twenty-four to thirty-five, move constantly closer in their declining fertility,* black teenagers (now three times as likely as their white contemporaries to become parents) and young Hispanic families will continue to be left farther behind, "dished out" of the chance to get ahead, not least because education, skills and work experience become ever-less accessible to very young parents.

The anxious middle class has always been less fertile than either richer or poorer Americans. Historically, our class/fertility graph has fairly well held the shape of an hourglass— with the mobility-minded strivers in the wasp-waisted middle, appropriately enough. But for the past decade and a half the hourglass has been inexorably sliding into a pyramid. Most of the reasons for this change in shape are well known by now: later marriages, more divorces, greater educational opportunities for women (and many more taking advantage of them), but especially, since the 1960s, the phenomenon of women entering the labor force in unprecedented numbers—and staying there.

The base of the pyramid represents, as we have seen, in part increasing sexual activity among adolescents of all classes and at earlier ages. More unhappily, it shows that the *results* of this activity—live births, individual and aggregate—are both more numerous and weigh more adversely upon those already handicapped by age, income and race. Between 1971 and 1978, nearly one million black single-parent families joined those Americans at the very lowest income

---

*In a study that revealed the "remarkably similar" rates of childlessness between black and white couples when age, age at marriage and duration of marriage are controlled, the authors predict disappearing differentials as whites and nonwhites become more alike in their experiences and characteristics, e.g., middle class.[14]

level.[15] Almost all of these "new poor" were in households headed by women. And of these women, three-quarters had been teenage mothers.

The worst news about the widening base of the class/fertility pyramid is the experience gap between the immobile childbearers at the bottom and the "others," those who are traveling light and moving up.

ALL OUR CHILDREN*— OR "THEIRS"?[16]

The experience gap between poor parents and childless achievers forms another gulf—in many ways more profound than income, job or education—between the haves and the have-nots. Moreover, the Great Fertility Divide may become far more divisive than other disparities between rich and poor.

THE END OF THE LIBERAL PRONATALIST CONSTITUENCY

As anyone who has donated time to "good causes" knows, both charitable impulse and liberal egalitarianism are based upon alternating currents of empathy, guilt and self-interest. When, however, there are steadily fewer parents among the chil-

*The Great Society programs—and those of the Kennedy years—with their emphasis on childrens' services, reflected among other "values" the unquestioned belief in the inalienable "right" of Americans—rich and poor—to have many children. My informal "child count" of those involved in the administration of these programs reveals a demographic profile characteristic of prosperous Baby Boom parents; few working wives among them, and typically three to four children. President Johnson, obviously an anxious child of the Dustbowl Depression, was the exception in his "Stop at Two" family size.

In contrast, among other attacks on New York City's Mayor Edward Koch, the accusation by welfare rights and other groups that he was "antipoor" was presumed proven by the preponderance of childless members of his administration, both married and, like the mayor himself, single. It was taken for granted by those protesting the mayor's policies that childless professionals could have no concern for poor parents or their children.[17]

dren's services constituency of such appeals,* and when the increasing mobility of this group is, in their own view, predicated on postponing children—now or forever—it is easy to guess what will happen to this traditional "target group" of middle-class "empathizers." They will become another past chapter in social history.

What commonality of experience—hopes, needs, expectations—can a two-career couple share with a poor single mother of three?

A widening polarity of class-as-experience, moreover, will inevitably expand the Proposition 13 mentality, in which graying taxpayers on fixed incomes will not tolerate being dunned for the school bills of other people's children. Except now the rebelling taxpayers are apt to be tanned and blonde.

"I don't want to hear the yells of kids on tricycles when I'm sleeping late on Saturday morning, and I really don't want to subsidize them either." Thirty-three-year-old Sandra Lembeck's weekend mornings are undisturbed, although her taxes still support invisible children. The former Chicago schoolteacher-turned-investment analyst lives with her husband, a shopping mall developer, in one of California's childless "planned communities."

Eleanor Akers is forty-five, the wife of a corporate lawyer, mother of four and lifetime "neighborhood activist" on Manhattan's Upper West Side, long a hotbed of liberal causes and politics. She was seeking support for a "mixed income" day-care center whose subsidy of poorer working parents was to be eliminated by city budget cuts, and was shocked by the response.

Declared one young professional wife, "We're putting off having kids until we can afford quality child care. So, while

---

*The media's much touted Baby Boomlet of 1982 seemed to involve women of high achievement and visibility (Jaclyn Smith, Faye Dunaway), whose one "token" child proved they could "have it all." Typical of these new mothers was literary agent Amanda ("Binky") Urban, 35, who spoke of the "embarrassment-of-riches syndrome. . . . You have an overflow of love and money that you just want to share with another person."[18]

I'm generally sympathetic to poor working mothers, I can't buy the idea that I should work to support *their* baby sitting services." To which she added, by way of defense, "I mean, aren't contraceptives free, if you're low-income?"

Selfish is selfish, we may argue. With children or without. But there is a difference here that spells many fewer advocates for those children now being born into poverty.

The suburban mother, Park Avenue matron, or Upper West Side volunteer activist of yore, sitting comfortably in the sun watching her toddlers in yard or sandbox, might well feel stricken by the thought of the less-cared-for children of the poor—especially of the working poor. However, the young working wife, postponing—or possibly never having—children, is unlikely to feel torn by guilt or sympathy for those who, heedless of social and economic consequences, reproduce, assuming others will foot the bill.

Indeed, a recent study of a representative sample of voluntarily childless couples found that, in contrast to their image as liberated individuals and politically progressive, childless couples were "more conservative than those who follow societal norms concerning procreation." The researchers' explanation for this unexpected conservatism is that "greater conformity on social issues" was a way of compensating for the still-prevalent view of childlessness as deviant;[19] in other words, "we-may-be-weird-but-just-in-one-respect."

The final evidence of the Right-tilting tendencies of the Baby Bust generation—the cohort with the largest numbers of college-educated working women in our history—is the shift of these twenty-five to thirty-four year olds from Democratic to Republican party affiliation.* For a generation, the political alignment of this age group had been 56 percent Democratic and 30 percent Republican. In 1981, the same young adults had realigned as 44 percent Democratic and 43 percent Republican.[20]

---

*This is the same age group who mobilized behind the New Deal and Great Society programs, and, more recently, created the New Democratic Coalition.

THE "NEW NATIVISM"

In a less self-consciously democratic era, nativists used to worry about pure American stock being overwhelmed and America overrun with swarthy foreigners. Publicly and in print—during that period before World War I which coincided with the peak of immigration to this country—genetic jingoists deplored the tendencies of the urban immigrant poor and of southern blacks to reproduce themselves, while Americans of Anglo-Saxon ancestry were not stocking their gene pools with sufficient numbers of progeny. Scholars in quantitative disciplines did not try to cloak their racial anxieties in the neutral language of science. An article in the *Journal of the American Statistical Association* of 1914 is titled, "The Decadence of the Native American Stock."

Even an early and recently revived heroine of obstetrical care for poor rural women had a none-too-secret nativist agenda. Mary Breckenridge of Kentucky, the pioneer of midwife training, describes in her letters the urgency of improving the prenatal care of mothers and saving the babies of what we now call Appalachia. Their high infant mortality was threatening to turn the region's pure blond, blue-eyed Anglo-Saxon stock into an endangered species.[21]

The "new nativism" expresses similar worry over the reproduction gap between rich and poor, but in language far less genteel. "To take all the genetic superiors out of the world is to leave a world of moribund morons behind,"[22] was the jeremiad of a forty-four-year-old New York banker, complaining of his wife and "other intelligent women" who continue to postpone childbirth.

GOOD NEWS
—OR MORE ROOM
ON THE SLOPES?

What will happen, as the best educated, most successful or most aspiring Americans have fewer children or none—leaving fertility to the least favored?

According to one demographer's scenario, everyone will be better off. By the 1990s there will be more jobs, less crowding and crime—benefiting everyone, but especially the poor, since the new job opportunities will include entry-level positions. The "trickle-down" effect promises that the space created by the non-procreating will make upward mobility easier for the offspring of their more fertile contemporaries—regardless of parents' age, race, or numbers of children. Once the slopes are less crowded, so this theory goes, more people can move up—if not to the top, at least further along than is presently possible. And they may need less "human capital" to get there. This is the "young adult scarcity" model.

To extend this bright picture further, "manpower shortage" even for entry-level jobs encourages expansion of day care, better vocational and on-the-job training, with craft unions more "hospitable" to minority youth, men and women. In short, there will be a "second chance" for those on the other side of the fertility gap.

This scenario is more cheering than convincing. Much as we might like to think of a socially self-correcting dynamic of demography, the diminishing population of under-eighteen-year-olds is already telling us it isn't so, by creating problems in basic services. There are fewer schools in shrinking cities receiving fewer resources to serve poorer kids, for example. Increasingly, the educational dollars will go "where the market is," namely adult programs to expand Dale Allen Viveros's continuing education in the humanities.

Fewer of "us" does not promise more for "them."

CHAPTER
NINE

COMING OUT
AND
MOVING UP

3 p.m.
You're island hopping again.
Friends at every port.
(Somehow, you
just seem to
know all the
Key people).

The words on the page are a poem. But even more lyrical is the image—two heartbreakingly handsome young men, running along the beach where a seaplane has just deposited them. They're gorgeous. They're happy. They're rich. They're on holiday. They know everyone. (But they have each other, when "everyone" palls.) And, as if life wasn't unfair enough, this full-page Bloomingdale's ad reminds us:

Style:
Some people have to work at it
...but then you're not some people.

*An excessively logical reader might wonder whether doing battle with Bloomie's on Saturday isn't "working at style." But never mind. Who's logical, when contemplating an eat-your-heart-out ad like this?

Who is that lucky "you"? (A final clue, for those who might have spent the last decade shipwrecked on Tierra del Fuego. The key is those "Key people." Get it?) The gay male consumer. Or in Bloomingdale's code: "Saturday's Generation." Too busy being successful on the job to shop weekdays, and with too much exciting nightlife to shop on Monday or Thursday evening. That's for secretaries!

Is this ad pure fantasy? Wishful thinking? Or down-to-earth demographics?

"We're everywhere," the rallying cry of Gay Activism for over a decade, wouldn't have held national (read media) attention for more than ten seconds, if the "we" were a nationwide network of welfare mothers. The "we" is the average gay male household of 1.4 persons, found by a Los Angeles-based marketing firm[1] to enjoy an income 50 percent above the national median. And since money isn't everything, not even in Consumerland, the same researchers noted that 70 percent of their sample are college graduates, of whom almost 84 percent—again, double the national average—vote regularly. Another study calculated that gay men control 19 percent of the disposable income in the United States.

The *Advocate*, a biweekly magazine in newsprint format, which claims the largest circulation (just grazing 60,000) of any gay publication, sponsored its own demographic profile of readers. They came up with a similarly heartening picture of gay affluence, and more important, to gladden the hearts of advertisers, of discretionary income and spending habits. With an average household size of 1.8 members, disposable income among *Advocate* readers is "inordinately high," with 36 percent of their sample earning more than $35,000. Sixty-eight percent were employed full time by others, 19 percent were self-employed, and 4 percent worked part-time for an employer.[2]

Indeed, as the handsome, mustached, banker/executive types in a full-page *Advocate* ad announcing the survey results point out: "the average reader is a lot like . . . us": editor Robert I. McQueen and publisher Peter G. Frisch.

Frisch is thirty-five, has an annual household income of

$50,000, and along with the other member of his household owns a Jaguar XKE, a Honda Accord, and a Fiat station wagon. He skis, swims and stays in shape at a Nautilus fitness center with clubs in four cities. He shops at Neiman-Marcus, Bloomingdale's and Bergdorf's. Last year he saw over twenty-five films and vacationed in the Caribbean, Mexico, Key West and Maui. His colleague McQueen, thirty-eight, has an annual income of $45,000, purchased thirty books last year, spent $50 monthly on wine, $1,200 on camera equipment, acquired a stereo system for $1,700, entertained at home or out fourteen times a month. He plays a Yamaha CS-50 music synthesizer and composes on his Knabe piano! In home appliances, a "significant number" of *Advocate* readers are a step ahead of their superconsumer editor and publisher. Fifteen percent have videotape recorders (38 percent report intentions to purchase one soon), while 8 percent have home computers. Perrier "prevails overwhelmingly" as the favorite bottled water.

However, the typical *Advocate* reader is no improvident spendthrift. Approximately four out of ten subscriber/purchasers own "real property" as an investment, while the same number invest in corporate stocks. For anyone skeptical of the *Advocate* image of gay consumer power as statistics "cooked" to be self-serving, other sources confirm a picture of an upwardly mobile, upscale market segment worth wooing.

The *Wall Street Journal* credited advertising from such solidly unhip enterprises as real estate and financial services for boosting the circulation of *After Dark*, a New York-based, predominantly gay publication. That advertising hiked the circulation from forty-nine thousand to ninety-four thousand in three years.[3]

As with all power—political, physical, or economic— the real test of strength is never the knockout blow; it's winning without having to use it, otherwise known as winning through negotiation. According to *TV Guide*, three major networks and numerous independent producers pay Newton Deiter, Los Angeles psychologist and head of the Los Angeles-based Gay Media Task Force, to appraise programs with "sensitive" material either in production, or as pilots. Like the

National Urban League monitoring the black "image," Deiter's role is to check for gay "negative stereotyping," but not just lisps or limp wrists. Esther Shapiro, producer of "Dynasty," snipped a scene where sensitive son, Steven Carrington (described by the program press release as "searching for his sexual identity and thus in conflict with his patriarch father") sobs at the end of the program.

Describing an "orgy of overcompensation," *TV Guide*'s Richard Levine points to the gay cop on a "Lou Grant" episode who "lifts weights, practices target shooting, coaches a soccer team and drinks beer—all in the first ten minutes of the show."[4]

Lest anyone be persuaded that the media's belated inclusion of homosexuals within the Television Code's broad fairness doctrine is disinterested, Levine is prompt to attribute the sudden enlightment to the "implied pressure of millions of gays around the country willing to march on local affiliates, *the majority of them possessing the kind of disposable income TV advertisers lust after*" (author's italics).

GAY MEN: VICTIMS OR MOBILITY MODELS?

Images of island-hopping and two-car households are not welcome to many gay activists. To politically conscious homosexuals, as to their heterosexual counterparts, especially on the Left, consumer power, as a way to win minds and hearts, is distasteful at best, dangerous at worst, and in the middle, unrepresentative of the lives of many gay men and women.

Activists in the forefront of the struggle for gay rights— a battle focused specifically on outlawing those millstones of mobility, job and housing discrimination—publicly denounce images of homosexual high life and saber-rattling consumer power brokers as giving aid and comfort to the enemy. Enemies of gay rights will be prompt to ask why "they" need such legislation since, unlike blacks or women, gay men are so well represented in the most economically rewarding and high status occupations? Envy is a dangerous emotion, once aroused, and many political strategists summon the specter of a Gay Conspiracy backlash: "the Moral Majority marching into your neighborhood,"[5] as one journalist put it, in an orgy of repression, a *Kristallnacht*, against those rich-faggots-who-control-everything.

So while media—gay and straight—hype gay success, thereby, in the words of the old Cadillac ad, hoping to breed more of it, many radical gay men, and most gay women, focus on homosexuals as victims.

Studies of gay men in the work force, especially, paint a somber picture of discrimination, fear, and underemployment: not getting the job at the entry level, being passed over for promotion later on, dishonorable discharges, job "tracking" of gay men into low pay, low status female "ghetto" jobs. Massed at the bottom of the occupational ladder are lower white collar and service jobs—or only slightly better, librarians, nurses, social workers, elementary-school teachers. Noting the evidence that gay men are probably better educated than the rest of the population, sociologist Martin Levine concludes that their "over-representation" in these "feminine" jobs "signifies that they are not able to convert education into high income or high status occupations." Citing Gallup poll figures, Levine goes on to show that even in such undesirable jobs as elementary school teacher, there is more discrimination against gay men.[6]

However, Canadian sociologist Barry Adam argues that things get worse toward the top. Using dummy applications to Ontario law firms, Adam found that those young men and women who, under a form heading "personal background" made known their sexual orientation "for reasons of self-affirmation," were least likely to be called for an interview.[7] Questions remain, though, as to exactly what Adam's sample of Toronto law firms found less desirable about the "self-labeled" gay applicants.

One New York lawyer, prominent in liberal causes, explained: "I wouldn't favor any prospective associate who under 'personal background' volunteered information about his/her sexual preferences—whether it was a conversion to chastity or a belief in sex for procreation only. That kind of 'self-labeling' always has a tinge of fanaticism about it," he said, adding that "in any case, it signals a preoccupation with the personal-as-political, a Moral Minority attitude, that doesn't promise the kind of professional detachment we look for." Other researchers claim, though, that fear of homophobia in high status professions has a "chilling" effect on the aspirations of young gay men. Of eighty-nine respondents surveyed in a 1973 study, 32 percent felt "homosexuality set limits on their ambitions and imposed restrictions on their choice of career or advancement."[8]

The way in which homosexuality acts to set these limits is complex and by no means self-evident. "Lots of gay men have trouble competing in a straight male world,"[9] notes writer Andrew Kopkind, suggesting that the process is as much one of self-selection into traditional gay/feminine down-scale jobs as it is of discrimination—actual or feared.

Strangely enough, no research on gay men in the work force has studied their role in those "integrated" fields notably hospitable to, or uninterested in, the sexual preferences of employees. They embrace: the media, including publishing, advertising, and public relations; retailing; architecture; the cultural world—where the pay isn't high, but the status is heady—in museums, art galleries, and foundations.

Silence about the gay presence in these hospitable and high-status occupations has other implications. Acceptance in fields requiring talent and taste, argue some writers, meant moral and political co-option. Gay "self-exploitation" was rewarded if "they" did not broadcast their sexual preferences.

"The idea of a special refinement among gay men as their best quality has been a legacy of conformity and acquiescence to the very class that would reward their arts and talents for their personal silence," writes Seymour Kleinberg in his moving autobiography, *Alienated Affections*. "Like other minorities eager for mobility and status," Kleinberg explains, homosexual men have exploited themselves. And he compares the "elegant bondage" of gay men to slaves who will not leave

the plantation because they have nowhere else to go. "Unlike
the oppression of blacks and women in America," Kleinberg
concludes, "ours has been a diffusive and confused injustice. We share with them a history of emotional disability,
like those who saw choice as a luxury and security as necessary."[10]

There is growing evidence, however, that "nontraditional" occupations like real estate and construction already
show more than a token gay male presence. Describing a
Dallas gay disco favored by go-getters on the way up, *Texas
Monthly* reporter Michael Ennis observes that a group of
fraternity men from Abilene, barely out of college, "had already reached professional status as pharmacists and accountants, even at their tender age." The patrons of the "happy
hour" at a still more stylish gay bar/disco/restaurant are divided between typical young Texan entrepreneurs—"the kind
of men who can look you square in the eye and close a million
dollar deal with a handshake that leaves your fingers throb-
bing—and young professionals with that unmistakable al-
ready-most-of-the-way-up-the-ladder look."[11]

Is demography destiny for gay men? Or discrimination?

As is true for childless heterosexual couples, two paychecks and no kids describe a household with higher disposable income than most American families, especially if both
adults have college or graduate degrees. But these parts of
the equation alone don't guarantee any chartered seaplanes,
ferrying you and a friend from key to key. Access to the right
jobs, followed by opportunities to move up, write the script
for occupational mobility.

If patterns of discrimination are as pervasive as sociologists Levine, Adam and others suggest, what do the paychecks in those two-income gay households do to alleviate the
immobilizing effects?

Some gays are self-employed, like the 19 percent of the
Advocate sample. They are often owners of stores, restaurants
and other service businesses in what Dr. Levine calls the "gay
ghetto."[12] These small entrepreneurs, in turn, facilitate mobility by hiring other young gay men who, on acquiring skills

and experience, may move from waiter to assistant manager to striking out on their own—the time-honored way of businesses training competitors. Many other gay men, however, have to be among that 68 percent "white-collar professionals/technical/managers" happily claimed by the *Advocate* publishers.

The real issue is not numbers, or percentages, or median household income, disposable and discretionary. The real issue is image: its value and political role. Will it help or harm gay rights to portray an "oppressed minority," victims of discrimination with more limited choices of housing, work, and with less job security than their straight counterparts? In one view, mobilizing the conscience of civil libertarians as well as less activist, more-closeted gay men and women, requires victims to arouse a strong sense of injustice. But defenders of "upscale," upwardly mobile, gay glamor feel that the gay as victim further injures the already "stigmatized." Baring wounds in public, the constant reminder that gays are second-class citizens, may be the surest route to staying that way.

Competition, moreover, is keen for what is left of liberal sympathy. Poor minorities are getting poorer. There are ever-growing numbers of indigent homeless elderly, abused children, and undereducated young people. The sympathy vote is shrinking, while its constituencies grow.

COMING OUT AND MOVING UP

Betty Williams, parent and community activist in a northeastern ghetto, has worked successfully with the district school superintendents—black and white—for many years. She was pessimistic about the incumbent Dr. John McKay, young, black and committed, because "he's gay. So he just can't relate to people in the community." Significantly, it wasn't McKay's Harvard M.B.A., his title of "Doctor," not even his expensive English suits that suggested to his constituents that he could no longer identify with the ghetto blacks he grew up with. His homosexuality is considered a badge of affiliation which, superseding earlier "primary group identity," signifies a definitive break with his class of origin.

Despite at least one well-known gay man among the heroic "first generation" of the civil rights movement leadership, there is an indisputable homophobe bias in black culture. In part, this is explained by the fundamentalist beliefs of that "old-time" religion, still a major cultural force in many black communities. Then too, black machismo, the more intense as the black male has been kept powerless, has often found it easier to focus on a more vulnerable and more visible enemy than the economic and political might of mainstream white society.

Younger black leaders like Eldridge Cleaver called homosexuality "the work of Satan," while the Reverend Jesse Jackson termed it a "tool of white oppression."

Yet in a very practical, political sense, Betty Williams was right. How many "oppressed minorities" can a person belong to? To "stand up and be counted" on more than one front means never sitting down, or giving up any other career goals for the life of a full-time activist.

Betty Williams knows, too, that for an upwardly mobile young man like John McKay, his "old" community—what the sociologist Max Weber called his "community of fate"—demands that he constantly look back. Gay is where he's going: his community of choice. In his new community, individual mobility is applauded. His success sheds luster on his mentors and peers. His new friends, record executives, editors, fashion designers, regard him as a "real saint."

A more visible focus of anger, resentment and envy than the John McKays, commuting out of the ghetto at 5 o'clock, are the new "in-migrants": prosperous gay white men associated with a process known as gentrification.

From Boston's "Southie" slums to Philadelphia's South Street to San Francisco's Haight—the news is about neighborhoods rescued from terminal squalor by a vanguard of gay urban pioneers. They don't need playgrounds or safe schools. They can live with the winos and acid freaks exposing themselves under the soon-to-be-Georgetown'd lampposts. What they do need and want: health food stores, record shops, smart saloons and cozy neighborhood "locals," follow in their wake, often owned by the "new" residents. Soon thereafter come the middle-class straight couples, young professionals, along with real estate developers and speculators, carving condos, duplexes and high rental apartment units from the remaining bargains. The neighborhood has been "turned around," its poor black residents turned out. And who gets blamed? The gay vanguard, who are rarely the ones who benefit from the real estate boom.

"I'm black, I'm fat and I'm gay," announces Lindley Charles. "So, I've got three *big* strikes against me in this society." Like many in all three "stigmatized" categories, Lindley has a self-protective *spritz* of jokes about his "multiple handicaps." He recounts his life and hard times in the lilting voice of his Creole ancestors. Lindley grew up in New Orleans where his grandmother "slaved her entire life as a hotel chambermaid, but insisted on teaching all of us," Lindley, his three sisters and brother, "French." It was their only link with a fabled, privileged past which *certainly*, Lindley underlines, had nothing to do with the impoverished present.

When their parents separated, Lindley's mother, who had been a schoolteacher before her marriage, did waitressing, housecleaning, anything she could get because, "I mean, we were *poor*. Just a meal ahead of welfare," is the way he describes the family circumstances, adding that with public assistance in Louisiana, the difference between welfare and starving wasn't too noticeable.

"I would probably have come out in high school," he states, "because there were other gay boys there. And certainly they were 'the better element,' at least not into stealing cars and housebreaking. But these guys were obviously going to settle for very low level work," and he was afraid that the gays in his school would hold him back. "Mobility has always been highly important to me, but even more crucial is *not* falling back into poverty."

After his graduation from a Catholic college in California,

Lindley started graduate school in social work. Then he met his "Family," whom he describes as a racially integrated group of gay professional men: a bank officer, a department store executive, an artists' agent, a couple of television producers, and several high school and college teachers. The "Family" do not live together, but they see each other essentially all the time, although many have non-Family lovers. Most important, though, are the ways in which "we function as a family, everything from helping each other to find jobs and housing, to financial support." One member, Lindley recalls gratefully, came to New York with him to help him find an apartment, introduce him to "Family friends, generally get me settled." And when, around Thanksgiving, he wrote a letter mentioning how homesick he was feeling, he found a round-trip plane ticket to California in his mailbox a few days later. Through Family contacts, members are hooked into the gay network anywhere in America, which means "jobs wherever you have gay people working," and he mentions a New York department store where the Family is especially well connected.

In their ten-year study of San Francisco's gay community, *Homosexualities*, Kinsey Institute reseachers Alan P. Bell and Martin Weinberg found that a majority of black gay males felt that homosexuality had helped rather than harmed their careers[13] providing, by extension, a boost to their social mobility as well.

Race, Lindley Charles reflects, seems less important in the gay community. And although he thinks class may count more, the definition is different. "It's not so much what your father did or where you went to school, but more 'Can we communicate? What kinds of experiences can we share?'"

THE PRINCE AND THE PAUPER

"Now, Made in the Suede...for Dad," reads a cheeky, double-entendre copy for Saks Fifth Avenue's Father's Day advertisement. But Saks's knockoff of Bloomingdale's "Saturday's Generation" doesn't suggest any revival of *Life with Father*.

Pops is upper-class WASP, a preppie turned network vice-president. The "son," with his close-set eyes, prominent cheekbones and suggestion of cauliflower ears, is certainly Latin, with a possible touch of Indian. Together they illustrate a theme of homoerotic literature, a fantasy and often a fact of gay life: the Prince and the Pauper.

Describing the compelling attraction of working-class youths for upper-class men, literary historian Timothy d'Arch Smith offers several explanations: an "inferiority complex preventing them from enjoying the rigors and responsibilities of a love affair with an intellectual equal"; the greater "sexual frankness and uninhibitedness promised by lower-class young men and the safety factor—they could be shaken off if they become too demanding." Most crucial to the Prince-and-the-Pauper romance is the older man's mentor role: The "laudable drive," as the very British Mr. Smith puts it, "to rear the boy from his menial environment into a better life wherein he could share the heritage of art, literature, the sciences, and eventually take his place as an equal, despite the fact that he had risen from the ranks."[14]

And who should be the first American interpreter of this theme (in disguise)? None other than Horatio Alger, expelled from Harvard for unspecified misdemeanors, then hounded from his Brewster, Massachusetts pulpit in 1866 for "boy love."[15] His revenge was to become the best-selling celebrant of the self-made man, of the newsboy whose virtue, intelligence and ambition are discovered and rewarded by a rich and powerful older man.

"Vic really educated me," Mike explains. "I've done more and learned more in the six months I've known him than in the entire rest of my life." Small and lithe, his dark skin and straight black hair are the legacy of Mike St. Clair's Seminole Indian father, a coast guardsman from Florida who settled in Brooklyn with his Polish-American bride. One of eight children, Mike dropped out of high school eleven years ago, when he was seventeen, mostly because he was "too scared" to take the board of regent's test required for graduation.

The other reason he left school was to join the navy. If he enlisted as a "lifer," Mike was advised, the navy would operate "free" on a congenital malformation of his jaw. It was good advice. A couple of thousand mess and boiler details later, followed by three months in a U.S. Navy hospital, and Mike's jaw was perfect. He returned to his old after-school job in the supermarket "full time." And he has been a night stock clerk there for the past ten years.

Mike still lives in Brooklyn with his first lover, a druggist's clerk. They are now "just good friends."

"I think I would have known I was gay even sooner," he reflects, if he hadn't gone to all-boy schools, first parochial then vocational high, followed by the navy. "I never had to be reminded that I *really* wasn't interested in girls and I was too scared to seem interested in boys." In the tough neighborhood where he grew up, where he still works and lives, "it isn't anything you'd want to broadcast."

Mike St. Clair thinks, though, that being gay is one reason he is such a good worker. "Because I might think I could get away with more if I wasn't...like the straight guys...whose attitude is 'so what if the work ain't done or not, as long as you can get away with it.' I might think, deep down, that even if they find out I'm gay, they might also say, 'So what? He's a good worker.'"

Six months ago, Mike met Vic Firulli, a television producer, and Vic's lover of ten years, Roger Felsner, a journalist and editor. Vic and Roger were the first professionals that Mike had ever met. "It used to be my fantasy," he confesses, "that I would meet people like that." In fact, he had once wanted to be a television cameraman, "just so I could be around guys like them. And here I am, their friend! Just before I met Vic, I remember saying to myself: I think I need a coach. I need someone to push me. I know I could never do it myself."

Vic Firulli was doing it himself, until he got derailed. He was paralyzed for a dangerously long time by coming out, doing drugs, discovering class consciousness—all at once. Vic was born in a northern New England mill town where his Irish-American mother, one of ten children, had worked in the plastics factory from the time she left school in the 6th grade to the month before her first child was born. Shortly after World War II, Vic's father, an Italian immigrant who had worked in a foundry before he was drafted, reenlisted: "He just couldn't seem to make it in civilian life."

Despite the steamy July morning, Vic Firulli wears a long-sleeved, plaid cotton shirt and tie. His style is carefully nondescript, so anonymous that he is hypnotically arresting: Lenin in Levi's. The hair, neither long or short, the beard neither trimmed nor scraggly. With his steel-rimmed glasses, he still looks the SDS activist he was fifteen years ago.

In the early 1960s, Vic moved with his family to a western Texas army base. "I already knew I was gay. Well, I didn't actually know I was *gay*. I knew I was different."

That was when he discovered Wally in "Leave It to Beaver."

"Wally was my hero. He made it O.K. to be different, to be studious, honest, sensitive. Always helping his little brother in fights. Just a *wonderful* person."

In Vic's sophomore year in high school, the Firullis moved back to New England. Living off the base as civilians was "very rough economically." And with buying a house, the family was in "way over their heads."

Marie Firulli went back to work in the plastics factory, which meant that Vic, as the oldest child living at home, had to take over the responsibility for seven brothers and sisters.

At the time, he had two after-school jobs. As soon as classes were over he had to rush to the hospital where he was a cook's assistant. Then at 8 P.M. he started work at a hamburger joint, coming home at midnight.

Armed with two scholarships, a loan, plus the money he had saved working all summer, every day from 6 A.M. to midnight, Vic arrived at the state university where "I went into real shock. A lot hit me at once, starting with the class thing." He suddenly realized all that he hadn't yet learned from his few middle-class friends at home: the university was very expensive for out-of-staters; most of the guys on his floor were rich kids from suburban New Jersey. "They had all this *stuff* in their rooms, cameras, stereos, framed pictures. And they went out to eat all the time." Vic's worst memory of these years is the shame and terror he felt about his parents' first and only visit. "This was their real proud day. The first time ever anyone in the family had gone to college and here it was their son they were visiting... who wouldn't even let them see his room. Instead, I tried to hustle them off to places where we wouldn't meet anyone I knew."

Now he enjoys being with his family. "I have no problems anymore about the way they look or talk. Or with their values. They're just fine."

Vic realized he was gay when, as a premed scholarship student, he got the bursary job of assistant trainer of the athletic teams, taping sprained ankles. His first affair, with a fellow activist, came when he plunged into the antiwar movement. Like Vic, his lover was also working class, but much more politically sophisticated. He brought Vic into the SDS, encouraged him to read Marx, Hegel and Marcuse.

"The gay thing, though, was really starting to take its toll on me," Vic recalls. "That, plus staying up night after night, putting out pamphlets on Kent State." He began getting dizzy spells and tics, taking a lot of Valium. At that point, "I just threw everything away. I didn't go to medical school, I quickly became a leftist hippie, who didn't have any real direction." The only positive thing about this period was that after "coming out in a small way to friends and co-workers in the Movement, the dizziness and anxiety attacks stopped." He no longer needed the Valium. "Life started making some sense," even though he still didn't know what he was going to do.

Part of the question was answered for Vic when he moved to Boston. It was there, he realized, that "being gay—more than being middle class, or even having middle-class values— gave you entrée to people who had money. Sex brought you immediately into circles of rich men, men who could take care of you. So that's what I did. That became my career. Hanging

—211—

out with wealthy gay men." He met them through Philip, his first "real lover" after college. Philip had a friend, an older man, who, as Vic describes him, "was taking care of a lot of young gay activists. He would offer us his house, Heartbreak Hotel we called it." He fed us, kept us alive. He became our protector. "That's when I realized that there were gay people with money who, *because* you were gay, were going to take complete care of you. It's an old boy network, entirely based on sexuality. Just the way the 'other' old boy network is based entirely on class."

His middle-class skills, the ability to maneuver in social situations, the college education, were that much more valuable, as "insurance. So, they didn't feel I was some cheap hustler." Hustling was the only way Vic could survive. "I became paralyzed by just the thought of the 'real world,' of going out and getting a real job. I had completely lost the desire to do anything. My old 'heavy work ethic,' just evaporated. Maybe," he reflects, "because the energy that once fueled it had gone into being gay...the life."

Vic became the lover of a millionaire, heir to a chemical fortune. "He was very nice. He gave a lot of money to left wing and gay political groups. I deliberately sought him out because I heard he was rich. I couldn't have admitted it at the time. But that's really the way it happened. I figured he was a likely candidate for protector, so I called him up."

Ten years ago, Vic met Roger. "Just in time," he says matter-of-factly. "My life was going down the tubes." Roger made him see what was happening in each of his alliances with rich men. "They were exploiting me sexually. I was exploiting them financially."

Roger is well off, but not really rich. "He works like a dog, reads and writes constantly, and volunteers what's left of his spare time to political causes—gay and others. So much of my education comes from Roger. Not the superficial stuff: wines, food, ballet, antiques, but the kind of probing he does, his analysis of social issues, the connections he makes." Roger supported Vic for a time, but "soon he was forcing me to think independently again. He made me get out there on my own, get my own job, start taking care of myself again."

"He was like the best kind of father, the best kind of mentor," Vic says of his lover and friend, fifteen years his senior. "Helping me to help myself." Finally, Vic started getting work in radio, then television. "Building my own career, my own contacts, with real achievements."

He is beginning to notice that an old boy network is emerging among gay professionals—especially in the media. Vic calls it a "crossover network: "Gay and Old Boy Ivy; one based on sex, and one based on class.

"There's a whole generation of Ivy League gays now who are my age: they've known each other since college, have the same friends, same experiences." Vic sees "how much easier it is for guys I know with that background. Jobs just seem to get offered to them. First of all, they just *know* so many people."

As Gay Culture becomes more institutionalized, Vic continues, there is a different type of person coming out. "Before, it was people like me, people who had no money or power or status. People who had nothing to lose. But as Gay Power gets stronger, more talented, upper-middle-class men can come out. And among his generation of thirty-five-year-olds, "that means people with good jobs. They may not march in Gay Pride parades, appear on TV panels, but they lead gay lives. They have a house on Fire Island, they see only other gays." There's a lot of class mix on that level of the gay world. "Middle-class values and attitudes are very available to a poor kid working in that milieu."

Like to a local Vermont boy. Carl was a dirt poor farmer's son who came out, moved to San Francisco, became a baker. "It's unbelievable," Vic says, "how fast and how far he's come in changing class values. Now he knows food and wine, takes literature courses at San Francisco State. He's an entirely changed person, because all the things that interest him have changed." Yet, what's really different about him—and many of the kids in his generation—is that he has absolutely no money, and no desire for any. "It isn't this guy's income that has changed from the days, not long ago, when he was driving a tractor, but his values and aspirations. Coming out didn't make him richer, but it made him middle class."

Hustling, says Vic, is still the quickest form of gay mobility. The Twinkie syndrome, Vic calls it. Whether he is a "plain twinkie" (just a gorgeous hunk), a Blond Bombshell, or a "talking twinkie," the gay hustler is different from the straight model. Because the gay hustler uses hustling to rise above being a hustler—that's the Twinkie syndrome. "The hustler career is a way to get out of your class without going through what I had to go through: schooling, feeling ashamed of your family, acquiring those middle-class values in a slow, painful process."

Like Eric Mundt. Legendary "fancy hustler," as Vic describes him, whose international Circuit Queen career in the 1960s included such protectors as a famous Italian film producer, a famous American fashion designer, a famous Russian ballet star, and hosts of other less famous—but even richer—lovers. Eric Mundt's career, says Vic, is the perfect example of Twinkie mobility. "He used the hustling, the goodies, to change everything about himself: accent, mannerisms, values. Then at the age of thirty, this little hayseed-turned-hustler became a self-respecting professional; he left the world, got a Ph.D., and now he's a tenured professor and gay activist."

Eric Mundt is still blond, still handsome enough to conjure up the other life, when "It was all yacht cruises around the Greek isles, and weekends in Morocco." But the gray in the hair, thickening around the middle, the baggy chinos and slightly faded cotton turtleneck suggest that preoccupation with Youth and Beauty (at least his own) is now ancient history. Nor is there anything in his narrow nineteenth century row house in a gentrified section of Philadelphia to visibly recall the glitter days. Paintings by artist friends mix comfortably with the mementos of more modest travels. Stacks of student "blue books" share coffee table space with offprints of articles by colleagues. "I was never one of those kept boys who was out to get a lot of money," Eric notes matter-of-factly. "I never, for example, accumulated stocks or asked for presents of real estate, which were commonplace."

His father, a sometime station master, was mostly a career alcoholic. The family was so poor, Eric recalls, that he couldn't afford the dime to use the local swimming pool. "There were so many things I couldn't do, but thank God, reading wasn't one of them." The library card was free and the local branch didn't require carfare—"a major consideration for any outing."

From the age of twelve, Eric knew that if he wanted to go to college, he would have to put himself through. So armed with a full scholarship, he headed East. Echoing every poor boy, Eric chronicles the loneliness and fear, the snobberies endured—of being a pleb among the preppies. "It was traumatic, terrible, not just my clothes and accent, which were awful enough, but the academic part. The kids from good schools not only wore blazers and button-down shirts, but they had read Homer and Dostoyevsky." After a few months in a freshman humanities course, Eric wrote down the names of twenty-one authors mentioned—"not by the professor, but by students." He had recognized only three: Eisenhower, Einstein and Jesus Christ. He learned the other eighteen names, and read their books, bought a blazer, "redesigned" his speech, developed ironclad, rigorous study habits and won every prize and medal available. He also became the lover of a boy two years ahead of him. The affair lasted until the older student decided that a doctor needed a wife, and broke it off in preparation for medical school.

It was only after graduation that Eric discovered the gay world right in the same city. After a brief career as an actor, he became, at the age of twenty-two, a "famous international kept boy." Faced with his thirtieth birthday, Eric decided it was "time I had a career...a real one." Teaching occurred to him. The professional life, with lots of books and free time, always seemed ideal. And, Eric had realized "on some level" that academe was a more welcome place for gay men than other professions. As he became politicized through Gay Activism, he has moved further to the Left. Now he has little good to say of corporate America or business—or the rich generally. "Most of what they do seems unethical and immoral. It's take, take, take."

The need for a Gay Network is, with Eric, an article of faith. "I think that any member of an oppressed minority has the obligation to help others in that minority... in whatever field, in whatever way he can." His "strong conscience" on this issue is, Eric feels, "part and parcel of my own working-class background." In his experience, there is more homophobia in the middle class than in working-class people. "Middle-class men," Eric declares, "are almost always insecure, and when they're gay, they feel that much more threatened by the 'majority community.'"

THE PARTY

The guest of honor is an expatriate journalist and writer of advanced age. Home for her first visit in several decades, she will never leave again. Dazed, she sits in state at the entrance to the "crush": a reception honoring the reissue of her first and only novel, published obscurely half a century earlier. Buzzing cheerfully, the other guests, her contemporaries, circle around her. They are all wonderfully preserved, beautifully dressed in dark suits by the great couturiers of our time. They admire each others' hairstyles and tasteful afternoon jewelry. Absent is the sour, nervous envy, the mean measures of success that percolate through most literary gatherings. They're the happiest women I've ever seen, observes a journalist, one of the handful of men in the vast, crowded reception room. Why, he wonders?

Why? They're happy because they're rich, well connected and free, an international lesbian circle convening to celebrate the survival of one of their own.

Liberation for most, it seems, came after marriage, a mercifully brief error. Free at last and well-off forever, on to a life of travel, cultural pursuits, spas for the preservation of health, leisure for the cultivation of friendship and love. The only closet they ever needed was the one for their Chanel and Patou suits. "Everyone" who could possibly matter in their lives "knows." No one they could possibly want to meet would care. The only stigma afflicting them is, inevitably, age spots.

Madame, la signora, la vicomtesse have no need to come out of the closet. They have never been in one. What could Lesbian Liberation or "oppressed minority" mean to these women? Since leaving their husbands, no one has ever oppressed them. Because no one has the power to withhold or confer what they need or want.

THE PARADE

On a parade perfect day, they are marching. From Christopher Street where Gay Liberation was born of police brutality, up Fifth Avenue. A block shy of the Metropolitan Museum of Art, they will turn into Central Park for rest, refreshment and, inevitably, speeches. Rhythm and spirits are sustained by two gay men's marching bands (one with a sprinkling of women), crisply in step. In perfect sync, silver batons streak through the air, are caught effortlessly in the midst of cartwheels and complicated disco steps, to the cheers and applause of thousands lining the streets behind the police barricades.

Nowhere is that American impulse to voluntary organization—the impulse which so awed de Tocqueville—more striking than in the groups of these gay and proud paraders. Many, it would seem, have organized along every conceivable "axis" of their lives: "Gay Christian Science Social Workers and Fathers" reads one placard. Each religious denomination bears its banner: *Dignity* (Roman Catholic), followed by *Integrity* (Episcopal), and the Jewish *Gay Havurah*. The professional groups are heavily concentrated in the "helping" professions: nurses, teachers, social workers and librarians. Absent are the conspicuously successful or celebrated. No stars of stage or screen. No fashion queens or disco darlings. And unlike San Francisco, no fabulous floats. No hydraulically powered penises, majestically rising and descending.

Yet this is not a Poor People's March either. Most marchers are white, and by every detail of visual evidence completely middle class.

The gay women are, in every sense, marching to a different drummer.

Gay women are mostly poor women. Sixteen percent are estimated to be mothers,[16] making them members of another poorer community: single female heads of families. Most have marginal jobs.

Many marching today are lesbian feminists. It is apparent that they have rejected middle class, male, capitalist definitions of what is "feminine," beautiful. To be thin through diet is part of the same cultural straightjacket as corsets, padded bras, false eyelashes—the "degrading artifice" that male capitalism has used to pacify and subjugate women.

In the rush of the liberation movements of the early 1970s, dance critic Jill Johnston came out, in a book with the proud title *Lesbian Nation*.[17] Like the "other America" discovered in the same decade, the Lesbian Nation, too, was invisible, and it has largely remained so.

As gay men are increasingly visible, and more *visibly* mainstream, gay women at every socioeconomic level remain, for varied reasons, a "hidden population." The most hidden of all are the most successful—and worldly. The most "closeted" are those gay women likely to be out every night—the well-known fashion editor, banker, politician.

Like single women everywhere, the relative poverty of most lesbians keeps them in the shadows. Life on the margins of society doesn't make it to the "life-style" pages very often.

In a four-year study of San Francisco's lesbian community, anthropologist Deborah Coleman Wolf of the University of California describes those working-class neighborhoods congenial to lesbians as characterized by low-rent housing and "the possibility of maintaining a kind of anonymity." Relative poverty and its frequent correlate, "a built-in degree of transience," mean that "most of the women live in old apartment buildings, or small low-rent houses. And unlike the gentrifying gay men often living close by, very few women in the community own their own homes."[18]

In a state where not owning an automobile makes one a social quadraplegic, most women in the San Francisco lesbian community, according to Wolf, were without cars, dependent upon physical proximity or public transportation to see friends or travel to and from work. Once inside these modest low-rent interiors, Wolf noted that most of the tenants seem to own very few things. If they move, they are likely to leave some of these behind since "too great an attachment to material possessions is thought to be a remnant of capitalist thinking." Characterized by marginal incomes and impermanence of relationships, high turnover in the lesbian community has another explanation. Many women fear that if the landlord finds out they are gay, they will be asked to move, so new housing is often sought, especially if the owner is a gay woman.[19]

Hostility toward lesbians as tenants is confirmed by Kinsey researchers Bell and Weinberg. Their ten-year study of the San Francisco gay community found landlords disinclined to rent to women whom they believed *might* be gay. Whether from experience, prejudice or rumor, landlords believed lesbians to be "careless about rent payments, poor housekeepers, contentious about repairs and disturbingly noisy tenants." Because of these perceptions, the researchers describe many lesbians as forced to live in nondescript suburbs that require commuting* as well as having to accept "unattractive living conditions"[20] even if their financial circumstances might normally enable them to afford better. Many women in Wolf's study were on welfare (Aid to Families with Dependent Children) and most lesbian mothers "except those few who work full time at professional jobs, have to contend with insufficient financial income."[21]

"Hi! I'm Gerry!" reads the big orange and blue button that is part of her uniform at the car-rental agency.

Geraldine Fisher, thirty-three, is pale and plump. Her strawberry blond hair is cut in a shaggy style. Almost all of

---

*Bell and Weinberg don't say whether this group owns cars, or whether these "nondescript suburbs" are served by public transporation.

the furnishings in her immaculate two-room apartment in a shabby warehouse section of Santa Monica belong to Gerry's two children, Becca, six, and Sam, three. The worn convertible sofa in the living room is for Ma.

Gerry dropped out of college in her junior year to marry a graduate student in business administration. Then five years later she dropped out of marriage to live with her lover, an assistant teacher in her daughter's nursery school. "Coming out," coincided with a political shift to the Left that began with Gerry's growing distaste for her husband's work as a junior executive in an aerospace corporation. "I had never been any kind of activist in college at all. It was the realization that we were living—and pretty well, too" on the sales of fighter bombers and missiles that made her realize "male supremacists, white supremacists, class supremacists were all the same thing—all on a death-dealing power trip—where women, gays, the poor, and Third World people were all seen as 'trash.'"

The "deal" with the children's father meant that Gerry asked for no child support, in return for his agreement not to make a custody issue over her lesbianism. His feeling was that he might as well write them off early, because of the antimale, anticapitalist upbringing they were going to get. But she believes "that's really a rationalization. I don't think he ever cared that much about them. Two kids are what every red-blooded male corporate clone is supposed to have." Like two arms, two eyes, and two cars.

Gerry, her two children, and her lover moved to a communal house in east Los Angeles. Of the twelve women, about four were mothers. The rest were either the mothers' lovers or single women who liked kids and the familial atmosphere. Most of the women were terrific, "sharing, supportive, sweet with Becca and Sam." It was her own "middle-class upbringing, at least that was what everyone kept telling me," that ultimately made the living arrangements "unworkable." Gerry is very neat.

When Gerry finally left, the affair with her lover ended. Gerry is still mourning the relationship and her failure at communal living—she figures both are her "fault. I had no trouble 'giving up' a lot of the perks of middle-class living," like having no money, or nice things, and doing low-level work for the movement. But she realizes that personal habits and the way she feels children should be raised make that kind of collective life impossible for her.

The bind, of course, is that without the shared expenses and housing, it is terribly hard to make ends meet. Ironically, because of the increased expenses of living on her own, she can no longer afford to do the very low paying political work she preferred—running a feminist bookstore. The only job she could find without a college degree or secretarial skills that even begins to cover basic expenses is her present rent-a-car desk. She is worried, though, that the cut-off point of the day-care fees will be lowered, meaning that she will earn "too much" and be unable to afford the program. Without the full-day session she could not afford to work full time. The last resort, one that she has successfully resisted so far, is returning home to her family, in a prosperous Portland suburb.

Her father, an insurance executive, and mother, both college graduates, keep urging her to come home with the kids, go back to school and get her degree. They never mention the lesbian issue. Their "deal" is they would pay for her to finish at the university. The kids would go "to the nice suburban nursery and first grade with the other nice suburban kids," and maybe, "Ma will straighten out and marry another nice M.B.A." But "they won't subsidize or even help out 'my present life.' It's always 'deals,' isn't it?" She is determined to hold out if she possibly can.

"If you have a college degree, you can get a better job than if you don't have one—unless you are a lesbian who has come out,"[22] notes novelist Rita Mae Brown, author of *Rubyfruit Jungle*.

Brown's observation is confirmed by evidence of the downwardly mobile lesbian, earning less and doing lower-level work than either her education or "inherited advantages" of parental status would indicate. Although a representative sample of a largely "hidden" population is impossible, two small studies point to the same conclusion. Researcher Robin Leonard interviewed 237 lesbians—closeted and "out"—in the New York metropolitan area work force. Compared to the national sample of white men and women, their educational level was exceptionally high. Of Leonard's respondents, whose median age was thirty-two, 26 percent had "some college," 41 percent had earned a B.A. or the equivalent, while 27 percent had graduate degrees. Their average income, $14,343, was well above the national average for all women, $9,257.

But, the highest percentage "out" (41 percent) earned the least. The income of full-time employees whose sexual orientation was known to supervisors and co-workers was under $7,000![23]

In a survey of the attitudes, opinions and sexual development of 205 homosexual women drawn from several Illinois urban areas, the authors also studied their respondents' occupations and earnings. Although 46 percent of the subjects' fathers were owners, managers or professionals, "very few of the women had professional positions" (not even in teaching). Most were in sales, clerical or general worker classifications (55 percent), with 45 percent of the sample earning less than $8,000. And this despite the similarly high educational level of the women, almost two-thirds of whom had college degrees or beyond. Interestingly, 66 percent of this sample were only children, a group (whether men or women) whom other research finds to be above-average achievers.[24]

The big question is *why*?

Do publicly identified lesbians earn less and work in low-status occupations because of discrimination and/or harassment on the job, or for other reasons? One politically active lesbian points to "other reasons." "Gay professional women tend to invest most of their energies in their career. They may not be closeted in the sense of hiding their sexual orientation, but they won't be politically active or 'public,' either." In contrast, the lesbian activist will often *choose* the kind of low-level, low-paid "shit work"—as a member of the San Francisco lesbian community described her job—that allows her to save her energies for political volunteer activities; or work for those same organizations, which also means working for pennies. The politically active lesbian feminist is also likely to be younger than the older professional "gay woman," which demographically translates into lower earnings.

Robin Leonard observes that younger professional women will often choose nonprofit work—the lowest paid within their field.[25] She points to gay lawyers who will opt for public interest, preferably feminist law, or lesbian doctors who prefer to run a women's health center.*

Finally, there is no lesbian analogy to the Prince-and-the-Pauper romance of gay male mobility. Indeed, for radical lesbians or lesbian feminists, that scenario would be as politically incorrect, as distasteful, as the notion of a lesbian Twinkie! Both are part of the ideology of middle-class male superiority and power.

"Class divisions and behavior," writes Charlotte Bunch, lesbian feminist and editor, "come from male-dominated society and it is absurd for us to perpetuate them... if middle-class women remain tied to male class values and behavior, we cripple our growth and hinder the development of a movement that can free all women."[26] (Things get fuzzy when Bunch and writers like Rita Mae Brown urge "sharing the advantages, skills and knowledge"[27] that are the birthright of middle-class privilege—without imposing the "values" that come with them.)

It may be that the "how to" part gets too problematic. Perhaps it's impossible to end class division without co-opting individual members of the working class into the middle class. As several gay men and women have observed, most lesbian

---

*No one can explain why lesbian couples, 84 percent or more of whom are childless, unlike their male counterparts, do not seem to benefit from the "gay advantage"— two paychecks and no dependents. Or why lesbian households own few possessions or assets in common.

couples are same-class couples, with less mix of social background, and even age and race, than is found among male homosexuals.

Nevertheless, gay women do help each other, especially in fields where there is a "critical mass," as one lesbian activist explained, like social work. When there are sufficient numbers of gay women in supervisory jobs, as well as other levels throughout the organizational structure, the hiring or promotion of one gay woman by another is less likely to put the first at risk. Significantly, though, social work is one of the female dominated, low pay and status occupations.

In other fields, there will be too few women—gay or otherwise—in a position to hire and help their own. With token representation in most organizations, a gay woman who was "closeted" would attract suspicion, while for one who was "out" to hire another gay woman could jeopardize her job or credibility, in what one gay male executive described as the "There-he-goes-hiring-another-queer" syndrome.[28]

And unlike gay male enterprises, successful lesbian-owned businesses are so few in number that the same ones are cited by women across the country: two record companies located in California, and dedicated to "women's music." In addition, for many gay women, allegiance to broader feminist goals often competes with, rather than complements affiliation with radical lesbianism. As one highly placed magazine executive, socially but not professionally "out," explained: "I tend to think in terms of hiring a woman, if and when I can. Next, I would give preference to a woman whose active feminism became apparent in the interview. It wouldn't occur to me, though, to hire a journalist or accountant because she's gay. I know gay men do it all the time, but I feel there is a moral difference between trying to recruit able women—vastly underrepresented, especially on the management side of publishing—and giving preference to a gay woman." Another lesbian historian explained this conflict between lesbianism and feminism as "starving" gay women's instituions.

For example, there is not a single, professionally produced gay women's publication—no lesbian *Advocate, Christopher Street, After Dark* (and certainly no slick soft-core magazine like *Mandate*). No gay *Ms*. Most lesbian publications—many with beguiling names like *Sinister Wisdom, Green Mountain Dykes* (Bennington, Vermont), *Out and About*—are modest affairs, offset or even mimeographed with the made-by-loving-hands-at-home look of a PTA newsletter. Largely regional, they are minuscule in circulation and ephemeral in life span. Why don't gay women, estimated by sociologist Martin Levine to number between three and four million in this country, support a national publication?

In part, back to basics, and the relative poverty of most lesbians who enjoy little discretionary income relative to gay men. Second, the competing demands of feminist causes, including publications. The closeted, high-status gay women are reading the *New York Review of Books*, the *American Lawyer*, the *Wall Street Journal*—or maybe *Town and Country*. They are not spending their discretionary income on *The Empty Closet*. Finally, separatist movements are always doomed to remain marginal, and nowhere will this marginality be more apparent than in members' occupation and income— in short, by two out of three basic measures of class. The "overeducation" and underemployment of many lesbian feminists, their overendowment of "inherited advantages" relative to present circumstances, underline the downward mobility that attaches to sexual politics as social segregation.

For, though we do not choose our sexual orientation, we do choose its social context, the political (or apolitical) meaning we decide it should have, in the way we live.

IV

AGAINST
THE ODDS

CHAPTER
TEN

BLUE-COLLAR
BALANCING ACT

"I ran because I like to win," Barbara Corsi Meara says. But there was another reason. "I wanted my father to be proud of me. He never even came to watch me run. Not once. Because I wasn't number one!" Tony Corsi, rowing champion, hunter, fisherman and, until recently, laundry truck driver, has reason to see his pride on the line. His father, a Sicilian immigrant, spent most of his life in his adopted country, "away in college." And Nonno Corsi wasn't sent up for any petty crimes, either! Assault, attempted murder, and finally murder kept him in jail for most of his youngest son's childhood. Bobbie's father was brought up by three older brothers. One of them was always sure to be "beating on him, and I mean beating," she emphasizes, "with broken bones," by way of discipline. Tony Corsi learned his lessons well. His three daughters were beaten, "hit in the face" regularly for anything or nothing. "If Pops just didn't happen to like your tone of voice." Bobbie Corsi Meara admits that for years she hated her father. She still can't forget or forgive him, although she knows he "loved us—especially me." He took Bobbie hunting, taught her to shoot and row.

Between shame and defiance, she admits to beating her eleven-year-old stepson. "I can't help it," she says matter-of-factly. "Now they call it 'child abuse.' But that's the way Italian families have always raised kids."

When her father had a bypass operation a few years ago, the laundry he worked for claimed it was a coronary, the result of a chronic heart condition. He hasn't worked since, and receives no benefits or social security. Fortunately, Bobbie's mother, a "crack secretary" before she'd had the kids, "was able to find a job." But dependency on his wife, her "having to go back to work," has been a "terrible blow" to this proud, combative man.

In the first circle of working-class suburbs, Bobbie's community and others like it have been described as the "white noose around inner-city Detroit."[1] Where second generation Poles, Italians and Irish moved, leaving the old city neighborhoods, with names like Hamtramck, to the new black migrants from the South. Her new house, on a street of new houses in a new subdivision built just before Detroit's depression, has a foyer/sun room, dining area, living room with deep chairs and matching sectional sofa circling a smudgeless glass coffee table. Bobbie has worked at the auto engine plant for a decade, from the month she graduated from high school at eighteen, to just days before Theresa's birth, four weeks ago. "Boy, was I *overeducated* for where I ended up."

When Tony Corsi found out that his daughter intended to go to the local university "he just hit the roof." His firm belief that "girls don't go to college" was reinforced by what was happening in those years on campuses throughout the nation. To Tony Corsi, college meant, "weirdos, peaceniks, and longhairs burning the flag."

Even though "with the couple of jobs I always had," Bobbie wasn't planning to ask her father for money he wouldn't have given her "even if he had it," she was still "too scared" to cross him. And her father's rage on the subject of higher education exceeded his anger about anything else except sex.

So she placated him on both counts by finding "the perfect boyfriend, short hair, no beard, no jeans, creased trousers," and married him right after her eighteenth birthday. The marriage lasted three months. It was, Bobbie thinks, her only way of saying to her father, "I'm a big girl now." When she was married, Bobbie had already been working "on the line" for almost a year. Looking at the white-collar jobs she could have had after graduation, like working at Sears, she "went instead for good dollars; the auto plants were paying more than five an hour and in '69 that was big bucks for a kid just out of high school. There were the kids I knew who were in college, in their ragged jeans, without a dime to spend, and here I am, waving at them from my fancy car, earned by putting spark plugs in a machine all day. God, what a dope!

"Six years on the line will make you old real quick, like nothing else." Contradicting those analysts who have described the "moving serpent" as creating catatonic robots, Bobbie insists that the line is "not just montonous, it's *stressful*. If you can believe it, you're under emotional and physical stress all the time; your feet are killing you, standing on steel grating or cement, in pools of oil or coolant. You just live for that stupid twelve-minute break every two and a quarter hours. Even if it's not a physically hard job... it's just knowing that the next hour will be exactly the same as this one... and that tomorrow will be just the same again." Shortly after her divorce Bobbie married Phil Meara, who had been working next to her on the line.

A large and amiable man, Phil Meara gives no hint of the disappointments which, his wife declares, have dogged him from an early age: from the bogus correspondence course in diesel mechanics that the U.S. Army encouraged him to "slave over," to the coronary bypass operation which knocked him out of a county sheriff's job on the eve of his appointment. Instead, his dreams of public service have involved him in the local volunteer emergency squad.

With seniority, Bobbie Meara was able to move from the despised assembly line to running a complex piece of machinery. But this work, preferable in its freedom from quotas, speedups, or direct supervision, has other drawbacks: "Boy, when you're trapped behind that machine and that's all you can see. It's suffocating."

For Bobbie, the most positive change between the line

and her present job is the opportunity for protest: "The line never stops, but you can break the machine.² You can get away with it twice a week. No one can prove you did it, because you know that machine better than anyone. You become part of it."

Rage is one reason for breaking the machine; the other is a few hours of freedom. Here, the goodwill of the foreman is essential. "You learn how to be real cheap, real quick." Bobbie claims that she was a slow learner, that it took her five years "to learn to play up to these guys. To wear my jeans tight, sexy tee-shirts. 'When I get divorced, you'll be first, honey,'" she purrs, in fake, sexy basso. "*That's* what you gotta say to some shrimp that comes up to your belly button. You gotta build up their stupid egos. Then when you break the machine, they let you relax while it's being fixed. You won't have to clean up the garbage."

For a brief moment, it seemed as though Bobbie Meara would triumph over probability, to become one of the few unskilled workers to move to a skilled trade. In the late 1970s, under government pressure, the company established a crash program to train minorities for the coveted jobs of master electrician. Affirmative action was invoked to reduce the interminable apprentice route. "The idea was to get blacks and Mexicans into the 'trades,'" Bobbie reports, "but legally, they had to include women as minorities. That's how I got in. When the program began, it was me and two black women. The rest was all black men and chicanos. Until the white guys got mad, and they had to let them in, too. I studied like hell, let me tell you. My husband never helped me. He didn't want me to pass. But I did! I was the only 'minority' left at the end." At the end of the program Bobbie Meara also discovered that she would need thirteen years seniority to be hired as a master electrician. The slowdown in the industry had started; hiring was frozen. The lists were four years behind. Six more years to go. By that time, she figures she will probably have another baby, have fallen into "your typical woman's rut. Where I'm just not going to start a new career at thirty-four."

Across the living room, tiny Theresa rocks gently in her infant swing, her gaze fixed on the bright brass fittings of the fireplace. A Mayan temple in miniature, its intricate brick-work rises from orange-carpeted steps. At the summit, sliding panels of black glass protect a fire, forever unlit. ("We should have connected the fireplace to the thermostat," Phil Meara says apologetically.) Now, a fire would make the living room unbearably hot. The altar behind the glass screen remains clean, cool and dark.

"To get this house, we worked overtime every day, seven days a week, for a year and a half." On the very last day— when overtime was eliminated due to the industry slow-down—it was ninety degrees outside in the humid Detroit September. She was working in the "grinder," the hottest place in the plant. "It must have been over one hundred and ten degrees inside. I just collapsed." But it wasn't only the heat; the medical diagnosis was "physical and emotional exhaustion." Bobbie was out of work for two months. Then she got pregnant.

"I'm ashamed to tell people what I do. Whatever I earn, however good I am at my job, I'm nobody, a factory rat!" She is determined that Theresa will go to college.

"Phil and I are trapped," Bobbie says.

Trapped is no metaphor. They are, literally, trapped. "We can't live on one income." Even if they could sell the house—which in Detroit's present economy, and with current mortgage rates, is unlikely—any small older house now costs $50,000, more than they paid for their large new one. The rent on their once "cheap" apartment is higher than their monthly mortgage payment. "So where would we go?" Then there is the seniority. The security trap. Bobbie Corsi Meara realizes she's lucky. Her ten years of seniority means she's still employed, unlike 200,000 other Detroit auto workers, one-quarter of the auto industry—some of whom were laid off with a few months less seniority than Bobbie. "I've only got twenty-one more years to retirement. I'd be a fool to leave."

"Getting laid off in '73 saved my life," George Ritchey says. "Otherwise I'd still be in that plant today, doing as little work as possible, just living for the daily drug break."

An only child, George Ritchey's parents came to Detroit in the 1940s from rural Illinois. His father's family had emigrated from a farm in Scotland early in the century. His father is a "straw boss" for one of the two major Detroit dailies, overseeing the shipping of the bound newspapers onto the trucks. His mother's family is Latvian, "but they're really Poles. And I always tell people I'm Polish. When I was in high school, I liked being Polish better than being WASP. Besides, at that point I wasn't even talking to my old man."

In junior high and through high school in Madison Heights, he wanted to become a police officer. ("Don't ask me why," he says, "probably TV.") But the "ideal was still there" when he graduated and he enrolled in the local community college which offered law-enforcement-related courses. That changed his mind. At the same time, he got interested in electronics, taking courses first at a 'tech' school, before trying another community college for computer courses. Somehow, even though he picked up an associate science degree along the way, the "things I was good at and liked doing, didn't seem to add up to anything. Probably because nothing inside my head was adding up to anything at that point." So he was a gas station attendant for "Monkey Ward" and a few other "nothing jobs" before the big money and the assembly line claimed him.

"Those were the days of high living, in every sense. Here I was at nineteen, making more than ten dollars an hour"— twice what his father was earning. If his younger co-workers didn't live in a van, like George, they lived at home. Either way, low overhead and no families to support meant that they spent it all on drugs and booze. From the minute they punched out, they partied all the time. Al Nash, an auto worker turned sociologist, describes this "daily drug cult," involving thousands of those younger, disaffected auto workers, Baby Boom

—234—

children hired by the industry in the late 1960s, as the "problem which neither management or the unions, each for their own reasons, liked to admit existed."[3]

"Guys went out to shoot up or get high at break or lunchtime, but you didn't have to go outside to buy," George says. "There was dealing all over the plant. You just had to turn around. Anything you wanted was right in the aisle. It was Alice's Restaurant!" More than the monotony, noise and dirt, it was soon discouragingly clear to George that there was "absolutely no room for advancement" for production workers in the auto industry—stoned or unstoned.

Laid off in 1973, he went to a small town in western Michigan to find a job. For a while he worked for a large local foundry. Then, as the recession dug deeper into the region's economy, that job dissolved. For a year he "did fine," collecting Michigan's generous unemployment benefits, living in a cabin in the woods, and "just hanging out." Then he met Sandy, his future wife, and his life started changing. "She did some leaning on me to get more schooling, find some direction to my life." They moved to Ann Arbor where, with a shock he discovered the class system. "You're either rich or poor in that town," he recalls sourly. "The university was rich; the rest of us were the proles. Second-class citizens, or maybe even second-class human beings."

The local community college did manage "to really fire me up" about electronics. Moving to Minnesota, George found a job with a computer manufacturer, "where I really got into it—from top to bottom." Where, for the first time, he started working day and night, where "he just couldn't seem to learn enough or do enough." Then came the "big divide." He was offered a job in management. George Ritchey is now plant manager and supervisor of another small electronics company with thirty employees, eighteen of whom report to him. As one of three executives—the others are two brothers who own the plant—George runs the production and shipping facilites. The "big divide" in George's life—the move from labor to management—created another area of father and

son conflict. "Now I was management. I had become 'them.'"
At the same time, as a fervent believer in the work-hard-
and-you'll-succeed philosophy, Jack Ritchey had to admire his
son for succeeding. "It was very hard for my Dad, and it still
is."

In his pioneering study of the industry, *Automobile
Workers and the American Dream*, sociologist Ely Chinoy
interviewed sixty-two factory workers in Lansing, Michigan
in the late 1940s, to reveal their frustration, their "anomie,"
as well as their aspirations. At that time, forty-eight of his all-
male respondents hoped to leave factory work and become
self-employed.[4] For most workers today, the reality principle
has dramatically altered that ambition. Gene Brook, director
of the Wayne State School of Labor and Industrial Studies,
thinks the economy, and the general conservatism of most
workers, if they kept their jobs by virtue of seniority in the
massive layoffs between 1979–1982, will conspire to keep
them on the assembly line. Few will aspire to self-employment. Also, they are well aware of the high failure rate of
small businesses. Like George Ritchey, Bobbie and Phil Meara,
accumulated seniority and future retirement benefits all argue
for living with present discontents. Friends and ex-fellow
workers on food stamps, others setting off for the Sun Belt in
hopes of a job, are reminders that frustration is a luxury.

Though he still feels uncomfortable about the envy and
resentment, George Ritchey is sensitive to his father's genuine
fears for his only son. To the older man, it is just "unthinkable"
to throw away the security and accumulated seniority of "being
union." To him, management and working "on your own" are
equally "chancy." When Lee Iacocca is fired, he can't file a
grievance. That's the "union mentality. That's why my old
man got stuck."

Shortly before 8 A.M., George starts seeing sales repre-
sentatives from companies that either already do business with
the plant, or would like to. The rest of the day consists of
checking orders, tracing shipment delays, meeting with his
principals, adjudicating personnel problems, trying to keep

on top of the nonstop flashing lights on his phone (and the pink message slips piling up) and "general troubleshooting." A conversation not related to work is "really exceptional" in the course of his day. Now his men are out on their lunch break, from two to two-thirty. George himself "almost never has the time" to stop work, not even for thirty minutes.

By the time he arrives home from the plant at night, it is usually near 9 P.M. Too late to see his two-year-old daughter and too exhausted for a real supper, he can "just about stay upright long enough to grab a sandwich and a glass of milk" before falling into bed.

Aware that he is "hooked, like everyone else," on a rising standard of living, George Ritchey knows that the punishing workday has also purchased "all the goodies"—the new house, boat, two cars, hi-fi system.

Although he equates getting fired with getting ahead, George readily concedes that "other factors" account for his expanding ambitions and high expectations of success.

Despite his "denial" of his father, George knows it was "something he drummed into me; the idea that people have to make choices, be willing to sacrifice good times and short-run pleasures for getting things later in life."

As manager, he sees in his workers little of the lust for work he rediscovered in himself. "Most people," he observes, "just weren't brought up to cope with the pressure of working all the time." Most people see little prospect of reward for such sacrifice. Others define reward differently.

When Nathan Eldredge was sixteen, he wanted to be a lawyer. But the teachers in his high school, located in Detroit's south-east ghetto, "more or less let you know what your potential was. And it was made clear to me that I wasn't college material." At the time, he wasn't all that disappointed, because no one else that he knew in his graduating class of 1962 went further—"at least, not at that period of their lives." Neither Nathan Eldredge's father, who had come to Detroit from rural Alabama in 1937 to find factory work, nor his mother, had gone beyond 8th grade. That six of their eight children completed high school was regarded as "really coming up."[5]

Nathan knew that as soon as he finished school, he'd have to look for a job. So he felt lucky when, a month after graduation, he was hired by one of the largest auto plants as an assembly line worker. He has been there ever since—for seventeen years. Half of his life.

Nat Eldredge sinks into the velour depths of his favorite chair; his long legs, stretched out in front of him, almost clear the width of the tiny living room. The last rays of a hazy Detroit sunset pierce his wife Leona's collection of cut glass. It was the union, Nathan says, that changed his life. Yet he is inclined to see chance as the real agent of his career as an organizer and activist.

As union work absorbed more and more of his interest, energy and aspiration, it became clear to him that he "needed to develop more skills, be able to articulate, to know what I was doing, what I was talking about." Very shortly after winning that first-rung office of "union rep," Nathan was beginning to feel that the "contributions I could make were being stifled by my low level of formal education." Then he discovered that the union local would pay for a six-week program at the Wayne State Labor School, where evening classes combined nuts-and-bolts reading and writing skills with courses in labor history. Nathan spent the next five years—dawn hours, evenings and weekends—writing papers and reports, until one amazing June day, he had a B.A. from the local liberal arts college that had grudgingly agreed to accept a few "nontraditional" students each year.

Doing four years of college at night and on weekends, after a full day shift at the engine plant, "didn't seem hard because it really tied my life together," Nathan says. "It was an extension of my days as a working man and union rep. It taught me that everything I was doing fit into a larger scheme, into history."

Since then, he has completed some work toward a masters degree in adult education, but studies had to be interrupted when he was named to serve on the union team during the last contract negotiations. "We would be going around the clock," he explains, "two twenty-four hour sessions, followed by eight, ten, sixteen hour days, so it was school that had to go."

Word got around about this "rep" who never seemed to stop working, who spent endless time helping more bewildered or less literate "brothers and sisters" fill out forms, explaining benefits, unraveling red tape, who could persuade some of the most cynical and disaffected younger workers that they should get more "involved"—and who was the person local newsmen surrounded during the wildcat strike at the plant. Word of Nat's organizing talents and "leadership potential" had reached, he was told, the highest cenacles of Solidarity Hall. The union had suffered a loss of credibility, due to recent wage give-backs, layoffs, the what-have-you-done-for-me-lately-besides-collect-my-dues attitude of younger members, along with accusations of slackened "commitment to civil rights and social justice." Nathan Eldredge became of "particular interest" to the international leadership. That was when his troubles began.

Nathan was approached about the possibility of a staff job at the national level. Those who had their eye on him for some time were especially eager that he become a full-time organizer. Nathan had to say no. A national organizer is on the road for months at a stretch, on indefinite assignment. With his recent marriage, he had acquired three young step-children. He was eager, finally, to "put down some roots."

If he didn't want to travel, that was all right. There were other, maybe bigger possibilities in store for him. He was sounded at length about his political ideas. What they really wanted to know, he realized, was "how reliable was I?" Somehow, it should have been clearer to him what "reliable" meant. At the time, though, he was still thinking of it in *his* terms— not theirs; as in "how willing was I to do what I was told." He was not, as it turned out, supposed to run for president of the local against the incumbent—the guy who, after all, by his own account had recommended Nathan for higher office. An international "rep" was delegated to tell Nathan that interest in him came "straight from the top." What that interest might mean to his future in the union depended on, well, how "dependable" he was. It wasn't that Nathan considered himself a righteous fanatic, or self-appointed policeman of the local. It was just that irregularities seemed to come to his attention. Such as evidence of the amount of money local officers of the union were being paid.

As might have been expected, Nathan's efforts to "bring this into line" became a "very sensitive subject." Especially when he entered an appeal, which resulted in a hearing before the review board. And right after that, it came to Nathan's attention that the local's deficit spending, on a month-by-month basis, amounted to over a million and a half dollars more than they took in. When Nathan reported this to the international union, and the secretary-treasurer looked into the situation, his local ended up in receivership.

Happily, these were not the bad old days when shooting messengers bearing Nathan's news would have made waves only in the Detroit River. Anyway, hadn't his union, with its proud reputation for probity and progressive politics, been in the vanguard of the struggle to end the "bad old days," of gangsterism, racism and "deals"? However, the same emissary who had brought word from on high about Nathan's future returned with an oblique notice that hearts and minds had changed: "You can't just go around fighting everybody, Nat. Sometimes you just have to back off." The leadership was disappointed with Nathan's insistence on entering an appeal—going public—and ignoring communiqués from "the top," discouraging this line of action.

So Nathan really had no choice. "I couldn't be part of any program on that basis." Which leaves him caught in the classic dilemma: if you won't, or can't, play by their rules, you end up out of the game—not representing anybody.

When layoffs take place, the number of reps drops along with the workers in a given shop. With whole shifts eliminated, "there was," Nathan notes evenly, "an opportunity to remove people for political reasons" through committee decisions rather than by an election. And that is how, at present,

Nathan Eldredge finds himself "back at work," repairing his machines, "doing my job and my thing." His "thing" is still education: his fellow workers', his kids', his own.

Community for Nathan is his Political Caucus.

Beginning as the first "third party" the local had ever seen, the first to have an integrated slate, the caucus has come to mean much more to Nathan than a political issue. "We work together, we keep educating ourselves, we keep each other honest," he ticks off slowly.

They share a belief in what trade unionism should be and, at least sometimes, a faith in what it can be still: a process of educating and informing, and most important to Nathan, a process of participation, of "openness."

Even more necessary for Nathan, the caucus stands in challenge to one of his most painful discoveries: that "everybody in the union hates education; the leadership doesn't want members who know anything, either about filing grievances, or enough about politics to know when they're selling out. And the reps and shop stewards, who know a little more than the rank and file, don't want any competition for their job.

"There's never been any question in my own mind," Nathan insists. "I'm working class and I always will be." The point of more education has never been "to make me middle class."

But for generations of Americans, from ghettos black and white, that has indeed been "the point of education"; "the Great Lever upward," as a nineteenth century black editor wrote,[6] the passport to the middle class and to professional status beyond. The very adjective "higher," as in higher education, pointed the way to "rising in the world," leaving behind lower-class origins. What kind of a man struggles for all that schooling—studying nights and weekends—in order to end up still an auto worker, just like his father? The classic definition of failure in America.

Nathan Eldredge is well aware a of cluster of contradictions at the heart of his choice of class, the gulf his schooling has created between him and some of his fellow workers. The smallest slight, or misunderstanding, is taken as proof "I've gotten above myself, that I look down on them." He admits freely, moreover, that there are "several rungs of working class. There are guys I socialize with, have a beer with after meetings, whom I wouldn't have in my house, wouldn't let them meet my kids. So I'm not sure that my class solidarity takes precedence over other things." He knows, too, that being working class in the American automobile industry is—while you're still employed—to have little in common with Marx's proletarian slave who "produces palaces and lives in hovels."

"I'm not knocking success," Nathan declares. "We all want to do well, especially for our families." He is prompt to point out that "doing well," the $30,000 he was earning when "things were better," along with his wife's salary as an administrative secretary, made it possible for them to "drive around until we found the neighborhood we liked, with the schools we wanted." In post-1960s Detroit, the most race-sensitive city in America, Nathan would never deny that the Eldredge family income greatly reassured their new neighbors.

The very act of self-definition, of choosing to be working class, is already elitist—or aristocratic. That, of course, is the most profound contradiction of all. Most of us stumble upward, downward, or stay stuck behind one machine or another: Vyadec, manifold intake, Cuisinart or Concorde, obediently jumping for the carrot before it's offered to someone else. Choosing to be working class, for Nathan Eldredge, means simply that "more" is not enough. "More" means remaining a factory rat, condemned to live out Hegel's definition of slavery as Thinghood.

With his own future as uncertain as the future of his city, Nathan knows that what he has been trying to do, he and his caucus, "looking to provide people with a sense of freedom, where they know they don't have to be dictated to or held back by someone else," is a remote goal. But if he can't do that, or if he gets laid off and has to go elsewhere, he thinks that maybe it's time to do something "radically different—like grow flowers for a living; something where the tension is not there, where you don't have to get into antagonistic relations with people."

Going beyond his present situation, or circling back to it, he is ready to reinvent himself through his project—the existentialist definition of a hero.

Halfway up the hill from the harbor, Arturo Duarte's house, a square of ochre stucco, sits solidly on a corner lot. Swirls of perfectly raked black and white stones carpet the front yard and meander toward the door, flanked by two palm trees— "the oldest and tallest on the block," their owner proudly notes. Inside, prune velvet curtains shroud the windows, shielding carpets and upholstery from the dazzling sunlight of southern California. From every surface—end tables, coffee tables, and floor—rise massive lamps. Thrusting or spreading forms of carved wood, blown glass with captive bubbles, arabesques of wrought iron, each is crowned with an expanse of vellum shade, the diameter of a child's starched petticoat. Yards of thick fabric—the drapes with their heavy lace undercurtains, the gold pile carpets spread with throw rugs, the suite of living room furniture, each chair a sheltering cave of avocado tweed—shore the house against remembered gales of Gloucester winters, forty years past.

Arturo Duarte was twelve years old in 1913, when he first accompanied his father, a dory fisherman, to sea. In those days, the Portuguese were already so well entrenched in the Gloucester and Provincetown fishing industry that, as Arturo recalls, "All orders on board were given in Portuguese. When they dropped the dory over the side, even if the skipper was a Yankee, he always said: 'Vai con deus.'" Of the ten thousand Portuguese who had settled in Gloucester by the turn of the century, Arturo Duarte thinks that about 90 percent were, like his father, fishermen. He doesn't need a sociologist to tell him that his countrymen clustered in "ethnic enclaves."

"It was a closed society. We all lived on what was called Portygee Hill." Indeed, by 1880, an observer had noted of the hill, formerly called Point Lookout, that "rows of homes owned exclusively by Portuguese fishermen, lined the newly laid out streets." Largely from the Azores, like the Duarte family, these fishermen forged beginnings in this country unique among new arrivals. Unlike other immigrants, who purchased steerage passage, the Portuguese began "almost without exception"[7] working their way across on the New England fishing fleets. "They became part of the work ethic," as one chronicler of Portuguese migration notes, "before they ever set foot on American shores."[8] Many were rewarded and moved from crew to captain's quarters, commanding schooners out of Gloucester for the Grand Banks.[9] Unlike his more prosperous kinsmen, whose houses in Gloucester and especially Provincetown boasted lace curtains and clocks, Joachim Duarte could never seem to do more than "just get by." Despite fishing haddock and cod "day and night," Arturo recalls, his father never achieved that saved-for and slaved-for goal of every man he knew: to buy his own boat and become self-employed.

So while other boys played hookey to go swimming during the first warm days of spring, Arturo would get his work permit to leave school, often not returning until late September.* "We couldn't come back until the ship was loaded." Even with the help of his two sons, times were getting harder—not easier—for Joachim Duarte. Fish got scarcer and finding them became more dangerous. "We used to have to go out further and further from Gloucester, to the Grand Banks, the Georges Banks—even up to Nova Scotia."

João (John) Santos is Arturo Duarte's oldest and closest friend, since their arrival in California as young men four decades ago. A large and round bachelor, "Tio Johnny" is the licensed joker of the family. Tio Johnny reminds Arturo that in Gloucester, "they never did get a good price for fish, because the price all depended on the weather, and the Gloucester weather was the worst on the entire coast." The only decent money to be made in those days was out of Province-

---

*As late as 1960, the educational level of Portuguese-speaking foreign born was lower than that of any nationality reported except Lithuanian.[10]

town, where the fishing was not far from the sandy beaches, and it wasn't as hazardous if a storm came up.

The Jewish holidays were a special cause of celebration to the Portuguese fishermen. Demand was so intense for the carp and yellowtail needed for gefülte fish, that they had to engage a broker at the Fulton Fish Market in New York to transact their business. Tio Johnny, at sixteen, was the agent "back home," who checked the accounts. "The older guys were all suspicious of me, though, because I could read and write and they couldn't." Unfortunately, Seders in New York and Boston were not sufficient to support the growing numbers of Portuguese earning their living from the sea, especially when the Great Depression struck the rest of the New England economy.

So they began the great move west.

Sociologists call the special movement pattern of groups like the Portuguese "chain migration." John Santos describes this process in sailor's terms. "Folks went where they had an 'anchor' already. An anchor was, first of all, information. When somebody left Portugal, they'd send word back about how much better Gloucester was. Then someone from Gloucester would get anchored in Provincetown, and we'd hear about how much easier it was there. Then we started hearing about California."

The Duarte family was especially receptive to the tales of blue skies and warm weather from their California "anchors," two uncles who had traveled directly west from the Azores. After "some quack doctor" had cut the joint of Joachim Duarte's finger to remove a splinter from a log that had caught in his net, his father's hand went numb in the cold. Fishermen were forbidden to wear gloves to pull in the nets. Gloved fingers caught in the mesh meant that "if there was anything broken and the net went down, you'd go with it." Unable to use his bare hands, Joachim Duarte could no longer fish.

The move west was a wrenching decision. Joachim and Evalina's house was almost paid off, after all these years. The three children were grown and ready to settle down, and just before the finger had festered, "Dad had finally been able to buy a boat, the Isabel." There has never been a moment of regret, though. As soon as the Duarte family, leaving one married daughter behind, arrived on this hilly spit of land near San Diego, Joachim found that the warm and sunny climate "cured" his finger. He got a job immediately on the tuna fleet. Arturo found work right away, too. And what his father hadn't taught him about fishing he learned from Tio Oliviero, one of the California "anchors;" like sailing and "surf fishing for sword."

Between father and sons, "We was in the chips! Boy, were we making money," remembers Arturo happily. In 1929, this dramatic improvement in the Duarte fortunes and those of thousands of Portuguese New Englanders who followed them in the next few years, was hardly typical of the rest of America.[11] They were not only doing much better than those who stayed in bleak Gloucester, but better than many established Californians.

For, although the prosperous Portuguese farmers inland were already a byword among California immigrant groups, they were outdone by their industrious fishermen kin, aided by the new canneries, with their related industries and services. "We were always good for twenty, maybe thirty dollars a trip; and this, mind you, for only seven to ten days out in the mild southern waters." His father, who received shares at $90 on the tuna boats, was "making a ton."

They kept on coming, more "anchors," attracting more émigrés from New England. Tio Johnny, orphaned at eleven, arrived with an older brother and sister-in-law. Back East, his brother had skinned fish for a living—"pulling bones" it was called. He worked "awful hard" just to survive.

Arturo Duarte is prompt to point out: "Nobody's family ever had to do without." There is no stronger or prouder tradition among the Portuguese-Americans than self-help. The "underlying factor of brotherhood"[12] as one chronicler notes, both informal and institutional, expressed in the mutual aid societies that sprang up in each settlement, made public assistance unthinkable. Going on welfare was considered a disgrace to the community as much as to the individual or family.

"Other boats always took in the guys with bad luck. A place would be made for them. Everybody was always prepared to divide the shares up another way."

How do people so intent upon prospering reject that first article of faith of those who prosper: that for some to succeed, others must fail? How does sharing become a commonplace, the unremarkable fact of everyday life? "We just had the custom," says John Santos.

Unknown to the welfare rolls, these Portuguese Californians are, however, almost as sparsely represented on the rosters of another public facility, higher education. For them, the achievement of middle-class economic status has created little of the educational and social aspirations which most other immigrant groups have focused so intensely on their children. The same strong family ties that have yielded the lowest crime rate of any ethnic group in America, also stress the family as the "primary economic unit"—as practitioners of the dismal science say. Success is measured in terms of the total income of all working members of the household.[13] And in this equation, pro-family equals anti-education. Coming to this country for economic advantage—rather than religious freedom, political liberty, or educational opportunity—Portuguese parents frequently judged more schooling to be in direct conflict with greater prosperity.[14]

The high school dropout, as one writer noted, is not necessarily considered a failure by his parents. Rather, he or she is a dutiful child contributing to the good of the family.

"Portuguese boys do more like the old man," Manuel Captiva, a retired Provincetown dory fisherman, told a Federal Writers Project interviewer in 1937. "Some of 'em get these ideas to go to high school. Don't do 'em no good as I can see...."[15]

This attitude toward education seems to have changed hardly at all. If anything, easier money has offered a more seductive alternative to more schooling. Bachelor Tio Johnny thinks that pressure to leave school came not from parents but from older kids. The average Portuguese father wants to give his children what he never had, "like fathers everywhere." But then, "the older kids would spoil the younger ones, show them good money, cars, clothes, so the younger brothers would drop out of school to go fishing."

Youth is no obstacle to big earnings. An egalitarian tradition holds that all hands get an equal share of the catch. If the fishing is good, Arturo Duarte points out, "a crew could make $26,000 on *one month's trip.*"

It is impossible not to feel admiration, envy—even awe—for these hardworking, self-respecting citizens, sharing with and caring for their own. They are not afflicted by the qualifying adjective "status" that sociologists have invented to describe the miseries suffered by those on the move: status striving, status anxiety, status discrepancy. Snug in their stucco villas, they cut the Great American Pie their way. No eyes bigger than stomachs, or psyches. They have never waited on the admissions committee of the local country club, or for their son-the-doctor too busy to visit, or for promises of Portuguese Power from homegrown demagogues. What these early Sun Belt migrants came for, they got: good money, a kindlier climate, an easier life. And ignoring every lesson on How-to-feel-like-a-failure-in-America, they have stayed off that endless escalator of "rising expectations."

Yet what does this warm "ethnic enclave" do for—or to—aspiring, gifted young people? Is it, as sociologist Andrew Greeley has suggested, a "mobility trap," discouraging ambition, stifling aspiration, atrophying talent? Where would that "social construction of reality"[16] come from, that would allow a fifteen-year-old biologist to see him or herself a fellow of the Salk Institute, glimmering distantly twenty miles down the coast? Individual aspirations only betray, upsetting everybody "and for no reason." Why, John Santos wonders, would anyone "want to go to a strange city"—to study, work or raise a family—when "they got everything here." He and his neighbors know that talent encouraged, ambition fanned involves loss, rejection and pain. The family is diminished, not enriched in any sense, by children who keep score by surpassing their parents.

Let other parents take pride in the achievements of far-away children. "Me, I like to have the boy on my boat," said Manuel Captiva, "then I know where he is, what he is doing."[17] His California kinsmen, with their house on the hill, two cars, and portfolio of stocks, would have no argument.

CHAPTER
ELEVEN

GETTING
THROUGH
THE NET

Every January for twenty-nine years, the Seventh Regiment Armory at Park Avenue and 67th Street has hosted the Winter Antiques Show. For nine days, the home of the National Guard is transformed. Decorators, carpenters, florists, along with seventy-three dealers in art and antiques have carved from this cavernous space an Imperial Russian dining room, Irish Georgian library, Louis XV salon and many early American farmhouse kitchens. In this enticing bazaar, where casual visitors and avid collectors jostle for a better look at Coromandel screens, cornhusk dolls, diamond-encrusted snuffboxes and Revolutionary War muskets, the scent of potpourri mingles with the sound of baroque music.

Four floors above, the air is dense with disinfectant. In the gymnasium, on cots whose new mattresses are still wrapped in plastic, fifteen men lie or sit quietly. All of them are black. They are part of the first contingent of twenty-five homeless males whom the city has agreed to house in temporary shelters. The entire busload arrived late Friday night, after a black-tie preview for the opening of the show. During their stay at the armory, the men will receive three hot meals, fresh clothing, adequate shower and toilet facilities, as well as recreational programs.

Interaction between the armory's two tenant groups will be minimal. Participants and visitors to the Antique Show use the Park Avenue entrance, while guests of the city enter and leave by a side door. The space between these two doors, separating the unwanted homeless men from the consumers of these coveted objects is the distance between the top and the bottom of the American class structure.

Whether or not we accept the definition of "underclass"[1] for a mixed population of homeless aged, young families on welfare, long-term drug addicts, youthful career criminals, mentally and physically disabled, their presence forces us to confront the ugliest reality of class in America. For some, a place at the bottom is a life sentence.

The most predatory—or pitiful—of the poor, they are also the most visible, whether on the streets or in the media. Yet the newly discovered underclass comprise less than 10 percent of the population classified as being under the poverty line.

Who are the poor? There are approximately 30 million of them—or us. Thirteen percent of our population.[2] The poor are those whose low incomes or no income make them eligible for public assistance. Contrary to popular belief, many have always worked. Most work sporadically, when they can find jobs. Some have never worked. An estimated 25 million are recipients of public welfare programs, either in the form of money or in-kind, transfer payments such as food stamps, Medicaid, and public housing. Disproportionately, they are the old and the young—especially the young, who comprise over half of all welfare clients. These children and their mothers receive payments through Aid to Families with Dependent Children, which accounts for more than 66 percent of public assistance. The mothers comprise the more than 50 percent of single "female heads of households" with an income at or below the poverty level. Of this group of mothers, more than three-quarters were—or are—teenage parents, with children born out-of-wedlock.

Neither the welfare or working poor are a static, unchanging, readily identifiable population. They are a fluid, dynamic changing stream of individuals and families.[3] Their welfare status may be only a day or week to help them through a family crisis, or it may last a lifetime. What makes the difference? Luck, pluck, "genetic pool" resources, human and material? Choices made—or not made?

Does anyone choose poverty? There are some high-status choices associated with becoming poor. (Remember St. Francis?) The religious, artistic or pedagogical vocations were, until recently, tantamount to a vow of poverty, which is why they were considered the "nobler and needier" professions.

Nevertheless, poverty, for the masses of the poor, spells only "pariah status."[4] To be thus stigmatized—in a society that values success above all—seems hardly credible as a conscious choice. In reality, though, life is a series of trade-offs. For many people, other choices may be more painful than poverty. As liberal economist Kenneth G. Boulding points out: "Many operators of small farms, residents of depressed areas and others with low income know (or have reason to believe) that they can make more money elsewhere. Yet for a variety of reasons they choose to live where they are and be counted as poor. . . . Much of this poverty is voluntary in the sense that opportunities to obtain higher incomes are foregone."[5]

"Don't, for God's sake, suggest that poor people could just choose *not* to be poor," warned a sociologist on the Left, "or that they choose Public Assistance over work. Not unless you want to see more welfare families without fuel next winter, and the Food Stamp Program slashed further." Giving comfort to the enemy. One of the deadly sins in the theology of the Left. "Choice" like "merit" has been co-opted, demoted to a code word. "Free to choose" absolves "us" of responsibility for "them."

Therein lies the dilemma—and the crux of all debate about the poor: How is this responsibility to be divided? A legislative report urging expansion of Great Society social programs still acknowledged that "Individuals make choices for which they should be held responsible, at least in part. Some of their choices greatly affect their economic well-being: employment, place of residence, family size, family structure and parental support of children."[6] The tricky phrase here, of course, is "in part." Which part? And how much choice do the poor have, relative to the rest of society?

In fact, diminished choices are among the most cruel— and unjust—characteristics of poverty. To a poor man or woman, even the choice of life over death may be unaffordable.

A recent study of the cost-benefit method of assessing health hazards in industry (and who should pay for correcting them) found that the poor constituted the highest on- and off-the-job health risks. The working poor are those least able to choose a "safer" workplace. "Income," as the authors noted, "plays a central role in the trade-off of risks and costs, not because the poor are ignorant, but because they cannot afford risk avoidance." Residents of Triana, Alabama, the same study points out, "eat fish from the Tennessee River with levels of DDT fifty times the amount the Food and Drug Administration considers carcinogenic because many cannot afford anything else."[7]

The decision to leave a job, however hazardous, is never a simple choice. Such a choice may mean giving up a pension or losing a home. Being poor often means "being convinced of the necessity of performing dangerous work in order to earn a livelihood." You have to have more than "just enough" money to choose health instead.

The rich, in Hemingway's famous reply to Fitzgerald, may be different from you and me because they have more money. But the poor are different not simply because they have less.

"Hidden income multipliers" compound a dollar deficit, to add unequal access to consumer goods (where the poor get fleeced by poor quality and exploitive credit terms) and to essential medical and legal services. Poor neighborhoods most often spell substandard housing and schools, which in turn translates, in a skill-rewarding market, into low-level jobs or none at all.

Yet the poor, like the non-poor, make choices about their lives—informed and uninformed, by guess and by God, short-term and long-term, for themselves and their children—that powerfully affect their economic and social well-being. The very fact that these choices are, for poor men and women fewer in range and number, magnifies their significance. Decisions—about more schooling, more or fewer children, seeking a job, changing skills, finding help or another place to live—can dramatically alter "life chances" for the poor man or woman in ways scarcely imaginable for many Americans.

The creases left by too many anxious frowns shadow the friendly smile of Dolores Martinez. Yet she still looks a decade younger than her forty-two years. Of her five children, the oldest, Michael, is a student in the local city college, his brother has a scholarship to a distinguished art school, and the youngest, Nina, is a fourth-grader. Dolores's husband, a construction worker, died of kidney failure eight years ago. Since his death, Dolores has supported the family on a combination of his union pension, social security benefits and, at such times as the year her mother lived with them, on welfare.

Dolores dropped out of her New York City high school in the 11th grade. "I had done really well. But money was very tight the summer before my senior year." Her father, a caulker, was frequently unemployed as shipyard work began to dry up. "I had gotten a pretty good job at the supermarket, but we just needed more money than after-school work would have brought in."

Two years ago, Dolores went back to work as a teacher's aide in her daughter's Head Start program. She was excited by the free courses in early childhood education that were part of her training, and proud of the encouragement she received. "They kept telling me I should get my high school equivalency, go right through to the college degree and I'd have a teaching certificate." But she wasn't sure how she would manage studying and working only part-time, so she didn't pursue their suggestions. It seemed, at the time, like such a big decision, so much planning and effort for an uncertain future. One of her teachers was very disappointed. "She kept telling me I could do it."

Dolores now works as a switchboard operator in a nursing home. The salary, $8,000, combined with her other benefits, allows her to "just make it." She is such a good manager that, as she says, "The Department of Social Services kept insisting I was doing something wrong. When I went off welfare, because I was working, they kept telling me I couldn't have budgeted right. They would send me a check every two weeks because they said I couldn't possibly 'be doing my budget correctly.' But I was. We were all O.K."

She appreciates the helpfulness of Phil, her boyfriend of five years, especially his efforts to be a friend to her older children. At the same time, she resents their dependency upon him for everything beyond life's basic necessities. He provides the only "treats" they enjoy. Without him, there would never be a weekend away, a meal in a restaurant or any respite from the relentless cycle of job and housework.

Dolores is aware of and fascinated by the differences that separate her from the liberated middle-class women on television: women who can choose to enjoy pleasures on their own. "I love to see women who are making it without any men—with no male influences—just to be able to afford to go to a restaurant or a movie by myself or to travel alone—without feeling guilty because if I go, one of the kids can't do something. I love to watch 'Rhoda' and the 'Mary Tyler Moore Show.' That would be my fantasy life... the way they have company whenever they want—and yet, with those lovely large apartments, they can be alone whenever they feel like it. The way they can decide and make decisions and just go ahead and do it! I'm going to go to Milwaukee or Chicago because I've been offered a better job!... It's the freedom... I just don't have too many choices, especially ones that would make me more like them. But it's so easy to imagine myself in their place... at least while I'm watching."

Dolores's perceived lack of choice is real—insofar as it is real to her. Even with encouragement, she couldn't choose more schooling, leading to higher-paid, higher-status work. Moving elsewhere—even with the offer of a better job—is not treated as a real option.

Michael and Marty are both personable, articulate and attractive; they are also young, black and unemployed. Michael and Marty are two of the nearly four hundred thousand unemployed black youth in this country.* Unskilled, like most of their peers, their prospects are bleak—unless industry and government undertake a massive reinvestment in their future, which would also require, in the present economic picture, serious training for jobs that may not exist now—or in the future.

Part of the problem is the nature of the jobs that do exist. They aren't ones that street-smart kids like Marty and Michael want or are willing to stay with for very long: "I was working at the welfare office in the file room. All I would do is push a buggy around and collect files, and most of them would be old records and stuff, and I'd just have to take them in my little office, my own little room, and put them in a paper shredder all day, from eight o'clock to five o'clock."

So Marty, a high school dropout, quit this job and another paying $2.90 an hour, the minimum wage, that was also part of a job program—exterior painting and minor repair work on Seattle's many Victorian houses.**8 Interviewed by a young, sympathetic reporter on Seattle television, Marty knows just what he finds unacceptable about such dead-end jobs. "Everything they was teaching me, I could have learned going through *Life* magazine." His buddy Michael adds: "I don't need no training to dig a hole, or to carry no wood."

Both young men are quick to point out the inevitable equation: jobs with no training equal jobs with no advancement.

Leaving aside the predictable reactions of Left and Right

*Average figure for 1982. Bureau of Labor Statistics, April 1983.

**The kind of work that other young people drop out of college to do.

—257—

ideologues, most Americans will have mixed emotions on meeting Marty and Michael. Why should any kid, particularly one as smart and articulate as Marty, be content to shred paper or paint houses when he is obviously capable of learning and doing a variety of more complex tasks?[9]

Still, there is something hard to accept about the right-not-to-work, the right, as claimed by a high school dropout, to reject a job that fails to provide new skills or a "career ladder." The missing coefficient in this equation of dead-end-job-equals-choice-not-to-work is "need." These kids don't "need" a job that desperately, so if it's menial, boring or "doesn't go anywhere," they don't want it. There is public assistance at home and the possibility of bigger bucks on the street. "There's something out there if you can get it. Either way, like if you feel you don't want to work or don't need to work, you say: 'Well, yeah, I think I could do better out there.'" Besides, hustling has the excitement and suspense of high-stakes gambling. Or as Michael says: "You either go a month without making nothing, or you might make $500 in five minutes."

We tend to forget how fast and far we have come since the "work or starve" ethos and the sense of entitlement so clearly expressed by these two young black men.

Until the last years of the Great Depression, when New Deal legislation authorized the National Relief Administration to provide emergency rations of "surplus" food to the destitute, "work or starve" had been unquestioned as social policy for millennia. Charity or philanthropy was never considered a right. One of the 15,000 workers laid off by the Amoskeag Mills in New Hampshire in 1935, the depth of the Depression, recalled: "When that first truckload of food arrived, a neighbor called me down to get our family's rations. 'From the government,' she said. I just couldn't believe it."

Between disbelief in the miracle of "free" food distribution to destitute families and the belief, fifty years later, expressed by a high school dropout in his "right to reject" a job without built-in mobility, lies the most rapid shift of social values in the twentieth century.

S. M. Miller, a sociologist who has studied both occupational mobility and the problems of minority youth over
several decades, defines the change not as one of entitlement,
but as one of inclusion. "The poor have finally been brought
into the American mainstream—just enough to know—(especially younger people) that they are being 'dished out.'"
However, survivors of other "hard times" may well be mystified by the new "mainstream mentality" of Michael and Marty.
Americans old enough to recall the Depression remember the
desperate strategems and part-time work pieced together to
survive. The European refugees who arrived here in the 1930s
and 1940s included doctors who worked as kitchen help,
teachers who became nursemaids. Need was translated into
no-choice jobs for millions of Americans.

The real question to be asked of rejecting the "wrong"
work is not whether such a choice exists. We know it does.
But rather, what does it mean in terms of class? By holding
out for the right kind of job or training program, Michael and
Marty are refusing to be shunted to the bottom of the occupational—and by extension—class structure. They are saying no to the menial, low-paying, no-future jobs that their
fathers and thousands like them—black Americans and unskilled immigrants alike—accepted and most often kept for a
lifetime.

Moreover, in terms of income these young men will be
worse off than their predecessors in such jobs. The earnings
gap between low-wage work and most high-wage skilled labor
appears to be growing rather than closing. "Relative to the
average worker in society, the working-poor wage earner is
poorer today than he was twenty years ago. His relative income position has deteriorated":[10] and that is what class is all
about. There is another facet to Marty and Michael's choice
of refusing the only jobs presently available. By dropping out
of high school and from two jobs, Marty won't be a likely
candidate for any employer or job program. The jobs he wants
are selective, and too many kids want in. Besides the numbers
involved, there is a cost-effectiveness calculation made in any
"real" work situation. As economist Lester Thurow points out:

"For new workers and for entry-level jobs, it is the 'background characteristics' of the workers that form the basis of selection. Those workers whose backgrounds promise the lowest training costs will be hired."[11] Reliability, punctuality, a high school diploma, the "sign-off" of a satisfied teacher or supervisor, are assets to private employers and directors of public-sector programs who inevitably practice the kind of *triage* that writers on the Left deplore: "helping those most likely to succeed—those who made the right choices."*

"What would I tell those kids? Without a second's hesitation I'd say, move. Anywhere. Just get going and get out." George Ellis is an administrator in a federal agency and a black man. It is a long way from New York's Bedford-Stuyvesant neighborhood, where he grew up, to his spacious and sunny Washington office, overlooking the Mall. Ellis doesn't forget and doesn't romanticize. One of five children of a sporadically employed Brooklyn transit worker, his family was on and off welfare for most of his childhood.

"Three of us made it, two of us didn't. But the tragedy is one of my brothers who didn't—the brightest, most gifted of all of us. Just one miserable juvenile crime. He couldn't get away from that record. It always managed to defeat him." The boy of such exceptional promise is now a postal clerk.

"My future looked pretty dismal. I had just graduated from high school. There wasn't a cent for any more schooling. Somehow they weren't telling poor black kids about the free city colleges in those days. At least I never heard anything about them.

"I looked around and saw my older brother in and out of drug programs—and jail. The unemployment, the street crime—this was before the Bed-Stuy Restoration that got the Kennedys all involved. In the late 1950s, it was all downhill. I just knew I had to get out—and out meant anywhere else.

*Obviously, this is not true of supported-work programs for the "hard-core" unemployed, such as the Manpower Demonstration Research Corporation (MDRC) project described by Ken Auletta in *The Underclass* (New York: Random House, 1982).

"So I went to Manhattan—to the Lower East Side. I must have climbed the stairs of twenty loft buildings looking for work. Finally, I found a job in a candy factory. Now talk about dead-end jobs! That had to be one of the deadest. But in a way, that was what made me come alive. . . . I started looking around, thinking: What else can I do? Then I heard about the U.S. Civil Service and their exams. That's where I've been ever since.

"I just don't see myself as 'exceptional' in the sense of smart or talented. I do work harder than most people though. I guess my experience makes me a believer in 'merit.' That and getting out. None of the other things would have happened if I hadn't taken that first step, even though it was only crossing the river from Brooklyn to Manhattan."

George Ellis isn't talking about a mass migration of the poor to the Sun Belt. Rather, he is echoing a choice that could not be more classically and uniquely American: our deeply held belief that moving out is moving up. Upward mobility as movement—anywhere. Making it as leaving home. Never mind where you go.*

Upward mobility is also relative—how far you've come and what you left behind. We are compulsive scorekeepers.

"To the black family who left grinding rural poverty in Tougaloo, Alabama, or the Mexican migrant worker, dilapidated, substandard housing in Houston's Second and Third Wards may still represent a big step up," observes Rice University sociologist Chandler Davidson.

Elena Navarro was fourteen-years-old when she married. Luis, her seventeen-year-old husband, left the National Guard and they began life on the first of many isolated ranches in the mountains around Santa Fe.

---

*From the first settlements fanning out from the eastern seaboard in the late eighteenth century to Ohio and Kentucky, Americans have been on the move to "improve" their lives. Whether the rationale was free worship, free gold, free land, or the big city, the real lure may have been motion itself: the perception that in severing ties, casting off moorings, a young man or woman could not fail to rise like one of the new helium-filled balloons.

"He did light cowboy work and I worked in the main house. The jobs never lasted long because of his drinking. Our first child was born when I was fifteen. We got fifty dollars a month plus food. But the food was all potatoes and beans.

"Luis was one of those very macho men. He could go out and do everything. But I was always supposed to stay home. And until the other kids came along, I had to stay in one room. He wouldn't let me go anywhere or see anyone— not even my family. He was very abusive, very violent. If I didn't go around with my head down, I got beaten."

It took seventeen years and four more children before Elena realized her life would never get any better. "Then one night he locked me and the kids out of the house. It was freezing cold, but we walked the six miles into Santa Fe. That was it."

Small and plump, with short black hair, Elena Navarro looks, at thirty, like a Chinese schoolgirl. She no longer bows her head, though her eyes are still lowered much of the time. "God, was I terrified! I had no education at all. How was I going to support five kids? And then I was so scared of him. He could have one of his violent fits and kill us all. But I knew I'd never go back and I haven't. I filed for a divorce. I wanted to be sure I was legally free."

"For brutalized women, particularly for brutalized poor women, no decision they ever make will so powerfully affect class mobility as the choice to get out," notes a Louisville social worker and director of a YWCA Battered Wives program. "The gain in self-esteem and desire for economic independence provide a dramatic lever up. Most of these women are without skills but they are desperate to work. They don't want to be at anyone's mercy again."

After that icy walk into Santa Fe with her children, Elena tried to find a job. But no one needed a twenty-nine-year-old woman with five children, an eighth-grade education and no work experience.

"I would have done anything. I applied for work in a laundry and as a maid, but I never got a job. They would always take someone with experience. Then I heard that you could get work training through welfare. I went to the welfare people and told them that I needed help financially to survive, but that, mainly, I wanted to get into a training program so that I could learn to do something."

The first lesson Elena learned was to raise her head. The second was that she needed more schooling. Through the Work Incentive program (WIN) Elena studied for the high school equivalency diploma. "I didn't find it hard at all. In fact, I really enjoyed it. I'd always read a lot, magazines, books—anything I could find around the ranch house, I read."

The WIN component of welfare has had mixed reviews— depending upon the administrators, the region and the local employment picture. In the Sun Belt in the early 1980s, there were real jobs or further training for more professionally de- manding work at the end of the program, especially in health- care careers. A booming population needs hospitals. In a re- cent study attempting to predict the economic independence of the WIN program's welfare clientele, 302 men and 428 women were interviewed in New York and Chicago. Who makes it and why, were the basic questions informing the reams of questionnaires probing "orientations," values, atti- tudes, as well as documenting the education, work experience and family structure of the respondents. Predictably, women (all with families) were only 35 percent as likely to become self-supporting as men. Astonishingly, among the black, white and Hispanic respondents, years of schooling, previous work experience, even length of time on welfare, were less impor- tant predictors of succeeding in a "real" job than was the "expectation of economic independence."[12]

Two jobs, seven days a week as a nurse's aide in the city hospital and visiting nurse in a county health program are needed for Elena to earn $12,000, pretax income. Besides supporting herself and the kids, Elena's salary also contributes to mortgage payments on the substandard cinder-block house she and the children share with her father and alcoholic sister. They would certainly be eligible for public housing, thereby reducing this outlay in Elena's budget, but her eighty-one year-old father refuses to leave his home and neighborhood.

The big hurdle looming now for Elena is getting her RN, "so that I can earn enough from one job." She will need a loan, possibly from the Opportunities for Women program at the local college. Her optimism is guarded. "Going to school full time means working only part-time." She is uncertain whether a loan and only part-time employment will cover the tuition expenses, payments on the house, food and clothes for the kids.

Elena Navarro can see clearly how far she's come, and where she wants to go. She is acutely aware that every hurdle left behind gives her that much more choice. "I'm just getting a promotion at the local hospital, to supervisor of nurses' aides. Instead of hands-on nursing, I'll be evaluating patients' needs and delegating other people to meet them. Through that, I'm hoping to advance a little bit more, to get a little bit more experience. Then, if I get my RN, I'd like to do administration—make the system run better. I've done the hardest part already... I think."

Jobless, drinking and brawling, Tony Yoruba at twenty-six had lost his wife and children. A third-generation Texan, Tony's grandparents were Mexican and Yaqui Indians who migrated to El Paso during World War II. "My grandfather influenced the rest of the family—he really motivated them, through his example. He was such a hardworking man and so was my father." Tony's father was a machine operator for the Southern Pacific, but when he hurt his back a few years ago, at the age of sixty, "they moved him down to an easier job. Of course, his pay scale was lower, too."

His father's industry and effort seemed to make no difference. The roughest times occurred during Tony's adolescence. There were ten brothers and sisters and never enough money for shoes—or even food. "Things were very bad with us then. The school gave us breakfast every morning, and lunch too—if you were poor enough to be eligible. I guess we had no trouble qualifying." Tony's athletic ability seemed to promise a better future. "Without my interest in baseball I never even would have gotten to high school." Neither baseball nor high school would have happened without the encouragement and example of his adored older brother, Mickey, killed last year in an automobile accident. "He really got me into it because he used to play varsity football and box. I was so proud of him." Tony needed his brother's example. Mickey had finished high school and was supporting his young family with a well-paying job in the copper mine.

"None of the kids I grew up with went to high school. They either dropped out in junior high or they went straight to the juvenile detention center."

Tony attributes his family's pride to their Yaqui heritage. Along with athletics, "taking part in the Yaqui Easter ceremony of the Resurrection became an important part of my life." His sense of the "special" nature of the Yaqui ritual is both keenly historical and comparative. "This is the way of God—not like those Indian dances you see for tourists. Our ceremonies took place before the Spaniards came to Mexico. The Christian part came later."

Everything seemed to be coming together for Tony until the 11th grade. With the promise of a football scholarship to college for Tony, his girlfriend, Laurena, became pregnant. "What happened to both of us shouldn't have happened." But fifteen-year-old Laurena's father was old-fashioned. "Once you slept with his daughter, whether or not she was pregnant, you got married." At sixteen, Tony Yoruba dropped out of school, became a bridegroom and began looking for work. He took the first job he found, with a janitorial service, on a split shift. The job was so far from the young couple's home, Tony never saw his infant daughter awake. He found something closer, starting as a sander in an auto body shop. Besides ending the exhausting split shift, the new work allowed him to move up.

"After I did sanding for a while, I started taping, then spot painting. Then I got to mix the paint and paint my own cars. Here I was, seventeen-years-old, painting my own cars! I was amazed at myself, and a lot of people around me were amazed, because I used to do a pretty good job.

"My pay started at the same as janitor's work, $2.60 an

hour, but it was a steady job, and every time I moved up to something different, I would get a ten cent an hour raise. The people there were very nice to me—especially the foreman—he seemed to appreciate how hard I worked and especially that I really liked learning new stuff. So he gave me a lot of breaks."

Tony left the body shop after a year. Their second child was soon to be born, and he had to earn more money. "I didn't think about going beyond where I was, beyond painting cars. I just wanted to keep my family fed. I got a job working on a construction crew, earning about $4.50 an hour. That was really good in 1969. And I kept moving up. I started getting paid $5.00 then $5.50—until I was making $7.00 an hour.

"Then I lost my job. Construction slowed down a lot; they just stopped building. It was very hard to get a job—any job. I didn't have enough money to pay the next month's rent. My wife had to start working, as a waitress in a drive-in. That was a terrible blow for me—not to be able to support my family. And that was when everything started falling apart. I just couldn't seem to stop doing things I knew I wasn't supposed to do—like drink a lot and get into fights."

An even greater blow for Tony was his estranged wife's ultimate need for public assistance. "We never thought of going on welfare, my Mom and Pop would just never do that. If you're on welfare, you're considered.... No, you're not considered *that*, you're considered dumb if you *don't* get it."

Tony and Laurena decided to divorce—a *legal* divorce. "It was very sad for me. I missed my wife. I missed my kids a lot. I take them every weekend. I haven't skipped one yet." Unemployed for over a year, it was somehow the judicial decision, the cold language of liability that galvanized him. "I had to get back to work because I needed to give my kids child support. The court ordered me to and I agreed with that. *It was my responsibility.*"

For most of us, abstractions are automatically "empty." But emptiness may be relative to the plenitude of our other choices. It is poorer cultures that cling, like Tony Yoruba, to notions like *virtù*, courage and manliness.

As soon as he decided that he was the only one who could win back his family, Tony looked for work in earnest. But personality problems tripped him up. A more painful revelation, though, was that skills he had worked hard to learn and work that he loved were not marketable. No one cared that he could operate a forklift truck and was a fast and elegant bricklayer. Because no one was building anything. Another reason no one cared, Tony became convinced, was his "drop-out" status. "I began to see that whatever it was I wanted to do, I had to have that diploma. Not having it was always going to be an argument not to give me that job."

Having that "piece of paper," Tony discovered, also had "hidden multipliers." Psychic and real income potential.

For the first time in his working life, Tony found himself in a white-collar job, processing applications in the credit department of a large department store. "I enjoyed being nicely dressed all day. I enjoyed meeting different people. I especially enjoyed being clean while I worked. It was something entirely new for me. I could feel how even the lowest clerk enjoyed more 'respect' than anyone in working clothes — even the foreman on the construction crew. But I began to see this was 'surface stuff.' For me, it wore off when I saw the paycheck. And I didn't see anyone going anywhere from there, either." He has done well on the high school equivalency tests. Is he ready to try for the next rung? There is scholarship money available. Well-wishers know how to help him. Tony has thought about it. "A lot." It's his second chance, but he is finally not persuaded. Besides the "foregone income" how does he know that he will end up better off? What he really wants is to get his family back and like millions of Americans, "to own my own home." College seems somehow diversionary. He has decided on a job in the copper mines. "That's what my brother did, the highest paid work around here. Now that I have a high school diploma, I can choose dirty over clean."

If there is a net keeping out the many, if, as one of Studs Terkel's respondents discovers bitterly, the "system is rigged," why and how do some of the least favored among us get through? Are they "exceptional" in ways that are not very useful to others? Or "exceptional," to all of our shame, only in their small number?

In fact, no one knows how many of the poor, welfare or working, ever move up to the next rung of "stable working class." After hundreds of thousands of dollars, vast numbers of researchers, tables, charts and graphs, sociologist Christopher Jencks's sequel to *Inequality, Who Gets Ahead?*, concludes that he and his coauthors don't have those answers. Yet, to hear the story of any American who overcame obstacles of race, poverty, sex, geography, or "other," is to be convinced that individual "life choices" are the most powerful lever upward. Luck is clearly a close second in the difference between who gets ahead and who doesn't. If you are poor, the missed appointment, the lost busfare, the sick child can literally be the chance of a lifetime lost forever. That is the most cruel inequality of all: the brass ring may come around only once. A black New Orleans mother described the tightrope talk of momentous chance: "When I decided to go to school, I knew I had to cut out the other two jobs. All I had was welfare, because I didn't want to flunk. I didn't want to fail. I figured the door unlocked this one time; it might not open for me again. So here's my chance. I'm going to grab it and I'm going to do the best with it and I went to school the full year— twelve months—not missing one day, not one day. I slept with my books, I walked with my books. You never saw me without my books. Because I didn't want to fail."

Tony Yoruba's "informed" choice of work in the mines over lower-paid, higher-status clerical work or more schooling is not just a case of "lower-class value stretch."[13] His two ambitions, "to keep his family together and to own his own home," seem more plausibly secured by higher-paying work.

"Right" choices aren't necessarily those which propel an individual to the highest possible rung of the occupational ladder. Choosing "dirty over clean" was this shrewd young man's quick take on what sociologists call "status discrepency." The white shirt and tie get you more laundry bills than bank bills.

All outsiders, whether they are women in the corporation or poor men and women trying to move up, need and tend to receive help from insiders. There is nothing cynical or subversive about this fact. Until the happy day when there is a well-placed, old-boy or old-girl network for every ethnic group in America, and consequently no need for one, everybody, but especially the poor, "gets by with the help of his friends." Who those friends are makes all the difference.

British sociologist and welfare administrator Richard Titmuss, pointed to "command over resources"[14] for the poor as the crucial distinction between who sinks, who stays afloat and who moves up. Resources include material assets and inner strengths, as well as help close to home: family, neighbors and friends. But the most important resource may be powerful allies who act as mobility mentors.

This critical choice of mentor can also be a racial issue and cause of generational conflict. Elena Navarro sadly observes: "My kids feel very threatened by Anglos. I never felt that way. I think I got more help, more emotional support. When I think what I've been, and what I am now, it wouldn't have happened without the white doctor, the people in the job program. Because with the Mexican attitudes about the family, I think I stayed in the position I was in all those years because I never had anybody say: 'There's something better for you. You don't have to live like this.' The message was: 'It's the culture. If you're married, you have to live with it, no matter what, you just have to take it.' And I was young, so I said: 'That's the way it has to be.' I just took it for granted. So, I think if not for my Anglo friends I would still be married to that man, still be beaten up.

"But my children just feel totally negative—partly because of what they've experienced in school. They and their friends see everything racially, and if I try to tell them any different, they say: 'Ma, you just don't know anything.'"

Profound differences in attitude divide many minority parents and children on issues affecting choice, mobility and the Anglo or white communities. Those among the minority poor who are over thirty-five, that is, who came of age before the 1960s, are likelier to accept an individualistic and paternalistic model of mobility. To Elena Navarro's kids, on the other hand, their mother is naive, refusing to face the larger issues. They appear to be unwilling to adopt her philosophy and seek friends or mentors in the Anglo community who might be able to help them. In Marxist terms, they have rejected their mother's false consciousness, in favor of a class/race consciousness. Rather than be singled out as favored individuals for help, they demand that the social structure accord them rights too long denied.

V

WHAT'S NEW ABOUT WEALTH?

CHAPTER
TWELVE

THE
DESERVING
RICH

When Thorsten Veblen wrote about the "busy rich," he was, of course, indulging in irony at the expense of his favorite victims.

The rich were busy, in his disapproving view, doing nothing. Their busy-ness was a frenzied rush from one futile, frivolous activity to the next time-filling and time-killing appointment.[1]

Conspicuously consuming, for purposes of "invidious distinction," Veblen's leisure class was characterized chiefly by its inefficiency.* They were literally good for nothing, except to waste time and money. Veblen, who inherited a heavy work ethic from his Scandinavian immigrant parents, didn't hold it against the rich that they had more, but that they did less. Unlike contemporary social critics, Veblen had no agenda for reform, and certainly no prophetic visions of redistributing wealth through measures like progressive taxation, transfer payments, or guaranteed family income. He merely wanted

---

*No one seems to have noticed that Thorsten Veblen (1857–1929) was a near-exact contemporary of Frederick Winslow Taylor (1856–1915), the father of scientific management, who pioneered the use of time-motion studies to rationalize the labor process and increase productivity.

the rich to stop being lazy and shiftless, to earn their privilege and power by productive labor.

It wasn't the ill-gotten, but the ungotten gains of the leisure class that incensed Veblen, whose belief in the virtue of work makes Benjamin Franklin look like the playboy of the Western (new) world. The poor, according to Veblen, had a moral edge over the rich because, in his day, they worked so much harder, beginning in childhood and ending with the grave. When Veblen lived, no child labor laws, compulsory schooling, sick leave, disability or unemployment insurance, paid vacations or social security provided deferment, respite or retirement from the relentless exigency: work or starve.

Since Veblen's time, the rich in America have been transformed. More than transformed. Morally regenerated. In a new meritocratic society, it stands to reason that the rich, who have more of everything else than the rest of us, will have more merit, too. Unlike their predatory predecessors, the "lives of the new strategic elites," notes Princeton University sociologist Suzanne Keller, are no longer "characterized by luxury and material splendor, and more by special responsibilities and styles of work."[2]

Saved by the ethos of achievement, the need to succeed, the New Upper Classes in America have abandoned their amateur standing. The rich have turned pro.

THE WORKAHOLIC WEALTHY

To a woman, a man is a sometime thing, but for most self-made men, making money is a full-time activity, allowing few other interests. For the New New Rich, work is not a duty, it's a pleasure—for many, in fact, their *only* pleasure. Unlike their predecessors in this country (and many Europeans, even today), for whom work was a necessary evil, the New New Rich enjoy making money; it is what they do best. They do it all the time and they can't imagine anything more fun.

The term workaholic is a post-1960s hybrid, needed to describe a new social type: the successful American male who needs and prefers the activity of work even to its rewards.

The man who, given a choice of ways to spend time—over and above what is required to succeed—chooses to work.

"I get the greatest pleasure from what I do, from my business," declares Hunter Bolling, forty-five. By his own account, and most other peoples' too, his career is "one of the astounding success stories in America since World War II." The hero of the story is not shy about citing figures, either: $1,300 million in revenues last year. "It's been phenomenal," he says proudly.

But Hunter Bolling is quick to distinguish his own intense "pleasure in business" and its rewards from the "self-fulfillment ethos" of his young adult children. "I never felt I had any choice but to succeed. In the 1950s, that was the man's role: to be a husband, a provider and a success." Tall, dark and movie-star handsome, Hunter Bolling would be any casting director's ideal for a remake of *The Plainsman*—right down to his down-home twang. But instead of wearing buckskin moccasins, breeches and carrying a rifle, Hunter Bolling, sockless in tassled loafers, wears English twill slacks, a worn navy blue "alligator" shirt, and carries a Georgian silver salver bearing two tulip glasses filled with wine.

The genial southern host is not his usual role. In this most gracious and sociable of cities, Hunter Bolling, a grocer's son from a downstate farm hamlet, is proud of his prickly, loner reputation, his complete lack of interest in the usual involvements of the small city big rich.

"I've never been a member of any church," he declares, "any men's club in town, or any country club. I'd rather spend all my competitive juices in my business, get the slam on *that* court, instead of knocking myself out on some square in the sun." With the exception of his directorship of a local bank, Hunter Bolling serves on no boards. "Voluntary activities" have always seemed to him "a complete waste of time."

Politics, he says disparagingly, was one of the reasons he found his former profession and colleagues "so dull. That's all lawyers seem to know about—that and the law," he observes.

Hunter Bolling enjoys staying home, studying his art

books and particularly his auction catalogues. His aim is to "know everything *important* there is to know about Western American painting and sculpture." His own small collection boasts several fine works by Remington and Russell.

"I don't really have any community," Hunter Bolling declares. "Most people seem to feel a need for those kinds of associations, but I just don't happen to be one of them." Instead, Hunter's affiliation is with what he terms his "network of intelligence." First and foremost, his business associates.

"We've built up this tremendous thing together, and we're very close." Then, there are his relationships with people in the art world, but these he carefully distinguishes from friendship. They are, he notes judiciously, "built on mutual interest."

His relations with this network—museum people, dealers, a few other collectors—has been such a learning experience, so "enriching," Hunter says, that he has become impatient with his role of "knowledgeable consumer," just an amateur.

"Hell," he says, "I know more than most of those guys by now. I'm thinkin' about becoming an art dealer myself."

Homer MacFarlane, fifty-eight, is hard put to tell you exactly where he grew up. "All around the southwest is the best I can do." By the time he was sixteen, Homer, his mother and eleven brothers and sisters had moved a total of twenty times. Mostly in flight from landlords and bill collectors.

At seventeen, Homer moved out, supporting himself until he could join the army in 1942. After the war, with a brand-new engineering degree from Yale "courtesy of the G.I. Bill," he headed for Oklahoma and the assistant manager slot in a supermarket. Building bridges and dams, Homer explains, meant working for the government like most of his classmates.

"I've never had much use for governments, but I was interested in business, and supermarkets looked like a chance to get in on the ground floor of something new."

Thirty-seven years later, Homer MacFarlane owns the

largest chain of supermarkets (and the only group to be locally controlled) in the region.

"I love this business," he says passionately, in the raspy voice, punctuated by coughs, of a three-pack-a-day man: "I love every minute of it and everything about it." Interests? Homer MacFarlane thinks, lights his second cigarette, and gazes down at his trucks for the third time in seven minutes. None that he can think of. "I guess I'm a boring and narrow person." There is a glimmer of a crooked smile through the smoke. "That's what my wife tells me, anyway." To be "neighborly" and to please the patient "Mrs. M.," Homer *thinks* he joined the Golf and Country Club around fifteen years ago, when they first moved to Wildwood, but "if I've been there twice, it's a lot."

Although he announces himself proudly as a "true-blue conservative," the extent of Homer MacFarlane's political involvement is summed up in this way: "I vote and I pay taxes." He expresses cautious optimism that a pro-business president and administration might "nudge this country on the right track." But this remark is qualified. "I've never heard a politician yet who seemed to know what the hell he was talking about. They're all such a goddamned bunch of amateurs," he snaps irritably.

Supermarkets, he explains, "are a *highly* competitive operation with a *very* low profit margin. And if you don't keep your eye on the ball every minute—well, you're not going to be around very long. I'm better than I used to be, though. When I was building this business," he recalls, "I was in here most Sundays—catching up." Homer inhales deeply and glances down at the trucks again. Now that their operations are computerized, there is less travel and less paperwork to get through.

Oh, yes, that reminds him: he has a "new interest": computer programming. "Here I hire these M.B.A. kids," he says with gruff fondness, "to do all the stuff for me, and they tell me *I* should learn all about it." Every day, in his "torture chamber" down the hall, assisted by a technical staffer, Homer "works out." Makes more sense than golf, anyway.

Half a century after Veblen's baleful view of the idle, unproductive, wasteful rich—fit only to fritter away money and time—came the revised version of their unworthiness.

The adversarial update replaced Veblen's conspicuous consumption with inconspicuous (but pervasive) corruption—and on a scale unimaginable to the early muckrakers. In the 1950s, C. Wright Mills found his "power elite" characterized by the "higher immorality" and the "big grab."*[3] In his view, money was only—and always—a means to power,[4] a habit requiring ever-bigger hits.

Throughout the 1960s, exposés of further "influence peddling" demonstrated the extent of corporate power. Budgets for public relations and salaries of lobbyists had soared, in direct proportion to the dangerously declining quality and steadily rising prices of everything from automobiles to baby food.

Younger sociologists went further. Where Veblen had characterized the rich as a class of febrile and frivolous loafers, and Mills portrayed his power elite as having more and bigger "toys," with the means to indulge every caprice, contemporary writers like sociologist G. William Domhoff conclude that the new elites have no pleasures at all that do not involve conspiring among themselves—and corrupting others. In studies that delineate the "processes of ruling class domination in America," Domhoff ascribes this power of the "powers that be"[5]—the title of one book—to an elaborate overlapping and interlocking network of associations. From men's clubs to intermarriage, the country club to the Council on Foreign Relations, the power of money is constantly raised by the reinforcement of mutual interest groups—the dark side of de Tocqueville's delight in American voluntarism.

Writers like Domhoff have no patience with skeptics who

---

*Mills was far from consistent about the nature of their immorality. Generally, he takes the view that "they" seek to own or control all institutions, public and private, appropriating for themselves all the "command posts of power." But elsewhere, he excoriates the rich for being "irresponsibly apolitical."[4]

raise questions about what really happens* as a result of these gatherings of the filthy rich; the outcome of outings like the annual retreat of the Bohemian Club of San Francisco, or the less elite horsing around of potbellied rough riders, members of the Ranchos Vistadores, a mostly Sun Belt, mostly New Rich gathering of movers and shakers.[6] They're together, aren't they? is all we need to know. What further proof is required of their sinister plotting? And together means planning the appropriation of natural resources, the revision of the tax laws, the elimination of food stamps and the invasion of Cuba—all the while peeing into each others' ten-gallon hats!

The New Rich—even according to their sworn enemies—never take a day off!

Notably missing, though, from the adversarial and aerial view of the new power elite is any explanation of how they got that way. (Presumably, the route is from the Lower Immorality to the Higher, with floods of money automatically flowing in the "wrong" direction.) But friends, neighbors and kin of the self-made Americans—what social psychologists Richard P. Coleman and Lee Rainwater call the "Local-and-Regional-Legend Rich"—do explain "who gets ahead" in America. And their explanations are remarkably similar: fierce ambition but mostly "hard work." In their survey of "new dimensions of class in America," Coleman and Rainwater interviewed a hundred Bostonians and the same number of Kansas City residents—representing all socioeconomic groups—about every aspect of "social standing": objective and subjective; their own, their parents', their fellow citizens'.[7] When working-class people described someone they knew well who had achieved dramatic upward mobility, the reasons given to explain this success were almost always the same: "pure effort," "just plain hard work," "work, work and more work."

---

*Without first-hand access to these cenacles of higher immorality, Domhoff has to rely on newspaper files, and the accounts of disaffected former service employees.

Heroes of these dramas, the authors note, had "often worked two jobs instead of one. They had worked double-time whenever they could. They had not taken vacations. They had worked nights and weekends... especially if self-employed and trying to build the business up." Fueling this heavy work ethic was ambition—specifically directed to economic ends.

Of the most "astonishingly successful" of their acquaintances, Bostonians and Kansas Citians alike invariably noted "they wanted to make money—lots of it." They were always "money-motivated."

The biggest "surprise in this portrait of status change," to emerge from the research is how little weight was given by respondents, in explaining the new fortunes of their peers, to "talent," "natural superiority," "excellence of performance"—the supposed attributes of a meritocracy. In the experience of this representative group of Americans in mid-life, their society was even more open than a meritocracy, a system that still presupposes a "destiny in part prefigured by genes or a favorable childhood." From their friends, relatives, "a fraternity brother of mine," "a man who was a neighbor who started building houses," "three boys I knew in high school," respondents limn an *effortocracy*:[8] men and women working harder than they themselves might be willing to work, more single-minded in pursuit of the buck than they might happen to be, but otherwise, no more remarkable or favored by fortune.

Nor is this explanation of success confined to participants in the Boston/Kansas City study. Taking no credit for the achievements of her three sons, college graduates and professionals, Mae Clark, a black Detroit kitchen worker, noted simply: "They always been mighty effortful children."

"Self-choice" not chance or charm was the reason given by most Americans for the rise of others whom they knew well. Plugging their way to the top, working weekends and nights—just to keep the competition at bay—these are the new antiheroes of success. The Deserving Rich.

For the New Rich, there is no respite from achievement, no time off from striving. Conspicuous competence is not a goal, it's a reflex. The body's biorhythms are set on "excel."

To sociologist Talcott Parsons, himself prodigiously prolific, modern society was defined by its professional, rather than by its capitalist character. And in the age of professionalism—the era of expertise—amateurs, bumbling around the office, kitchen, garden, nursery or bedroom, are out.

"Stewart is no playboy," a Delectable Person was overheard describing her escort. "He's a heavy hitter on Wall Street, a drug dealer, a pimp—and a real pro at all three." For those with reputations to uphold, nothing is avocational. Hobbies (as in "Hobby Shops") are for retired accountants from Des Moines.

Only people from families who made it, can remain rank amateurs. On them it looks good. Like George Plimpton. As patrician putterer and professional writer, Mr. Plimpton has the best of both worlds. A more "contemporary" contemporary of George Plimpton is Ted Turner. Nothing is out of his league. No sireeee! Whether its skippering the America's Cup winner in 1977 or taking on the networks in the Satellite War Between the States. If he wasn't so busy being the William Paley of the Piedmont, Ted Turner would obviously be pitching for the Atlanta Braves instead of just owning them.[9]

The aristocratic amateur is an all but extinct species.

"Excuse me," Abe Gray apologizes, blowing his nose operatically into a large blue handkerchief. The unnecessary apology—natural, humorous, diffident and arrogant—conveys every attribute of the upper-class American male. The self-deprecating style goes with the distinctly unstylish attire: an off-the-peg Brooks Brothers suit of indeterminate age and terminal sag, the cracked vintage English shoes.

No designer of creative office interiors has "personalized" Abram Gray's executive image. Behind Abe's scarred desk and worn leather chair hang two small oil sketches by Homer and Eakins. "My little souvenirs," as he describes them, the only works from his family's famous collection that did not go to the university from which every male Gray has graduated since 1809.

"My *present* wife is just finishing a doctorate in Far Eastern history for which she learned Chinese and Japanese. She's not interested in American art. It's too easy. Patty is only interested in mastering things that are terribly hard to do. She came from a *very* lower-middle-class family." Somehow, with the addition of "very," lower middle class has sunk to somewhere off the socioeconomic scale. "She grew up in a mobile home." That Abram Gray III would know—let alone marry—anyone whose social world had once been bounded by a trailer park requires a considerable leap of the imagination.

Patty should have attended Bryn Mawr or Radcliffe, but because the transportation was unaffordable, she had to turn down even the offer of full scholarships, going instead to the "very Southern belle" women's college close to home. Just having the "right clothes" meant holding "a dozen jobs all through school."

"I think what Patty wanted—and needed most to emulate about the rich girls she met at school—was a kind of perfectionism." But the focus of her efforts at perfection still, after fifteen years, mystify her husband. "Whether it's cooking, skiing, sailing, music, it has to be just right. Perfect. With no mistakes. She gets up at six in the morning," her husband reports in awe, to do the ski exercises that justify the expensive lessons. "Every new recipe is tried out a half dozen times *before* it is served at a dinner party."

Abe Gray is enough of a New Englander to admire his wife's strenuously self-improving character. Not even his Instamatic can catch Patty in any attitude except achieving. He glances at the folding silver triptych frame on his desk where snapshots have arrested a pretty young woman with dark bangs, crouched over skis, clutching an armful of sails, and in profile at the piano, her gaze fixed on the music stand.

Music making reminds Abe that Patty's need to plug

away at pursuits he associates with pleasure and relaxation, have not always been harmless. "I think it's been very rough on the kids...the ones we have together. Because they were always expected to have the same attitude toward music and sports, and of course, schoolwork and grades....I sometimes think that's why our son, who's away at school, arranges to get home very seldom.

"For Patty, if you don't achieve, if you don't work hard at everything, if you don't...'excel,'" says Abe, putting his wife's favorite word in inverted commas, "you won't stay on top."

THE PROFESSIONALIZING
OF LIFE AT THE TOP

What Patty Gray realized from her first weeks at Magnolia College, millions of strivers from "obscure" social origins have also discovered. Choosing life at the top, in terms of money and social standing, now means choosing to achieve and excel—in every realm.

The arduous self-improvement program for the upper-class-in-training can't begin too early. Successful graduates, moreover, will never have a moment to spare, ever again. Because the move from merely middle class to really rich now requires the professionalization of one's entire life.

THE CONSUMER TURNS PRO

Even in the matter of acquiring, that most basic American activity, the unskilled are becoming the underclass. Not because spending money is ever out of style. That ten-thousand-dollar watch, the sliver of lapis circled with diamonds, will unfailingly be admired, even envied. As will a four-million-dollar condo on Fifth Avenue, with sweeping views of the park (but not of the plebs at play).

The catch is that both the wristwatch and the pied-à-terre are, literally, up for grabs. And too many people these days can afford to grab these deluxe goods. As the frenzied demand grows, more lapis is sliced, more glittering towers rise. From the consumption point of view, invidious competition in consumerism added a new element of futility. When the bids were in, the chips down, any Arab, or his agent, wallets stuffed with OPEC Big Ones, would inevitably top that last wave of the pencil from the third row.

The final curse of the Consumer Class, though, is irreversible scarcity, the finite—and diminishing—supply of the most desirable assets, like oceanfront property (at least in places where other successful strivers want to join you).

Even travel to far-flung and exotic lands, once so costly and time-consuming as to exclude all but the very rich, has yielded its secrets to mass tourism. Watching turtles mate in the Galapagos, snapping zebras at happy hour from balconies in Treetops, Nairobi's resort-and-game preserve, are ordinary Americans of the upper middle class, salaried or self-employed, on three-week vacations. Gliding down the Nile is a retired oral surgeon and his wife from Ventura, California.

Consumerism, in its pure and innocent form, whether avid for durables like videocassette recorders or perishables, like travel, is a throwback to an earlier, more primitive stage of capitalism. As soon as Joan Didion, the Sacramento Spengler, took as her subject the American shopping mall,[10] it was ready to be abandoned to the Visigoths, e.g., the lower middle class.

CONSIDER THE CATALOGUE

Whether choosing a mid-eighteenth century Chinese Coramandel screen ($10,000) from the Horchow Collection, a Dallas-based mail order company that does a $40,000,000 annual business, or a genuine reproduction from the Nelson C. Rockefeller Collection, ordering a Scotch salmon from Shannon airport, or granny's cotton long johns from Sears, shopping by mail is a class act in itself. Matching illustration 14b with the desired size, style and color effectively eliminates all those who failed to achieve a combined score of 1,400 on their college boards (along with those nonaffluent Americans who do not have credit cards or checking accounts).

In fact, the upward mobility of the catalogue is a fascinating class study in microcosm.

Until the age of the automobile, Sears Roebuck and Montgomery Ward mail order catalogues were the only means of buying "store-boughten" consumer goods for most of rural and small-town America. Suburbia rerouted the next generation to the Mall,* which their grandchildren (who may well be unable to read a Sears catalogue) also use for "hanging out." The real second coming of this basic text came with the *Whole Earth Catalog*, which combined buying it with doing it.

First published in 1971, as of 1981 its four editions have sold a total of 2,350,000 copies.[11] This best seller of conspicuous consumer competence staked out a market of upwardly mobile, upper-middle-class students or young professionals-on-the-move. M.B.A.s pored over instructions for building geodesic domes and compost heaps. Inspired by the *Whole Earth*'s send-away-for-survival message, even the Old Rich invented new ways of not wasting their assets. Abby Aldrich Rockefeller, great-grandaughter of the founder of Standard Oil, with the help of a Swedish friend, developed and marketed a toilet that turned human waste into potassium-rich fertilizer, saving water, plumber's bills and producing, it was claimed, spectacular flowers and veggies. To order, only by mail.[12]

The Consumer Movement itself is upper middle class in its rank and file and upper income in its leadership.** Significantly, its goals are nothing less than transforming amateur suckers into professional shoppers. Prerequisites are required for this advanced course in spending wisely and well—as the Old Rich are trained to do from childhood. High levels of general knowledge, literacy, and free time are needed to secure the advantages of unit pricing, cooperative "bulk" buying, and comparative shopping—not to mention reading and understanding warranties and seeking legal redress for fraud.

*In upscale communities, the Mall has been reborn as the Galleria.

**One study places Ralph Nader's *real* earnings—as opposed to "official salary"—at $250,000 a year.[13]

TO THE SWIFT, THE STRONG, AND THE (ALREADY) SUCCESSFUL

He staggers past, eyes glazed, face contorted in agony, body awash in sheets of sweat, heaving and gasping. This man is a runner. After a punishing day in the office, followed by another fun-filled forty minutes in the subway, commuter train or traffic jam, he sheds his sodden business attire and, donning a sweatshirt—bearing the faded stencil outlines: PENN. PHYS. ED. DEPT.—he is off, to suffer some more.

When he was in college, Joseph Epstein recalled, athletes in training ran or jogged in order to improve their *real* sport: boxing, football, tennis or swimming. Why, wondered Epstein, given the mixed reviews about the effect of running on heart and general health, has this activity become an end in itself?[14] The answer is: it hasn't. Running is getting in shape for the Only Game in Town—Success. New Rich Readiness Training for the upwardly mobile middle class.

Supremely meritocratic, unlike polo or even tennis, running requires the lowest capital investment of any sport ever practiced: $35.00 for a pair of shoes (sweat pants and other gear are completely optional). No clubs, racquets, skis, greens fees, tow fees, dues or expensive lessons.

Yet, only the already successful run!

The average male marathon runner, according to Fred Lebow, president of the twenty-one-thousand-member New York Road Runners Club, is a "prime catch" for marriageable young women. He is "thirty-four-years-old, college educated, physically fit and *well-off* "[15] (author's italics). Why is he knocking himself out? Enduring agony, tendinitis, back problems, possible coronary failure? In the most obvious symbolism lies the most obvious answer.

This already well-off professional male is running—to get ahead. He is in training for the fast track, the real one. Getting and staying lean and mean today, in order to pull out ahead tomorrow. In a competitive market economy, running in place means falling behind. Not by chance are banks and brokerage houses prime sponsors of marathons. On a thousand soaking chests, their names and logos flash by in the summer twilight: Manufacturers Hanover, Bache, Halsey, Stuart. Getting up to speed—a favored Wall Street metaphor from the runner's vocabulary—then, pulling away from the herd.

The move from merely upper middle class to really rich means, first of all, full employment of your most valuable asset: you. Every muscle, sinew and brain cell in superpro shape— not to forget creative juices and hand-eye coordination. Professionalizing the amateur life entails leaving behind old notions that the work day ends when the office door closes. (Down that path lies the gold watch, not the *Fortune* 500.) Now is not the time to dull that competitive edge with a few beers, crawl into bed with a best-seller and a box of ginger snaps; not the hour to let finely honed analytic skills rust from disuse, reflexes go sluggish, muscles slack. The moment, as St. Paul reminds us, is now.

KUISINART KULTUR

The Old Rich, like Abram Gray III, can be "duffers": sloping home without so much as a jog. But the Rich-in-training cannot afford scuzzy surroundings or primitive skills. After panting in from the park, the young manager or entrepreneur-on-the-move is not "off" for the night.

When he opens the door of his post-Minimal pad, will he find Total Woman in black lace proferring fluffy towel and frozen daiquiri? Certainly not. Instead, handing our puffing pro a spanking white-bibbed apron for the night-of-the-long-knives stands...the Cooking Teacher. Or, sometimes, two of them. As described by Gael Greene, in that Bible of new money on the move, *New York* magazine, "Elegant but Easy" (two young women who incorporated their own culinary skills) turns corporate chieftains into professional quality chefs. "A man should have visitation rights to his Cuisinart," mourns Thayer Bigelow of *Time-Life* films. Right now, though, he has no time for nostalgia. Hired by host John Emmerling, head of his own ad agency, "Elegant but Easy" directs the chopping, dicing and sauteeing efforts of Mr. Bigelow, Colgate-Palmolive executive William Powell, and a kitchen of their peers.

No horsing around here. The menu for tonight's "Welcome to Italy" dinner will require the creation of "carpaccio and eggplant marinara through fettucine Alfredo, to steak pizzaiola and zabaglione." This menu is to be mastered between aperitifs at 6:30 and the sit-down feast at 10 P.M.![16]

"Elegant but Easy" is only the first stage of leaving Amateur Hour in the kitchen forever.

As Messrs. Powell, Thayer, Emmerling, et al., become more successful in the kitchen and the marketplace, they will not only replace the Cuisinart* that departed with the spouse, they will add to it a professional Garland or Vulcan stove, home sales of which have tripled in the last three years.

Purchasers of these commercial ranges are not families with seven children, looking to belt out meals for millions in less time. "This new buyer," noted one astonished stove supplier, is the "super deluxe professional cooker."[17]

With $1,750 in loose change and seven free days, more serious cooking students spend a week in Bologna or Venice, Italy under the culinary tutelage of Marcella Hazan. "An unusual mix of people come to Bologna," notes Signora Hazan. "Cooking teachers and novice cooks, jetsetters and housewives, food critics and novelists, surgeons, bankers, artists, entertainers, restauranteurs."[18] Here is where the semipro is able to rub shoulders with "food professionals" even while learning. Not to speak of the other "upscale" winners in "real life": the novelists, bankers and surgeons, an alumni association that will add luster to any future guest list.

---

*Obviously, male "singles"—whether confirmed bachelors or the newly separated— are not the biggest, just the newest, share of the booming professional food processor market. The Cuisinarts and Robot Coupes sold in the United States are still the purlieu mostly of women consumers. Their sales volume and dropping prices, moreover, also mean that, like other appliances, they have made strong inroads into the middle classes.

WHY IS THIS NIGHT
DIFFERENT
FROM ALL OTHERS?:
THE MERITOCRATIC MEAL

Unlike Europeans, who still today vigilantly maintain a separation of their private and professional lives, Americans have always mixed business and pleasure. By including wives and girlfriends, expense-account evenings on the town soften the reality that hours spent eating, drinking or watching hockey games are, in fact, an extension of the workday. Similarly, "taking care of business" in America has always included "entertaining" at home. Until the recent surge of women entering—and reentering—the work force, that "lovely wife" as hostess and social consort was deemed essential to male success.

In a society dedicated to upward mobility, having the Boss (or Big Client) to Dinner has long been accorded the status of mythic event. Its terrors, pitfalls, pratfalls, along with rewards, are celebrated in works as diverse as *Babbitt* and "I Love Lucy." The dinner parties of one New York couple, fashion designer Oscar de la Renta and his wife Françoise, staked out new frontiers in the professionalization of private life at the top. No mystery was made of the criteria for their coveted invitations. "Guests will find no failures at the de la Rentas' table," tabulated reporter Francesca Stanfill, in a cover article for the *New York Times Magazine*, which sent waves of outrage, anxiety and, according to some, despair among uninvited strivers.

For, like the de la Rentas themselves—a couple of modest, middle-class origins who together parlayed his designing talent into a $300 million business—their guests were self-made men and women. Described as "hardworking professionals" by a de la Renta "regular," novelist Jerzy Kozinski, guests like Henry Kissinger, Norman Mailer, investment banker Felix Rohatyn and producer Sam Spiegel did it all themselves.[19]

By their works shall we know them. A place at the de

la Rentas' meritocratic board signaled the social ascendance of Conspicuous Competence. Winning through achievement.

If you're not a winner, you're a loser. That is the message a fluid society with room (but never quite enough) at the top beams to those on the move.

Today, the furthest distance you can travel from the Culture of Poverty is the Culture of Prowess.

It's not just *nouveaux* striving to master *nouvelle cuisine*. The cooking mania among the "haves," observes one noted interior designer, "is only one piece of a terrific desire to be good at things that make you look useful. If it's gardening, they're going to tell you about every plant and cutting." "Let's grow that great geranium," exhorts socialite C. Z. Guest in her *New York Post* column,[20] where together with her books, she turns an interest in gardening into paid work. Somewhere between Marie Antoinette and Luther Burbank, Mrs. Guest has professionalized herself into the "Dear Abby" of the problem privet.

HIGH TECH AND
JUST FOLK (ART)

Serious minds tend to dismiss matters of style as mere fad or fashion. They're wrong. A late and great German art historian proclaimed, "Everything means something." And of course, he was right.

In the late 1970s, there appeared on the scene a back-to-basics style of home furnishings known as High Tech. Its artifacts celebrated the functionalism of factory, hospital, restaurant. The furnishings being shipped (directly from the plant) to the lofts, apartments, and town houses of the urban New Rich were, significantly, objects of mass use. Restaurant steam tables and wholesale butcher's freezers. A million miles of dark gray industrial carpeting and rubber tile flooring. Commercial steel shelves and factory lighting. These utilitarian, institutional fixtures were democratically Cheap—costing a fraction of the "to order" designs of whatever young Milanese hotshot was featured in the latest "shelter" magazine. Most important, if the hard edges, cool colors and tough materials of these wares didn't convey the odor of sanctity, they suggested the order of merit.

High Tech eliminated any evidence of inherited advantages, real or assumed, like family portraits or heirloom silver, along with inherited disadvantages—like no taste. High Tech was the ultimate statement of classlessness for the upwardly mobile New Rich, proclaiming them to be so proudly self-made, they had no past, only a mass-produced present. This serious stuff said: hardworking folks dwell here, living clean and orderly lives. People *worthy* of success.

Developments in computer technology, moreover, have given High Tech a new lease on home life. The home office of an international gold dealer, reports a design supplement, "has been integrated into a living and entertaining space...equipped with a telex, television, a commodity trading service monitor, a Reuters teletype, computer and electronic typewriter."[21] Question: Why can't this prosperous fellow afford a separate room for his office-at-home? Answer: He doesn't want one. These are the attributes of Expertise and Prowess. Class is Competence. Money is Merit. What does he have to hide?

Class is also power, as Marx reminded us. But since his time, the two have moved steadily closer together, linked by experience or skill.

In her recent survey of fifty computer owners, sociologist Sherry Turkle of the Massachusetts Institute of Technology found that consumers appreciated most of all the feeling of power associated with programming a computer. "When you program a computer, you feel a great deal of control and mastery."[22]

Those who would move from undifferentiated middle class to the deserving rich must be prepared for still further encroachments on the place once marked Private. In his transformation of a cavernous loft into a home-office, architect Janusz Gottwald was obliged to ask his bachelor client, a freelance consultant, "some fairly intimate questions." How important was it, for example, to have "privacy between his bedroom, guest room and office"? Not important at all was the reply. Should he have an early morning appointment with a client, any "friend who stayed the night" would have to get up and (presumably) out at the time her host rose—or else, charting a route behind the client's chair, crawl to the bathroom on her hands and knees.[23]

People used to be ashamed of being self-made. Their surroundings were supposed to neutralize, if not to deny, both past obscurity and present hustle: pedigreed silver, family portraits, mellow glowing veneers, porcelain with provenance. Now anyone who has made it is proud of it. But flaunting it doesn't require a return to the Sèvres dinner service, Queen Anne silver, Savonnerie carpet under your toes—all the stuff that shrieks Filthy Rich. Now, ambient virtue from a preindustrial past can turn tax advantages into a look of hardearned reward.

American Folk Art in a simple country setting takes the elitist edge off wealth. Providing a populist—not patrician—past for the self-made individualist, the charming furniture, toys, pictures and quilts, made by anonymous craftspersons are a form of nongilt by association. The whirligigs and pottery jugs, *fraktur* and faded samplers, hooked rugs and portraits of doomed consumptive children—all proclaim the American journeyman/millionaire, redeeming with hard work his own profits and the labor of artisans past.

We are of the same stuff, self-taught and self-made, their possessors tell us: surviving not through connections, special favor or interests, but by our talent, skill and merit.

It was bad enough when the rich just had more money, fancier possessions, and more control over people than the rest of us.

In the good old days, even when they became a "power elite," a "ruling class"—buying legislatures, manipulating the military, controlling universities and foundations, economic and cultural life—they did it only with dollars. Anybody with the Big Ones could do the same.

When they also work harder and longer, using scarce leisure hours to "professionalize" in unleisurely fashion the pastimes that used to be mere pleasure, hunkering down with auction catalogs, seed catalogs, computer systems, food processors, standing over hot (six burner) professional stoves, we're all in trouble. When they start beating out working pimps, art dealers, drug dealers, and master chefs, producing more prize melons and zucchini than a 4H Jamboree, what's left for the rest of us?

Moreover, how do we keep the "competence chasm" from widening in the next generation? From lisping his first words into the Telex, practicing "show-and-tell" on the customized computer system in daddy's "home-office-entertainment-center," son-of-international-gold-dealer will graduate to designing software in kindergarten, leaving *our* kids to stop counting when they run out of fingers and toes.

How to prevent the polarities between the totally professional, conspicuously competent Supremely Deserving Rich— and the Rest of Us?

Through a combination of high taxes and inflation, the gap between the middle class and the poor will disappear. From using all our energies to scratch for food and shelter, the rest of us, like those sad Indian tribes of Central America, remnants of the great Mayan culture, will have forgotten the arts and sciences we once enjoyed, without acquiring the new competence necessary for success. Only those living in Malibu, like Joan Didion, will know how to use a pastry marble.[24] The rest of us will know only from Sara Lee.

Since the 1950s, increasing numbers of Americans, one survey noted recently, derive their satisfaction outside of work.[25] By that time, sociologist Daniel Bell of Harvard gloomily observed in the mid-1970s, the basic American value patterns had begun to "run riot." Where the culture had once "emphasized the virtue of achievement, defined as doing and making, and a man displayed his character in the quality of his work," by the 1950s, Bell insisted, "achievement had been redefined to emphasize status and taste. The culture was no longer concerned with how to work and achieve, but with how to spend and enjoy."

The 1980s, however, have changed all that. As with other

cultural values, hedonism, the "fun morality," has gone into hiding, driven underground by the rush to success.

The New Rich have appropriated the work ethic. Their emulators are making sure that when *their* turn comes, when opportunity knocks, they will be more than equal to it.

Ignoring the dour prophets inveighing against narcissism, decrying the cult of the self, the meritorious rich and their middle-class contemporaries seeking to occupy a high place recognize that mobility, like merit, lies in rigorous self-improvement. You are your best asset—and possibly the only one. The one whose value, with effort, can always be enhanced.

If, instead of merely consuming, those in line for the top ceaselessly produce—muscle tone to manicotti, great geraniums and quality sex—they will be ready to join their peers: the Deserving Rich.

CHAPTER THIRTEEN

LIVE LIKE A RICH ARTIST

Asked to describe the most dramatic social change in her lifetime, a wealthy woman in Kansas City had one phrase to sum up the breakdown of class barriers: "More accepting attitudes toward deviants, like artists."[1] When, in order to be up-to-date in Kansas City, you have to accept deviants like artists, you can be sure they're not deviants anymore. Indeed, the matron from Missouri had her finger on the pulse of a significant class phenomenon of our time.

Once a social outcast, the artist has become a social lion, joining the upwardly flowing mainstream of new money.

A decade ago, a now-successful artist told his father, a machinist, of his plans to become a painter. Instead of the expected smiting of forehead and gnashing of teeth, his father, a Sicilian immigrant, was delighted. "Why not?" he said beaming. "You're a smart boy. Maybe you'll be *Time*'s Man of the Year—like that guy Rauschenstein."

"Come to New York," dealer Ivan Karp advised sculptor Duane Hansen, "and I'll make you rich and famous."*[2] Shades of Sam Goldwyn!

---

*Hansen came to New York and, although he stayed only a short time, he did become rich and famous. His eerily lifelike, life-sized subjects also experienced parallel upward mobility. Hansen's early pieces, cleaning women and construction workers, have progressed to "middle Americans"—tourists in Hawaiian shirts with a thousand dollars worth of camera equipment slung around their necks.

Lodestar of upwardly mobile artists, the white haired granddaddy and the first celebrant of the artist as celebrity/companion to the New Rich was Andy Warhol.

The upheavals of the 1960s, as critic Peter Schjeldahl observes, included "a burst of social mobility toward the upper levels like nothing since the early part of the century, shuffling people from show business, art, government, crime (drug pushing), fashion . . . into the deck of inherited, corporate and professional wealth. Warhol was plucked by this mini-revolution from the bottom of the heap and plopped without ceremony or initiation at the top."[3] Son of a Czech immigrant laborer, Warhol was also a creature of the 1960s "other" revolution: media. He controlled his own total production "factory"; Warhol film, videotape and later, *Interview* magazine. No one missed his or her fifteen minutes of fame, certainly not the creator. The Warhol Factory was there to immortalize. Heiresses to old and new fortunes vied for walk-on parts in the new Warhol Social Register—happening (as so much social history did at this period) right on camera! Accompanied by Jewish princesses and "real" princesses, First Ladies of fashion, stage, screen and White House, the portraitist and play-companion of Agnelli, Onassi and Sculls, moved with his subjects from Sun Valley to Newport, a Saint-Simon of the silkscreen. Old Virginia wealth gutted landmark mansions to accommodate outsize Warhol double portraits. Other patrons preferred "social icons"[4] of more remote authority, like Warhol's portrait of Mao Zedong.

"My father is a rabbi," explains Josh Gold. "When he came to visit us and saw how much of my time, emotions and resources I had invested in a painting of Mao, he found it very hard to accept."

"Joshua," his father had asked, "why do you have a big picture of this man in your living room? You admire him so much?"

"It's art, Pops," Josh explained. "You don't have to admire the subject." But Dr. Gold was not persuaded.

With his deep tan, white jogging shorts and tee-shirt, in

his all-white living room in a white beach house in Venice, California, Josh Gold is more than a continent away from the world of his fathers. Grandson of a distinguished Talmudic scholar, son of a rabbi, Josh is also a *summa* in history from Harvard and a graduate of Yale Law School. After a brief stint back home in a Cincinnati law firm, he moved west and into "commercial real estate development," a change which has, by local accounts, made him a millionaire many times over. The way to the top in a tough city and a tough business has left no visible signs. At forty-eight, Joshua Gold's face with its halo of dark curls is unlined; his blue-eyed gaze clear and childlike.

Enthusiasm—part undergraduate, part Hollywood—is the real source of Josh's youthfulness. Whether he is talking about his "favorite" professors at college (whose books he still buys and reads) or his "favorite" artists, whose work he collects, Josh is a fan.

The Golds began seriously collecting art almost as soon as they moved to Beverly Hills. "We've always been very visual people," Josh says of himself and his wife, Mara. Along with acquiring their first works of art in that period, the artists themselves began to play an increasingly important role in the Golds' activity as collectors. "In our old house in the city, we had our first dinner parties—for Robert Rauschenberg, Warhol, Lichtenstein. Those dinners were the high point of our life up to then. They were opulent, exciting events."

For Josh Gold, the social and aesthetic are inseparable needs—each happily fulfilled by collecting contemporary art. "For both of us, coming from our particular background, being involved with collecting, with artists and museums has been part of a social drive, too. A way of striving, of climbing. Maybe we do see this world as high society, or as bettering ourselves."

Josh and Mara Gold decided to leave Beverly Hills, its Hollywood squares and "opulent dinner parties," and with their two young sons went to live in Venice among their artist friends.

However, there are still lines separating Josh Gold's community of choice from his "other" community. "Because of my religious background, it's very important for me to uphold other values in my house that are different from those of our artist friends. So, I've never been able to go out drinking, or do drugs—or even stay out very late. It's just not part of my way of life." Still, values aside, Josh Gold has much in common with his "new" community.

Success, Josh admits, is what characterizes their artist friends, in Venice or elsewhere. "I guess we don't tend to meet the ones who haven't made it." The ones who have made it are those artists able to work with the Establishment toward goals like the new Los Angeles Museum of Contemporary Art, goals that will benefit "both the artists' community and the larger one." Successful artists, he observes, are very sophisticated and adroit, adept at working with politicians and what Josh calls "the economic and corporate forces" to achieve their own objectives.

When artists become successful, they start associating with other "communities," which Josh defines as lawyers, accountants, corporate people. "You get invited to these peoples' houses. Soon you start feeling more and more comfortable. Your host and *his* peers are part of your world now, and if you're shrewd and sensitive and articulate," Josh says, "you start adapting. You start learning their language."

"So here's this slum. Right? Venice. Zoned residential with one commercial strip. Fifteen minutes from the airport and fifteen minutes from Beverly Hills. It didn't take any genius to see that this was great land to buy, because you could just see the real estate boom coming."

Down the boardwalk from Josh and Mara Gold's beach house, past the smart bistros, discos, astrologers, Home for the Jewish Aged, improvised flea markets, black look-alike transvestites on roller skates, twirling in sync to the matching sounds from their headsets, Larry Neal, thirty-three, lounges, his long limbs stretching from the seat of a Barcelona chair. Padlocked iron gates cover the small windows pierced in the no-color cement of the vast, two-story warehouse, now his home and studio. An elaborate security system monitors the transition from the glare of the beach, the funk-sleaze and camp of the boardwalk *passegiata* to the cool elegance and functional working spaces within. The living room is almost without light. ("Let's stay here," Larry says, "I have a lousy hangover.") But the studio and separate exhibition space are luminous from a skylight above.

"Where was I?" Larry asks, returning with beers. "Oh yeah. The Venice land boom. Sooo, it didn't take any genius to figure out this was good land to buy... and dirt cheap. The problem was, none of us had any money then, in the late sixties. I kept telling other guys, other artists, to buy here," he recalls, noting that "we, the artists, were the first to see which way this place was going." One friend of his swapped his pickup truck for a down payment of $60,000 on a warehouse/garage. He sold it three years ago for $360,000. Today it's worth a million.

Even after Larry Neal started making money from making art, it took him a while to get wise to how to spend it. "At first, if you're a poor kid like me, when you start to make a few extra dollars, you do stupid things. You just buy fancy toys."

There were no toys, fancy or plain, when Larry was growing up in Lynn, Massachussetts. His father, "a real estate salesman, sort of," was "actually an alcoholic and a gambler... just sort of a deadbeat, loser kind of guy." When the family was still together, Larry, his brother and sister lived in "low-end tract houses. When my parents split, we were in slum public housing. I had a pretty miserable childhood. I used to go to school and borrow nickels and dimes from people for lunch money or a soda."

By the time he managed to graduate, "with a little trouble from the authorities in the meantime. Okay, I was a real hood," Larry and his five buddies jumped into his 1955 Chevy ("That car was *everything* I had in the world") and like millions of Americans seeking fame and fortune, they headed for California.

"Even as a kid, I was always doing art things. Everything I could draw or build, plus painting pictures—if I could get hold of the paints. When I was growing up in Lynn, there was never ever any thought of going to college. Anyway, I thought college was only for doctors and lawyers. I didn't know you could study art there."

Doing some odd-job construction work for a young architect and his wife, Larry was encouraged by them to try art school. "They told me about scholarships, portfolios—all that stuff. The first people in my whole life who ever gave me any helpful advice." At a commercial art school, where he made a brief detour, "guys would come in to give us pep talks about how we could make fifty grand a year designing Barbie doll outfits!" But a trip to New York and a visit to the Museum of Modern Art convinced him. "I knew I had it—right then and there! I was so naive and ambitious, I wanted to start showing with Leo Castelli right away." Instead, "the best dealer in Los Angeles persuaded me to start with the third best." Then things started snowballing and "I worked my way up to the best pretty fast."

He and another friend were in the vanguard of artists who moved to downtown Los Angeles. At this same time, "rumors were getting around that I was doing some pretty good stuff. A lot of people kept coming by." It was unbearable in the broiling city in the summer, so he and another buddy decided to go down to the beach and find some space. What they found turned out to be his home. Happily, his friend's family was "just so rich, a construction company is only *one* of his old man's *minor* interests. He sent a crew down here and they built this studio...dumped over fifty grand here ...*into a slum building that we were just leasing!*"

A decade later, Larry Neal is still incredulous at what rich parents will do for their children.

Soon after the move to Venice, Larry Neal found that "even though I was dumping a lot of money back into my art—materials, assistants—I was finally getting a surplus." Enough for his accountant to warn him against "being foolish" with his money and to think about investing. But this was the time when the "stock market started falling to shit and I thought, well, one thing I can really see and understand is real estate. So I said to my studio partner, the deal is obvious. We should buy some property.

"Through this black real estate guy, a real sleazy type, we found three houses in the middle of the ghetto. THREE houses for $35,000! Here we were, both scared to death just to *be* in the ghetto, never mind buying property there. But I decided, goddamnit, we're going to buy! We sold it for ten grand profit. BIG mistake," Larry groans. "Because if we had that today, we'd have made another fifty or a hundred grand, easy!" Talking about the ghetto reminds Larry to go outside and check his car, because earlier he had noticed some kids "hanging around outside." The Mercedes 350 SL is safe. The kids have goggled their fill of the sleek frosted silver car and turn to stare at the owner. Larry is tall, slender and muscular, in Levi's and a faded tee-shirt. His expensively cut corn silk hair falls across his forehead but does not obscure the Roman profile and large gray eyes.

"Hey, mister, you in the movies?" demands the shortest of the group. There is a flash of perfect white teeth. Larry Neal smiles. He has been asked this question before.

"Naw. I'm an artist."

The kids disperse. The man's jiving them.

The system of locks and security doors is renegctiated with Larry's bunch of keys.

"After that deal," Larry continues inside, "we bought a few little things and just kept them. This place is worth well over a million more than I paid for it."

This place meant taking in partners, some of whom are also his patrons. Even more valuable than their cash up front, though, was the way "my business associates taught me how to put together a general partnership." Then, with another limited partnership, Larry bought into "a group of buildings in New York," but this deal was mostly to have a place for himself there, "where I can just keep a toothbrush." Basically, though, "I really don't want to think about real estate anymore. Because it becomes consuming. With real estate, once you get into it, you start trading up—especially in California. Well, the next trade up was, like four hundred apartment units in Oklahoma City. I didn't want to do it. I get deals offered to me all the time. It's a kind of mental baggage."

One Los Angeles psychoanalyst who numbers many artists among his patients, claims that these new success heroes are "gigantically self-conscious about all of it...the attorneys, business managers, accountants, brokers. They go into capitalistic ventures with great reluctance. How could it be otherwise? This kind of activity goes against the tradition of art and the role of the artist."

"I got enough," Larry says with sudden finality. "I got what I need. I got what I want. And I even make a pretty good living off my art. It's almost frightening," Larry admits, "how well you can do on art. The sky's the limit. It really is."

Even Los Angeles and its New Rich are finally coming around to contemporary art. They're no longer stuck on Monet water lilies in the bedroom. But it took time. "New money," Larry explains, "has to drive it, fuck it, and eat it first. They gotta have a fast car, a flash house. They gotta feel comfortable with their wealth before they start buying art."

Larry Neal is not a fast worker. In fact, "I'm pretty slow. I take my time. But as soon as things get finished, there's always a dealer there, sucking it up. I've got dealers everywhere," Larry says wearily, "L.A., Houston, New York, London. They're such notorious crooks, anyway, always trying to cheat you out of nickels and dimes, no matter how many thousands you've made for them. The best thing about painting is that it's the easiest thing for me to do—much easier than real estate.

"I play tennis with judges, lawyers, people like that, almost every weekend. I really love to play tennis. I don't think they even *had* a tennis court in Lynn. Not in my neighborhood, anyway." So when Larry first moved to California, he took up tennis, "because that was *the* game out here. I meet a lot of successful businessmen. I also meet a lot of successful businessmen's wives. You're always meeting people's wives. And they got all this dough. And they don't have anything to do. So they go out and get cultured. They like art and all this crap.

"I've met rock stars, movie stars." There is astonishment in his voice. "All kinds of performers have this secret hidden thing: they'd like to be an artist. Not making music or films, but making ART. Everybody loves success and they really love a successful artist. Because that's the best of everything.

"No one would tolerate (he names a noted contemporary) if he weren't famous. No one would have him to dinner, filthy like he is. But it's part of his costume. They're not going to hang around with a guy who looks like a coal miner unless he's a famous artist. Frank Stella went around for—how many years?" Larry calculates, "without his front teeth, smoking those cigars. But famous artists deserve that treatment, just because they're artists and famous!

"I've seen so many people get involved with art and watched them change," Larry reflects. "Like one of the most clean-cut straight bankers I ever met. He was so square, it was unbelievable! He and his wife got involved with the old Pasadena Museum and they met Rauschenberg. Then this guy started showing up at museum openings in a red-white-and-blue suede cowboy outfit, with fringes hanging from his ass. Then the guy completely flipped out. Got into drugs. Got divorced.

"Art affects people; it changes their lives. I've seen lots of business couples get divorced because one got further out or further into art than the other. People come over here all the time. They say, 'This is so nice. This is the way I want to live.' Even when I tell them it's horrible to heat, you can't keep it clean. Hell, it's not even a safe neighborhood! They still love it. They want it."

"I looked around one day," Hilary Ross recalls, "and I said to myself, This is very boring. I hate this life. I hate the Upper East Side. I hate 72nd Street and Park. Nobody knowing my name. Everything delivered. The maid. The nurse. The charming apartment. This is too much. It's too rich. I can't deal with it."

Hilary Ross looks as though she could deal with anything, from dinners for fifty to magazine deadlines. Small and trim, with pepper and salt hair cropped—like her speech—for maximum efficiency and minimum waste of time on nonessentials. Her high energy is tempered by calm. She listens as intently as she speaks. Like most of the superbly organized of this world, there are no visible "organizers" in her white living room/office silvered with mirrors, no Rolodexes, no memo pads bearing the hortatory: Don't forget!

Hilary Ross doesn't forget.

"I felt guilty about all of it." A guilt made worse by tedium. "There we were, giving the same dinners that everyone else who had gone to Radcliffe and Harvard was giving. Our apartment was a carbon copy of everyone's in our building." The real epiphany, the last supper, so to speak, was a particular evening with an architect friend and his wife, a block away. "Suddenly I realized I was looking at *our* Mies chairs, *our* Empire sofa, *our* Baccarat glasses. And I said to myself, 'This is it!'"

That same week, Hilary bumped into an artist friend on the street who invited her down to see his new place—south of the Village. She came and saw and was instantly converted. She returned to share her revelation with her husband, Bob, a lawyer. "The one last way we can change our lives," she announced to him, "is to change the type of space we live in. We are too constricted, intellectually and sensually, in the way we live now." A few more visits to lofts of other artist friends in the newly reclaimed industrial area, Soho, convinced Hilary that what she glimpsed had been no mirage. "I saw people living with a freedom I didn't have. This is the way people live who don't care about material possessions.

"Let's get back to something more essential. Something that artists seem to have that we don't," she said to Bob. But Bob Ross wasn't ready to make the leap—especially with a young child. "In that neighborhood?" he asked. Besides, he wasn't bored by the way they lived. He enjoyed coming home from a day at the office or in court to the crystal, china and silver. And he didn't mind visiting friends whose apartments and weekend houses in Connecticut looked and smelled the same as theirs.

So they compromised. They bought a loft "to play in on the weekends. Our fantasy," is the way Hilary describes the all-white, huge bare space, which she and Bob worked on themselves. Where, on a Parsons table and five paint-splattered chairs, they had friends to dinner all the time for pasta. "People loved coming down. Miranda had birthday parties there, too, with kids roller skating all over the unvarnished floors."

"It worked," Hilary asserts. There was "immediate relief from all those uptown pressures. I felt great." This "extraordinary experience" proved what Hilary Ross had long suspected. Style was substance. At least for Hilary. Commuting back and forth between fantasy and reality was too much for Bob. He stayed uptown. Even on weekends. Alone in the loft with her young daughter, Hilary Ross was no longer the stylish young matron who did the occasional illustration for a fashion magazine. She now worked full time—anything and everything, to pay for the steadily rising rent. No more commuting. No more play-house. Work, family, food, space. Life itself had that beautiful integrity she had once envied from afar. Style, indeed, had become substance.

It's a fantasy life I lead, I admit it," Larry Neal acknowledges cheerfully. "That's what attracts people who can afford to do it. But it's a fantasy that you buy into—and still lead your other life. Not like Gauguin going off to Tahiti."

There have always been successful artists, ornaments of a princely entourage, the Renaissance painters of the Medici court, or like Rubens, baroque impressarios of their own grand entrepreneurial style. But that "burst of social mobility" since the 1960s also created startling shifts in the who-follows-whom story of class values.

Formerly, that *rara avis*, the rich artist, was one who celebrated the possessions and experience of the upper classes—at play or prayer—in his art, and emulated these (as best he could) in his life.

The poor artist who became successful displayed his new status by acquiring the established trappings of wealth. Once risen from poverty, Rembrandt lived like a rich Dutch burger, his house in Amsterdam boasting a "treasure room" to display his own collection. The American landscape painter Frederick Church, building his Moorish fantasy "Olana," emulated the life of the Hudson River landed gentry, only with flair, the patroon as pasha, while Mark Rothko, son of an immigrant Russian-Jewish butcher, marked "arriving" by the purchase of an Upper East Side Manhattan town house, like the ones owned by his patrons.

In the early 1970s, the Soho loft, once the cheapest of squatter's space (cheap because the illegal artist-tenant could be evicted at any time) became a symbol of, first, Romantic creative poverty, then of Romantic creative wealth! Propelled by the upward mobility of their tenants, the Soho loft and Venice warehouse were transformed from images of the artists' marginality—like the garrets of Grub Street and the *Vie de Bohème*—into models of urban "gentrification."

A century ago, the prosperous biscuit manufacturer might envy and even fantasize about Gauguin's escape to Tahiti. But neither he nor his son would have traded in life on the Avenue Foch for Montmartre's Bateau-Lavoir. Now West Broadway is the Avenue Foch of the hip bourgeoisie. Main Street in Venice is soon to be Rodeo Drive West, all because the artist has become the new American ideal of self-made success.

Hollywood caught on fast to the social significance of Soho, anointing the Prince of Prince Street as the new romantic hero. *An Unmarried Woman* (1977), one of the most successful films of the decade, beamed the loft-with-rich-artist-in-residence as a message of liberation and rescue (redeeming the sufferings of divorce) into every movie theater in America. So lowly are the origins of Rich and Famous Artist (Alan Bates), that his only childhood memory of life in the slums of East London is of his parents throwing herrings at one another during family fights! After a few years in America, land of opportunity, the hero inhabits a Soho loft only slightly smaller than the Astrodome, which, unlike that stadium, is padded with Persian carpets. Nor does this artist's work involve any Romantic agony. Like Larry Neal, making art for the painter-prince is a "natural activity," requiring all the concentration of changing a light bulb. While merrily pouring and dripping,* the artist chatters on to his lady (Jill Clayburgh) about a forthcoming trip to India. If that isn't temptation enough for the newly single woman, there is also his house in Vermont for the summer. (This artist has assets to spare.) But the heroine can't be bought by Soho security, trips to India, or rescue from August city heat—at least not by the final reel.

Two days away from their annual exodus to Maine, Adam Merrill and Erica Epstein still manage to seem relaxed and unhurried. Their only pressing constraint, they insist, is when Adam has to descend the five flights of stairs, hop on his bicycle, and collect three-year-old Julia from nursery school. "It's climbing back up with Julia that can take all afternoon," her father jokes.

Both thirty-five years old, Erica and Adam are painters, living and working in the same vast and sunny Soho loft. Once a factory, their block-through building makes the Merrill-Epstein half of the top floor the most spacious railroad flat in the world. Studio space unfolds into living and dining space to disappear into bedrooms. Outsized windows open every room to a dazzling architectural panorama of Soho's cast-iron facades.

"Lots of artists got married when their building went co-op," says Erica. To which Adam adds, with a wry smile, that loft "co-opting" and the required pooling of assets did more for marriage among artists than the joint tax return. "We were lucky," recalls Ricky Epstein. They had started with a "not very satisfactory place" next door. When loft prices started to skyrocket in 1976, they sold it, buying into this building, with enough profit left over to install the "basics," which include the standard "serious" Soho kitchen and the silky hardwood floors. "When we first came to Soho ten years ago," Ricky

*Both the technique and finished work of Alan Bates are those of successful painter Paul Jenkins.

points out, "we would have been embarassed to have a couch. Couches were bourgeois then."

Furniture is sparse, the large sand-colored sectional sofa an archipelago in the vast space. A low formica filing cabinet for drawings serves as a coffee table, which, along with a neo-Parsons table and four Mexican chairs in the kitchen does it for adult furnishings. The only other structures belong to or were made by Julia Merrill, a jungle gym and large house of corrugated cardboard "constructed and painted entirely by Julia herself," her father notes proudly.

"The couch is the only subsidy we've ever had from our parents," Erica jokes. "Mine weren't happy about my being a painter—instead of a doctor or lawyer like my older sister. They were even less happy about my marrying another painter. But they really couldn't stand seeing me without a sofa." Even without the sofa subsidy, though, the Epstein-Merrill household is doing better than just managing. Both Ricky and Adam are represented by first-rank dealers and have exhibited in one-man and group shows. For the last few years, their paintings have been selling to private collectors. More recently, Erica has sold several pieces to banks and corporations. In addition to painting, both have part-time jobs teaching and working in a gallery.

"I still feel poor," Adam confesses, even though he quickly concedes that their joint earnings place them "way above the national median income. I guess not feeling poor for me would be having a beautiful antique carpet."

"That's the only way you can tell artists' lofts from lawyers' and stockbrokers'," Erica adds. "The nonartists all have 'important' carpets."

"No," her husband contradicts, "the most successful artists have 'significant carpets,' too."

Success, visible, palpable, big time, big-bucks success—and the hunger for it—is what Adam feels "all around them. So many artists are obsessed with the fear that if you don't make it while you're young—that means under thirty—you'll never make it at all. It's the Brooke Shields syndrome in art,"

Adam explains. "Not just fashion models, but 'hot' artists are getting younger every year."

And with time so short, ambitious young painters can't leave promotion to dealers. "These kids," says Adam, marveling, "are so adept at marketing and promoting themselves." "Managing my reputation," is the way he heard one twenty-two-year-old describe this process. "They're knowing about when to trade up dealers."

Yet there is something about the "hot" young artists, the "hot" galleries with their promo machines grinding out the sizzle of instant fame and big dollars; the grab-it-while-it-lasts, unabashed, exuberant, shameless careerism that makes Adam feel out of step. "I worry," he says, "that instead of working, I should be hanging out somewhere, drinking with the right people." Lots of artists, as soon as they get a good review, make a point of calling the critic, asking him down to "see what I'm doing now," continuing to cultivate him. "I just can't do that with people I don't know," admits Adam. "I don't know how to exploit that kind of situation, go after success in that way."

What has changed even since the sixties, Adam thinks, "is media and Big Money awareness of this new 'hot' kind of success—*before* it happens."

"Careers have been developed," Erica adds, "on just the *rumor* of success, an aura around certain young artists that creates waiting lists for works nobody's even seen yet."

"It's not what the work looks like anymore, not even what anybody writes about the artist," Adam elaborates. "Not the 'painted' word, or the written word. Maybe not even the spoken word. Just a kind of jungle tomtom."

Adam Merrill's grandfather was a noted economist. His father is a printer/publisher of Western Americana. He is the third generation of his family to graduate with highest honors from the same distinguished midwestern liberal arts college. "In the value system I grew up with," he recalls, "you worked hard and the work was rewarded. Or even if it wasn't, in some tangible, immediate way, the work itself was its own reward.

I still believe that. I still believe that in art, to survive is to succeed. I always thought the best I could hope for was to be able to keep on painting. But recently, I've started feeling crippled by my own values."

Erica Epstein, though, is not ambivalent about defining success differently. "I want to paint without having to do other work," she declares without hesitation. "I want to buy whatever I want, without thinking about the cost. I want," says Erica, looking at her husband somewhat defiantly, "to be famous. Isn't that what it's all about?"

"I'm not morally, politically, or religiously motivated," asserts Larry Neal. "Sure, if you're an artist, you have to be for the lettuce pickers, the Chicanos, right?" But Larry owns that he doesn't meet many lettuce pickers in the course of his usual rounds. In Los Angeles, Larry Neal points out, "we don't see other people's problems. Because we don't see other people. I just jump in my car to get away. The people we don't see," Larry reflects, "made it just as easy for artists as for other property owners to vote for Proposition 13. Thank God," he adds fervently. "I've got property to protect, right?"

"What success means to me," asserts Stan Sieniewicz, twenty-nine, "is not having to ride the subway with blacks. I mean, those guys really scare me."

Small and pale, Stan Sieniewicz, "hot" New Wave multimedia artist, still looks like the most vulnerable kid in his old gang. "We were the ones goin' nowhere." The only other one of his old buddies who isn't in jail or driving a hack, he laughs, "is a vet!"

In his new studio, in the shadow of Wall Street, an assistant works on plaster figures to the sounds of an eight-track stereo. "Now I take taxis, for the first time in my life. But if I'm with my dealer, it's a limo."

Stan's dealer is known for bringing along young artists. "He makes sure you meet all the right people. He teaches you about food and wine. He really tries to help you develop your career. Yeah, he's not just out for the quick buck, like most of those guys."

For those just starting out or not yet lucky enough to have found a dealer/mobility mentor, the process of success is becoming institutionalized. In a course, "The Artist as Career,"[5] Professor Dale McConathy of New York University seeks to dispel the romantic struggling artist myth by giving artists "the basic skills they need to survive as small businessmen. It's very easy to see what the ingredients for individual success are." Professor McConathy tries to help his artist/students to rationalize these "ingredients" by forcing students to look objectively at their careers, to plan ahead for their survival. He brings artists to class who have fought the battle already. The end product, so to speak, of the course is to encourage each student to have a five-year plan.

"It's the artist in the gray flannel suit,"[6] mourned sculptor George Segal.

Trying to rationalize success, find its magic formula and "replicate" it, is nothing new in America. The do-it-yourself course on career management began with Benjamin Franklin. It's simply new to the artist's "career." Yet with all that money at stake, it had to happen. Leave nothing to chance—or even genius. With that infinite hunger out there for new talent, those endless Dallas dollars waiting to be spent on hot young artists, the only reason for failure is "poor planning," lack of "reputation management" as the serious twenty-two-year-old painter says. The artist's career can now be professionalized, the artist transformed from Bohemian to Gamesman!

"What I really hate," Stan Sieniewicz says vehemently, "is middle-priced, middle-class anything. Because it's what my parents sacrificed everything to be." Scowling, Stan recalls both his parents working all the time. His father took night courses in accounting which finally inched the Polish immigrant from machinist to bookkeeper to comptroller, "just so they could retire to a finky ranch house in Arizona. That's what it was all for—all that work. With no pleasure, no fun. Retirement," he says in disgust.

If he's not wearing old clothes or jeans for work, Stan has "six-hundred dollar custom suits. It's the two-hundred dollar stuff from Bloomingdale's that I wouldn't be caught dead in. And I love evening clothes. That's what's so great about Warhol. He made it O.K. for the artist to go out in black tie."

The sweet smell of success overpowering the smell of turpentine is not new to art or even unique to artists in America. After all, it was Picasso who insisted that artists, no less than other men, merely wanted wealth, fame and the love of beautiful women. The differences may lie, though, in whether that happy status is a "by-product," a reward, or an end.

One young woman, a second-generation art dealer whose parents represented some of the giants of Abstract Expressionism, insists that "the motives for making art have run amuck." She mentions the response of one of "her" artists to the question: what did he want to achieve? "My own plane," was the unhesitating reply. "So I can jet anywhere I want."

Jet-setting fantasies—or reality—even big-time entrepreneurial activity, may be less dramatic than the shift in attitudes that accompany modest property ownership. The artist as businessman or woman. The wave of the future.

Adam Merrill is keenly aware of the shake-up in his own values that occurred when he became a "co-opter." "Other owners defaulting become *your* problem. What do you do about an artist who is in arrears because he isn't selling pictures? It's just agony. You end up buying him out—at least that's what we did. Paying him to leave, then feeling guilty because it's such a relief when he does—as much a relief," he adds painfully, "to get rid of his failure as it is to find someone who pays maintenance on time. That experience also influences your next choice of buyer. You end up looking for someone you won't have to worry about. In other words, a certified success."

A lawyer, who is also a veteran Soho resident and attorney for many artists, observed that becoming a businessman or woman inevitably changes the way you see yourself in relation to your nonpropertied peers or artists without assets. "I have clients who tell me that they don't want to sell apartments in buildings they own to other artists—even applicants who have passed the standard fiscal vetting. They prefer executives or lawyers who 'enhance property values' as opposed to artists who 'lower' them."

WHATEVER HAPPENED TO
THE RADICAL ARTIST?

Since nineteenth century romanticism, at least, there existed a tradition of the artist as ally of the underdog. At the barricades in spirit if not in flesh. With the Industrial Revolution, a romantic identity with peasants and Greek revolutionaries moved closer to common cause. Both artists and the new urban proletariat *were* the underclass—the one as machinery, the other as window-dressing of capitalism.

Then as now, even if the social origins of the artist tended to be middle class, the choice of a life in art was a choice of downward mobility. Parents sobbed, and cursed at the awful news. Their child, in one stroke or several, was about to undo all previous family efforts to rise in the world.

Prior to the 1960s in America, anyone who "made art"* with the view of making money would have been declared, without hesitation, certifiably insane. When the choice of the artist's vocation and life was tantamount to a vow of poverty, there was no difficulty identifying with the poor. When artists were an underclass, despised and dismissed by good bourgeois or patronized, in all senses, by the more enlightened rich, artists had no problem identifying the Enemy or casting themselves in a revolutionary role—if only as fifth columnists.

---

*This "new" phrase with which artists now describe their activity is in itself significant, suggesting the democratization of art, no longer more exalted than other artisanal or industrial processes, such as making widgets or mud pies. The phrase "making art" entered the aesthetic vocabulary at the same time as "making money" became a real possibility and legitimate goal for artists.

In 1871, when Courbet was imprisoned for allegedly inciting a mob to tear down the Napoleonic column in the Place Vendôme, his actual guilt or innocence was not an issue.[7] The real threat to public safety was the artist's insistence that the cause of Art, the revolutionary Commune of Paris, the exploited urban proletariat were one. There was more economic truth than poetry to his belief. The same wonderful folks who were starving the poor weren't buying his pictures, either.

When Depression-hungry American artists were earning $23.86 a week painting post office murals for the federal Work Projects Administration, they were in the same boat, making the same money, as those laying roads for the Civilian Conservation Corps.

When did it all change?

The revelation of the Stalinist concentration camps, says sculptor George Segal, was the shock that turned many artists of the first Abstract Expressionist generation from the utopian belief in Marxist revolution. Disillusionment with Marxism became distrust of social abstraction generally. Belief in a collective Utopia was transformed into the search for individual salvation. Mainstream American art turned inward to seek the sublime, leaving an imperfect world to fend for itself.

At least one writer has seen unintended political consequences follow from the new apolitical art. Abstract Expressionism,[8] according to Canadian historian Serge Guilbaut, became the propaganda weapon of choice in the cultural cold war—with Jackson Pollock's drip paintings Exhibit A of freedom of expression unique to the United States.

Beginning in the 1950s, the message of American Abstract Expressionist art was spread throughout Europe, in U.S. State Department-sponsored shows, a visual counterpart of the Voice of America.

At this same time, another fortress emerged to ensure the assimilation of the American artist into the social and economic mainstream. "Once the Museum of Modern Art became a flourishing institution," points out Hilton Kramer, "that undercut the whole idea of contemporary art as an effective medium of social criticism." The artist as rebel, outcast or critic lost his or her relevance. Instead of philistine, academic, bourgeois culture rejecting the artist, the artist was now supported by museums, university galleries, art departments and critics. To any criticism the artist might have of society, the bourgeoisie responded, you're right (and we'll buy, subsidize, exhibit your work to prove it).[9]

Still, if the fifties and early sixties "domesticated" once-radical artists, stifling dissent with the media kiss of peace, it is strange, nonetheless, that the student movement of the next half of that decade and into the 1970s, failed to produce a generation of younger artists on the Left. "It didn't happen," claims critic Lucy Lippard, "because the radical painters and sculptors who should have been their teachers in art school weren't getting jobs—for political reasons. There was a vacuum of influence."*[10]

For Adam Merrill, who graduated from college in 1969—the height of the student movement—a vacuum of teachers is not the solution to the mystery of the disappearing radical artists. "There are no ideas from the Left. No programs to engage the artist. There are just poor people."

"Artists," insists James Rosenquist, "are still dangerous."[11] To whom, though, is the question.

Nobody's knees are knocking in the executive dining room at the Chase Manhattan Bank—decorated with works by rising young talent. Reviewing an exhibition of a group of young artists she called the Gowanus Guerrillas (after the redolent Brooklyn canal where they produced and exhibited their on-site "action pieces"), critic Kay Larson observed that "until art becomes pricey, it is usually pugnacious."[12]

Today, even the pugnacity of the not-yet-pricey has a made-for-the-media quality, as in the term "guerrilla action" for a work like *Crucified Coyote: He Died Because of Our Sins*, a fusion of nostalgia for the sixties (when every sit-in

*This was certainly not true of liberal arts colleges and universities, whose younger faculty members in the humanities and social sciences supported, when they did not actually inspire and in many cases participate in, student protest.[10]

was a guerrilla action) and media hype. For despite the furry pathos of the real-life subject on his wooden cross, there is a comfortably middle-class "Save the Whales" appeal to the protest, which absolves the viewer. (Do you know anyone who has crucified a coyote lately?)

This is not to say that art or its creators should be inspired by protest, politics, ideology or even sympathy for their fellow man. After all, Flaubert said it best: Noble sentiments make ignoble art. But it is no accident that in a period when artists became socially acceptable in Kansas City, courted and celebrated by the most socially and economically powerful forces in America, the Media and the Rich, it is crucified coyotes who died for our sins, not abused children, their unemployed parents, illiterate teenagers, or the discarded elderly.

What more fitting end to the saga of recent class change and choice in America? With the deviant, despised and dangerous element in society now socially acceptable in Kansas City, and envied, admired, emulated and rich on both coasts. The artist as the new Horatio Alger. Yet free of the stigma of crass new money. Aristocratic by election. Conservative through divine right of talent. Radical by tradition. Rich and famous by popular demand.

Living out everyone's fantasy, as Larry Neal notes, the artist fuses America's uniquely dualistic longings: the freedom of creativity coupled to the moorings of money and success.

CONCLUSION

As Americans, we may not believe in class, but we fervently believe in social-class mobility. If this sounds like a contradiction, it is one of many in this book. For if there is a single overwhelming discovery I made in the course of researching, interviewing and writing *Class Act*, it is the web of contradictions that characterizes both the class "system" and our individual responses to it.

Where class is concerned, now we see it, now we don't. We make choices—and are astonished when they have class consequences. We aspire to succeed and fear success. We deplore inequality and the high taxes required to make us all more equal.

From a loftier perspective, economist Fred Hirsch suggested that individual effort to move up may be worse than contradictory: macroeconomically speaking, such behavior is irrational. "If everyone stands on tiptoe, nobody sees any better."[1] Yet even as he makes this case for the social limits to growth, Hirsch concedes his own contradiction. The individual who wants to see better had better be on his/her toes.

Indeed, the virtue of standing on tiptoe for social and economic betterment is so ingrained in our value system, other researchers suggest—that those who do *not* make choices on this basis are seen as deviants. In this view, it is not the relative poverty of many divorced women or the sight of a college-educated young man driving a school bus that is so threatening to some Americans; the apparent choice of downward mobility denies an historic article of faith.

When I returned home from the last of my interview trips, a friend asked me a key question: Were those who moved up smarter than the "others," their friends, neighbors or classmates? The immobile, of course, are not my subject. And since I am not a sociologist, I used no "control group" to test my findings about those who had changed class.

Still, my ultimate conviction is that intelligence— whether defined as I.Q. or street smarts—is less crucial to moving up than another quality.

Imagination.

"I could just see myself..." was an opening phrase that constantly recurred in the self-description of men and women in the process of class change. "I could just see myself in that nurses' uniform," Elena Navarro said. Mike St. Clair, supermarket checker, "saw himself" with friends who were professional, before he ever met such a man.

Perhaps "constructive fantasy" is a better description for the process through which some people form an imaginative projection of the self in more desirable circumstances. "Constructive," because these are not the passive escape fantasies in which we all indulge, but plausible scenarios that function as dress rehearsals for choice and action. Those who stand on tiptoe not only see better; script in hand, they are seeing themselves on the move.

ACKNOWLEDGMENTS

For their help in sighting the myriad contradictions of class in America, I am grateful to the following social scientists: Steven Brint, Carol A. Brown, Chandler Davidson, Thomas Espenshade, Herbert J. Gans, Peter M. Gutmann, Suzanne Keller, Melvin L. Kohn, Martin Levine, Seymour Martin Lipset, S. M. Miller, Kristin A. Moore, Morton Paglin, David Riesman, Frank Riessman, Douglas Wolf.

In a class by himself, Andrew Hacker's contribution to this book could not be measured—even by him!

For kind permission to quote from the script of *Annie Hall*, I would like to thank Woody Allen and United Artists Corporation. Similarly, grateful acknowledgment is made to Paramount Pictures Corporation for permission to quote from *Saturday Night Fever*.

Others who shared expertise and opinion with me, or who helped my snowball sample roll along are Gene Brook, Mary Cantwell, Midge Decter, Celia and Henry Eisenberg, Louise Epstein, Jean Firstenberg, Charles S. Haight, Jr., Mark Hampton, Arlene Handel, Douglas E. Kneeland, Jean Hays, Hilton Kramer, Phyllis Lafarge, Robin Leonard, Al Levin, Lucy Lippard, Dale McConathy, Victoria Newhouse, Alexandra Penney, Mary Proctor, Jim Rosenquist, Peter Schjeldahl, George Segal, Diane Smith, Robert A. M. Stern, Michael M. Thomas, Arthur R. Tower, Matthew Wald, Alan Wurtzel.

Sallie Bingham, Elsie and Barry Blitzer, Bertrand Davezac, Joan and Eugene Goodheart were sources of help and diversion on my travels.

I am thankful to the fellows and trustees of the Macdowell Colony and especially to its director, Chris Barnes, for enabling poor writers to live like landed gentry.

I hope that I have profited from the knowledge and skills of my researchers, Beverly Burris and Jay Rosen. Greg Whittington performed heroic tasks of typing, aided in the final stages by Michael Cooper.

The professionalism and loving support of my agent, Maryanne Colas, sustained me throughout; Ellen Joseph was the editor worth waiting for.

My largest debt is to the men and women who shared with me their experience of class in America. In talking with them about aspiration and achievement, success and failure, I was often reminded of how harshly we judge ourselves and others. Only the people who love us for what we are, not for what we do, mediate the conditional measures of our worth. For this and much more, I am grateful to Frances Blitzer, Colin and Rachel Eisler, and to Halcy Bohen.

SOURCE NOTES

INTRODUCTION

1. David Potter, *People of Plenty: Economic Abundance and the American Character* (Chicago: University of Chicago Press, 1954).
2. Susan Sheehan, *A Welfare Mother* (Boston: Houghton Mifflin, 1976).
3. Robert T. Bower, *Television and the Public* (New York: Praeger, 1973); Ronald E. Frank and Marshall G. Greenberg, *The Public's Use of Television: Who Watches and Why?* (New York: Russell Sage Foundation, 1980) on the demographic differences among television audiences. For a dissenting view of "program attachment" as opposed to "disloyal" television watching, see G. Gerbner and L. Gross, "Living with Television: The Violence Profile," *Journal of Communications*, 26 (1976), pp. 172–99.

CHAPTER 1

1. Quoted in Stephen Birmingham, *The Right People* (Boston: Little, Brown, 1968), p. 340.
2. Richard P. Coleman and Lee Rainwater, *Social Standing in America* (New York: Basic Books, 1978), p. 3.
3. Max Weber, "Class, Status and Party," in *Class, Status and Power*, ed. by Reinhard Bendix and Seymour Martin Lipset (Glencoe, IL: Free Press, 1953), pp. 69 ff.
4. Vance Packard, *The Status Seekers* (New York: D. McKay, 1959). For a valuable discussion of how Warner devised his American "mix" of class and status, along with his critics' objections, see Ruth Rosner Kornhauser, "The Warner Approach to Social Stratification," in Bendix and Lipset, *op. cit.*, pp. 225 ff.

5. Harold M. Hodges, *Social Stratification: Class in America* (Cambridge, Mass.: Schenckman Publishing Company, 1964), p. 13.
6. Joseph A. Kahl, *The American Class Structure* (New York: Irvington, 1959), p. 12.
7. "Super Skiing: Upward Mobility on the Downhill Slope," *Cosmopolitan*, November 1976.
8. "Downward Mobility and the Baby Boomers: Has America Let Them Down?" aired on "U.S. Chronicles," Eastern Education Network, November 1982.
9. Coleman and Rainwater, *op. cit.*, p. 232.
10. Seymour M. Lipset, "Equality and Inequality," in *Contemporary Social Problems*, ed. by Merton and Nisbet (New York: Harcourt Brace Jovanovich, 1976), pp. 307–53; Seymour M. Lipset, "Whither the First New Nation," *Tocqueville Review*, 1 (Fall 1979), 64–99; Morton Paglin, "The Measurement and Trend of Inequality: A Basic Revision," *American Economic Review*, 65 (September 1975), 598–609.
11. Seymour M. Lipset. Personal communication to the author.
12. For the unequal impact of inflation on the poor, see Paul Blumberg, *Inequality in an Age of Decline* (New York: Oxford University Press, 1980).
13. Coleman and Rainwater, *op. cit.*, p. 232.
14. The functionalist argument was propounded most notably in 1945 by Kingsley Davis and Wilbert E. Moore, "Some Principles of Stratification," in *Class, Status and Power*, ed. by Bendix and Lipset (2nd ed.; NY: 1966), pp. 47–53; and, in a famous debate, attacked by Melvin Tumin, "Some Principles of Stratification: A Critical Analysis" in Bendix and Lipset, *op. cit.* (1953), pp. 53–58.
15. A "just meritocracy" is defended by Daniel Bell, *The Coming of Post-Industrial Society* (New York: Basic Books, 1973), pp. 443 ff.
16. David T. Bazelon, quoted in *Making It* by Norman Podhoretz, (New York: Harper & Row, 1967), p. 331.
17. Melvin L. Kohn. Personal communication to the author.
18. Podhoretz, *op. cit.*
19. Russell Baker, *Growing Up* (New York: Congdon & Weed, 1982).

CHAPTER 2

1. Coleman and Rainwater, *op. cit.*, p. 232.
2. Richard A. Easterlin, *Population, Labor Force and Long Swings in Economic Growth: The American Experience* (New York: Columbia University Press, 1968); and by the same author, "Relative Economic Status and the American Fertility Swing," in *Social Structure, Family Life Styles, and Economic Behavior* edited by Eleanor B. Sheldon (Philadelphia: J. B. Lippincott, 1973).
3. For the classic formulation see Kurt B. Mayer, "The Changing Shape

of the American Class Structure," *Social Research*, 30 (December 1963), pp. 458–468. America as a middle-class society is implicit in J. K. Galbraith, *The Affluent Society* (New York: New American Library, 1958); David Riesman, *The Lonely Crowd* (New Haven: Yale University Press, 1950); and William H. Whyte, *The Organization Man* (New York: Simon & Schuster, 1956). For a critique of the class ethnocentrism of these writers, see Richard Parker, *The Myth of the Middle Class* (Philadelphia: Liveright, 1976). As Parker notes, Riesman and Galbraith later "revised" themselves: in the preface to the 1969 edition of *The Lonely Crowd*, Riesman acknowledges that he had unduly emphasized the "upper-middle class affluent American."

4. Barnaby J. Feder, "New Twists in the Foreman's World," *New York Times*, May 17, 1981, p. 4.

5. Note: "best educated generation," Landon Y. Jones, *Great Expectations: America and the Baby Boom Generation* (New York: Coward McCann Geoghegan, 1980), p. 310.

6. U.S., Congress; Congressional Budget Office, *Federal Student Assistance: Issues and Options* (March 1980).

7. Joseph Minarik, quoted by William Severini Kowinski, "The Squeeze on the Middle Class," *New York Times Magazine*, July 13, 1980, p. 27.

8. Daniel R. Mandelker and Roger Montgomery, *Housing in America* (Indianapolis, IN: Bobbs-Merrill, 1973), p. 85.

9. Robert Lekachman, *Greed Is Not Enough* (New York: Pantheon, 1982), p. 58.

10. Note: U.S., Congress; House, *Report of the National Commission on Urban Problems*, House Doc. 91–34, 91st Cong., 1st Sess., p. 73.

11. Howard Husock, "The High Cost of Starting Out," *New York Times Magazine*, June 7, 1981, pp. 28–42.

12. Ellen W. Freeman, "Abortion: Subjective Attitudes and Feelings," *Family Planning Perspectives*, 10 (May–June 1978), p. 154.

13. Dr. Melvin L. Kohn, November 25, 1980. Interview with the author. November, 1981. Kohn's thesis on the relationship between parental occupation, values, and child-rearing patterns has been elaborated and refined in numerous articles since his classic work, *Class and Conformity: A Study in Values* (Homewood, IL: Dorsey Press, 1969). Other researchers have discussed class differences in child rearing, beginning with Martha C. Ericson, "Social Status and Child Rearing Practices," in *Readings in Social Psychology* (New York: Henry Holt, 1947), and including "community studies" such as Herbert J. Gans, *The Levittowners* (New York: Pantheon Books, 1967). Kohn is the only writer who goes beyond description to analyze parental expectations of children by the content of parents' work.

14. Gavin Mackenzie, *The Aristocracy of Labour: The Position of Skilled Craftsmen in the American Class Structure* (Cambridge: Cambridge University Press, 1973), pp. 68–94.

15. James J. Cramer, "Students: Smitten by Big Business," *New York Times*, April 25, 1982, p. 26.
16. April 11, 1982. Interview with Dr. Theodore Caplow, for the "Middletown, U.S.A." series, produced for Public Broadcasting System by Peter Davis.
17. "Fun morality,": Martha Wolfenstein, "The Emergence of Fun Morality," in *Mass Leisure*, ed. by Eric Larrabee and Rolf Meyersohn (Glencoe, IL: Free Press, 1958), p. 86.
18. For an analysis of the New Traditionalism, see Martin E. Marty, "Religion in America Since Mid-century," *Daedalus* (Winter 1982), 140–62. "Wholeness-hunger" and "restrictive vs. Protean personality": Theologian John Murray Cuddihy and psychologist Robert Jay Lifton, quoted in Marty, *op. cit.*, p. 28.
19. Kenneth Briggs, "Mainstream U.S. Evangelicals Surge in Protestant Influence," *New York Times*, March 14, 1982, p. 1.
20. Adam Clymer, "Poll Finds Nation is Becoming Increasingly Republican," *New York Times*, May 3, 1981, p. 1.
21. Kohn, *op. cit.*, p. 73.
22. Dr. Alvin Poussaint and James Comer, *Black Child Care* (New York: Pocket Books, 1976), p. 56.
23. For a portrait of the corporate executive as victim, see Earl Shorris, *The Oppressed Middle: The Politics of Middle Management* (New York: Doubleday, 1981).
24. *The Big Business Executive 1964: A Study of His Social and Educational Background* (a study sponsored by *Scientific American*, conducted by Market Statistics, Inc., in collaboration with Dr. Mabel Newcomer). The study was designed to update Mabel Newcomer, *The Big Business Executive: The Factors That Made Him: 1900–1950* (New York: Columbia University Press, 1950).
25. Report of the National Commission on Urban Problems, *Building the American City*, to the Congress and President of the United States, 91st Congress, 1st Sessions; House Document, No. 91–34, 1968, p. 73.

CHAPTER 3

1. "Adversary culture": Lionel Trilling, *Beyond Culture* (New York: Viking, 1965); used by his student Norman Podhoretz in "The Adversary Culture and the New Class" in *The New Class?* ed. by B. Bruce-Biggs (New Brunswick, NJ: Transaction Books, 1979).
2. Daniel Bell, "The New Class: A Muddled Concept," in Bruce-Biggs, *op. cit.*, pp. 169, 186. The definition is further elaborated by Daniel Bell, in *The Cultural Contradictions of Capitalism* (New York: Basic Books, 1976).
3. Andrew Hacker, "Two 'New Classes' or None," in Bruce-Biggs, *op. cit.*, p. 167.

4. John Kenneth Galbraith, *The New Industrial State* (New York: New American Library, 1967), chaps. 6 and 25.
5. Alvin W. Gouldner, *The Future of Intellectuals and the Rise of the New Class* (New York: Seabury Press, 1979), pp. 27 ff.
6. Peter Steinfels, *The Neoconservatives* (New York: Simon & Schuster, 1979), p 67.
7. Gouldner, *op. cit.*, p. 31.
8. *Time*, XLVII, January 21, 1946, quoted in Davis R. B. Ross, *Preparing for Ulysses: Politics and Veterans During World War II* (New York: Cambridge University Press, 1969), p. 108 ff.
9. Note: Keith W. Olson, *The G.I. Bill, the Veterans and the Colleges* (Lexington, KY: Univeristy of Kentucky Press, 1974), p. 77.
10. The President's Commission on Veteran Pensions, *A Report on Veterans Benefits in the United States*, Staff Report No. IX, Part A (Washington, DC, 1956), p. 143.
11. Peter L. Berger, "The Worldview of the New Class," in Bruce-Biggs, *op. cit.*, p. 53.
12. Nathan Glazer, "Lawyers and the New Class," in Bruce-Biggs, *op. cit.*, p. 94.
13. Midge Decter. Interview with the author, June 1981.
14. Note: A. James Reichley, "Our Critical Shortage of Leadership," *Fortune*, September 1971.
15. Aaron Wildavsky, "Using Public Funds to Serve Private Interests," in Bruce-Biggs, *op. cit.*, p. 151.
16. Steinfels, *op. cit.*, p. 288. For a critique of these "credentialed knowledge" holders as tools of the industrial-military complex, see S. M. Miller, "The Coming of the Pseudo-Technocratic Society," *Sociological Inquiry*, 46, (1976), pp. 219–21.
17. Hacker, in Bruce-Biggs, *op. cit.*, p. 71.
18. Robert D. Hershey, Jr., "Deregulation Cuts Lawyer Need," *New York Times*, June 1, 1981, p. 1, Section D.
19. T. Scott Fain, "Self Employed Americans: Their Number Has Increased," *Monthly Labor Review* (November 1980), p. 3.
20. This figure is derived from six large surveys of the American population conducted between 1972 and 1977 by the National Opinion Research Center of the University of Chicago (NORC). Cited by Everett Carll Ladd, Jr., "Pursuing the New Class," in Bruce-Biggs, *op. cit.*, p. 103.
21. Daniel Bell, "The New Class: A Muddled Concept," *Ibid*, p. 189.

CHAPTER 4

1. "Yes, You—A Fabulous Hostess," *Cosmopolitan*, May 1980.
2. *Ibid.*
3. "How to Be House Proud," *Cosmopolitan*, November 1977.
4. *Ibid.*

5. "Managing Your Expectations," *Cosmopolitan*, October 1976.
6. "Subtle Art of Timing," *Cosmopolitan*, May 1976.
7. *Ibid.*
8. "A Handbook for the New Executive Woman," *Cosmopolitan*, June 1977.
9. Linda Wolfe, *Women and Sex in the Eighties: The Cosmo Report* (New York: Arbor House, 1981), p. 45.
10. "In Praise of Money," *Cosmopolitan*, April 1977.
11. "Your Boss Woman Style," *Cosmopolitan*, June 1976.
12. *Ibid.*
13. "How Good Is Your English?" *Cosmopolitan*, January 1977.
14. "The Executive Spouse," *Cosmopolitan*, July 1981.
15. Arthur J. Vidich and Joseph Bensman, *The New American Society: Revolution of the Middle Class* (Chicago: Quadrangle Books, 1971), p. 121.
16. "Checking Out Waitresses," *Cosmopolitan*, August 1981.
17. "Foreplay and Good Sex," *Essence*, September 1981.
18. "Essence Women," *Essence*, September 1981.
19. "Marian Wright Edelman, Civil Rights Crusader," *Essence*, September 1980.
20. "Fashion in Jewels," *Essence*, September 1981.
21. "Abortion: The New Facts of Life," *Essence*, September 1981.
22. "Build on Your Success," *Essence*, September 1981.
23. "Self-Confidence: How to Build Yours," *Essence*, September 1981.
24. "Dealing with That Cheap Man," *Essence*, September 1981.
25. Alan Wurtzel. Personal communication to the author.
26. Paul M. Hirsch, "An Organizational Prospective on Television," in *Television and Social Behavior: Beyond Violence and Children*, ed. by Stephen B. Withey and Ronald P. Abeles (Hillsdale, NJ: L. Erlbaum, 1980), p. 91.
27. Harold L. Wilensky, "Mass Society and Mass Culture: Interdependence or Independence?" *American Sociological Review*, 29 (April 1964), p. 93.
28. Personal communication to the author.
29. National Urban League, panel at Conference for Better Cities for a Better Nation, "The Black Image in Motion Pictures and Television," August 6, 1978.
30. Herbert J. Gans, *Popular Culture and High Culture* (New York: Basic Books, 1975), p. 141.

CHAPTER 5

1. P. L. Berger and B. Berger, quoted in David Riesman, *On Higher Education* (San Francisco: Jossey-Bass, 1980), p. 85. The only other writer to have documented this as a voluntarist movement is Champ

Clark, "White Collar Kids in Blue Collar Jobs," *Money*, February 1976, pp. 33–36.

2. Midge Decter, *Liberal Parents, Radical Children* (New York: Coward McCann and Geoghegan, 1975), for the earlier phenomenon.

3. Note: Anthony Bailey, *America, Lost and Found* (New York: Random House, 1980).

4. C. Hess Haagen, *Venturing Beyond Campus* (New York: Columbia University Press, 1977).

5. C. Hess Haagen. Personal communication to the author.

6. Peter M. Gutmann. Personal communication to the author.

7. James O'Toole, "The Reserve Army of the Underemployed," Parts I and II, *Change*, May 1975, pp. 26–63; June 1975, pp. 26–61. See also Paul Blumberg and James M. Murtha, "College Graduates and the American Dream," *Dissent*, Winter 1977, pp. 45–52; and a reply, James Wright and Richard Hamilton, "Blue Collars, Cap and Gown," *Dissent*, Spring 1978; Rosabeth Moss Kanter, "A Good Job Is Hard to Find," *Working Papers* (May–June 1979), pp. 44–50.

8. Janet L. Norwood, "The Job Outlook for College Graduates through 1990," *Occupational Outlook Quarterly* (Winter 1979), pp. 2–7. Douglas E. Kneeland, "Young Drifters in America," *New York Times*, April 15, 1981, and personal communication to the author.

9. Jean Hays. Personal communication to the author.

10. T. Scott Fain, *Monthly Labor Review* (November 1980), p. 98.

11. Kenneth Noble, "Can Venture Capitalists Be Taught?" in "National Recruitment Survey," Special Supplement to the *New York Times*, October 12, 1980, p. 55.

12. *Ibid.*

13. Paul Lazarsfeld, "A Memoir," in Donald Fleming and Bernard Bailyn, *The Intellectual Migration* (Cambridge, MA: Harvard University Press, 1969), p. 277.

CHAPTER 6

1. Hugh Carter and Paul Glick, *Marriage and Divorce: A Social and Economic Study* (Cambridge, MA: Harvard University Press, 1970), p. 403. For further evidence of the positive relationship for men between socioeconomic status (whether measured by education or income) and marital stability, see also Paul C. Glick and Arthur J. Norton, *Marrying, Divorcing and Living Together in the U.S. Today* (Washington, DC: Population Reference Bureau, 1977), p. 9.

2. Andrew Hacker, "Divorce à la Mode," *New York Review of Books*, 3 (May 1979), pp. 23–26.

3. George Levinger and Oliver C. Moles, *Divorce and Separation* (New York: Basic Books, 1979), p. 149.

4. John F. Cuber, *The Significant Americans: A Study of Sexual Behavior*

among the Affluent (New York: Appleton-Century, 1965), pp. 100–131.

5. Jean Brody and Gail Beswick Osborne, *The Twenty Year Phenomenon* (New York: Simon & Schuster, 1972), p. 244.

6. Anthony Haden Guest, "The Mysterious Mogul of Lincoln Center," *New York*, May 5, 1980.

7. Robert Hampton, "Marital Disruption: Some Social and Economic Consequences," in *Five Thousand American Families: Patterns of Economic Progress*, ed. by Greg J. Duncan and James N. Morgan, Vol. 3 (Ann Arbor: Institute for Social Research, 1977), p. 165.

8. Richard Hoye, Los Angeles Department of Public Services. Personal communication to the author.

9. U.S., Bureau of the Census, "Money, Income and Poverty Status of Families and Persons in the United States: 1980 and 1981," *Current Population Reports*, Series P–60, Nos. 127 and 134 (August 1981 and July 1982).

10. Judith S. Wallerstein and Joan Belin Kelly, *Surviving the Breakup* (New York: Basic Books, 1980), p. 151.

11. Levinger, *op. cit.*, p. xii.

12. Jessie Bernard, *The Future of Marriage* (New York: World Publishing, 1972), quoted in Levinger, *op. cit.*, p. xi.

13. *Ibid.*, p. 135 ff.

14. Hampton, *op. cit.*, p. 185.

15. Leonore J. Weitzman, "Social and Economic Consequences of Property, Alimony and Child Support Awards," *UCLA Law Review*, 28 (August 1981), pp. 1181–1268.

16. Mary Jo Bane, "Marital Disruption and the Lives of Children," *Journal of Social Issues*, 32 (1978), pp. 301–07.

17. Hampton, *op. cit.*, p. 183.

18. Angus Campbell, *et al.*, *The Quality of American Life* (New York: Russell Sage, 1976) p. 420.

19. Levinger, *op. cit.*, p. 194.

20. Cited in Isabel V. Sawhill and Heather L. Ross, *Time of Transition* (Washington, DC: Urban Institute, 1975), p. 27.

21. Duncan and Morgan, eds., *op. cit.*, Vol. 4, p. 41.

22. Thomas J. Espenshade, "The Economic Consequences of Divorce," *Journal of Marriage and the Family* (August 1979), p. 622.

23. Note: Andrée Brooks, "Child Support: A Growing Problem of Non-Payment," *New York Times*, August 14, 1982, p. 24.

24. Judith Cassetty, *Child Support and Public Policy* (Lexington, MA: Lexington Books, 1978), p. 123.

25. *Ibid.*

26. Laurie Shields, *Displaced Homemakers* (New York: McGraw-Hill, 1981).

27. Wallerstein and Kelley, *op. cit.*, p. 108.

28. Duncan and Morgan, *Five Thousand Families*, Vol. 2, p. 81.

29. Wallerstein and Kelley, *op. cit.*, p. 25.
30. For documentation of the "domino effect" of poorer housing conditions, see Ruth A. Brandwein, Carol A. Brown, and Elizabeth Maury Fox, "Women and Children Last: The Social Situation of Divorced Mothers and Their Families," *Journal of Marriage and the Family* (August 1974), pp. 498–511.
31. Judith A. Kohen, Carol A. Brown, and Roslyn Feldberg, "Divorced Mothers: Female Family Control," in Levinger, *op. cit.*, p. 233.
32. Wallerstein and Kelley, *op. cit.*, p. 185.
33. Note: Cassetty, *op. cit.*, p. 60.
34. Colette Dowling, *The Cinderella Complex* (New York: Summit Books, 1981).
35. Andrew Hacker, *U.S.: A Statistical Portrait of the American People* (New York: Viking, 1983), pp. 112–15.
36. John Leonard, "New York Women," *Private Lives in the Imperial City* (New York: Knopf, 1979), pp. 27–29.
37. Hampton, *op. cit.*, p. 181.
38. Note: Brandwein, *op. cit.*, p. 506.
39. Alvin Schorr, "The Single Parent and Public Policy," *Social Policy* (March–April 1979).
40. David Greenberg and Douglas Wolf, "The Economic Consequences of Experiencing Parental Marital Disruption," *Children and Youth Services Review*, 4 (1982), pp. 141–62.
41. Wallerstein and Kelley, *op. cit.*, p. 282.

CHAPTER 7

1. Kathleen Rudd Scharf, "Teenage Pregnancy: Why the Epidemic," *Working Papers* (March–April 1979), p. 68.
2. Lloyd Bacon, "Early Motherhood, Accelerated Role Transition, and Social Pathologies," *Social Forces*, 52 (March 1974), pp. 340 ff.
3. Kristin A. Moore, *et al.*, "Teenage Childbearing: Consequences for Women, Families and Government Welfare Expenditures" (Washington, DC: The Urban Institute, 1979), p. 6.
4. W. H. Baldwin, "Adolescent Pregnancy and Childbearing," *Population Bulletin*, 31 (January 1980), p. 26.
5. Moore, *et al.*, *op. cit.*, p. 18.
6. Josefina J. Card and Lauress L. Wise, "Teenage Mothers and Teenage Fathers," *Family Planning Perspectives*, 10 (July–August 1978), p. 210.
7. P. Cutright, "Timing the First Birth: Does It Matter?" *Journal of Marriage and the Family*, 35 (1973), p. 585. Also, Card and Wise, *op. cit.*, p. 200.
8. Harriet B. Presser, "Social Consequences of Teenage Childbearing," cited in Baldwin, *op. cit.*, p. 26.
9. Moore, *et al.*, *op. cit.*, p. 18.

10. Frank F. Furstenberg, Jr., "The Social Consequences of Teenage Parenthood," *Family Planning Perspectives*, 8 (July–August 1976), p. 158.
11. Arthur A. Campbell, "The Role of Family Planning in the Reduction of Poverty," *Journal of Marriage and the Family*, 30 (1968), p. 238.
12. M. Zelnick and J. F. Kanter, "Sexual Activity, Contraceptive Use and Pregnancy among Metropolitan-Area Teenagers, 1971–1979," *Family Planning Perspectives*, 12 (1980), p. 230.
13. M. Zelnick and J. F. Kanter, "Reasons for Non-use of Contraception by Sexually Active Women Aged 15–19," *Family Planning Perspectives*, 11 (1979), p. 289.
14. Note: "1981 New York City Study": New York, NY: City Human Resources Administration, "Pregnancy and Welfare Dependency: A Research Note," No. AR (February 1981), p. i.
15. "Centers for Disease Control: Abortion Surveillance 1978," (Atlanta, GA, November 1980), p. 5.
16. Alan Guttmacher Institute, "Teenage Pregnancy: The Problem That Hasn't Gone Away" (1981), p. 27.
17. T. James Trussell, "Economic Consequences of Teenage Childbearing," *Family Planning Perspectives*, 8 (1976), p. 187. Card and Wise, *op. cit.*, p. 199.
18. K. A. Moore, "Teenage Childbirth and Welfare Dependency," *Family Planning Perspectives*, 10 (1978), p. 233; U.S., Social Security Administration, Dept. of Health and Human Services, 1977, *Recipient Characteristics Study: Part 1*, SSA Pub. No. 13–11729 (1980).
19. Baldwin, *op. cit.*, p. 25.
20. U.S., Bureau of the Census, "Fertility of American Women in 1980," *Current Population Reports*, P–20, No. 364 (August 1981).
21. New York, NY, Human Resources Administration, *op. cit.*, p. i.
22. Frank F. Furstenberg, Jr. and Albert G. Crawford, "Family Support: Helping Teenage Mothers to Cope," *Family Planning Perspectives*, 10 (November–December 1978), pp. 322–333.
23. Alan Guttmacher Institute, *op. cit.*, p. 9.
24. *Ibid.*, p. 11.
25. Zelnick and Kanter, "Sexual Activity..." *op. cit.* Also, "First Pregnancies to Women Aged 15–19, 1976 and 1971," *Family Planning Perspectives*, 10 (January–February 1978), p. 19.
26. Scharf, *op. cit.*, p. 68.
27. June Dobbs Butts, "Adolescent Sexuality and the Impact of Teenage Pregnancy from a Black Perspective," Paper Commissioned by the *Family Impact Seminar*, George Washington University, Institute for Educational Leadership, 1979.
28. Lee Rainwater, *And the Poor Get Children* (Chicago: Quadrangle, 1967), p. 25 ff.
29. Note: Dr. Willard Cates, Jr., Centers for Disease Control, Abortion Surveillance Branch, quoted by Jane Brody, *New York Times*, September 6, 1981.

30. Richard Wertheimer and Kristin Moore, "Teenage Childbearing: Public Sector Costs" (Washington, DC: The Urban Institute, 1982), p. 23.

CHAPTER 8

1. Fran Lebowitz, *Metropolitan Life* (New York: Dutton, 1978), p. 34.
2. U.S., Department of Agriculture, *Estimates of the Cost of Raising a Child*, Miscellaneous Publication No. 1411 (1981), p. 2 ff.
3. Thomas Tilling, "Your $250,000 Baby," *Parents*, November 1980.
4. U.S., Bureau of the Census, "Fertility of American Women: 1980," *Current Population Reports*, P–10, No. 375.
5. Charles Westhoff. Personal communication to the author.
6. Note: Lolagene C. Coombs and Ronald Freedman, "Premarital Pregnancy. Childspacing and Later Economic Achievement," *Population Studies*, Vol. 24, No. 3, November 1970, pp. 389–412.
7. Jean E. Veevers, *Childless by Choice* (Toronto: Butterworth, 1980), p. 25.
8. Note: Veevers, *op. cit.*, p. 80.
9. Thomas J. Espenshade, "The Value and Cost of Children," Washington, DC: Population Reference Bureau, Inc., 32, no. 1 (April 1977), p. 31.
10. Espenshade, *op. cit.*, p. 29.
11. *Ibid.*, p. 43.
12. Linda Silka and Sara Kiesler, "Couples Who Choose to Remain Childless," *Family Planning Perspectives*, Vol. 9, No. 1, Jan./Feb. 1977, pp. 16–24.
13. Note: Veevers, *op. cit.*, p. 88.
14. Note: C. Shannon Stokes and P. Neal Ritchey, "Some Further Observations on Childlessness and Color," *Journal of Black Studies*, 5 (December 1974), p. 207. Since this study, both black and white fertility have also declined 32 percent among teenagers, but the rate for black young women remains three times that of whites.
15. U.S., Bureau of the Census, *Current Population Reports*, Series P–20, No. 340 (1979), quoted in Andrew Hacker, "Creating American Inequality," *New York Review of Books*, March 20, 1980.
16. Kenneth Keniston *et al.*, *All Our Children: The American Family under Pressure*, Report by the Carnegie Council. New York: Harcourt, Brace, Jovanovich, 1977. Advocated a greater sense of collective responsibility for the nation's youngsters.
17. Note: Clyde Haberman, "A Hidden 'Singles Issue' Trails City's Hierarchy," *New York Times*, July 21, 1980, Section B, p. 1.
18. Note: "Media's Much Touted Baby Boomlet: The New Baby Bloom," *Time*, February 22, 1982.
19. Peter L. Heller, Yung-mei Tsai and H. Paul Chalfont, "Voluntary and Nonvoluntary Childlessness: Personality vs. Structural Implications" (paper presented at the American Sociological Association, 1981).
20. CBS/*New York Times* Poll, cited note, 20, chapter 2.

21. I am indebted to Sallie Bingham for this information from unpublished letters of Mary Breckenridge.

22. Linda Bird Francke, "Childless by Choice," *Newsweek*, January 14, 1980.

23. Richard A. Easterlin, "What Will 1984 Be Like? Socioeconomic Implications of Recent Twists in Age Structure," *Demography*, 15 (November 1978), pp. 397–421.

CHAPTER 9

1. Michael Ennis, "What Do These Rugged Texas He-men Have in Common?" *Texas Monthly*, June 1980.

2. *Characteristics of Readers of the Advocate*, Walker & Struman Research, Inc., Study No. 124–002, (Los Angeles: Walker & Struman Research, December 1980).

3. Roger Ricklefs, "Campaigns to Sell to Homosexual Market," *Wall Street Journal*, May 13, 1975, pp. 44–46.

4. Richard M. Levine, "The TV Industry's Gay Underground," *TV Guide*, May 30, and June 7, 1981.

5. Larry Bush and Richard Goldstein, "The Anti-Gay Backlash," *Village Voice*, April 8–14, 1981; also, Arthur Bell, "A Bunch of Gay Guys Sitting around Talking," *Village Voice*, June 24–30, 1981.

6. Martin Levine, "Employment Discrimination against Gay Men," *International Review of Modern Sociology*, 9 (July–December 1979), pp. 151–63.

7. Barry Adam and Douglas E. Baer, "The Social Mobility of Women and Men in the Ontario Legal Profession," *Canadian Review of Sociology and Anthropology*, forthcoming.

8. Levine, ed., Saghir and Robins (1973), cited in Levine, *op. cit.*, p. 159.

9. "'Gay men have trouble competing'": Andrew Kopkind. Personal communication with the author.

10. Seymour Kleinberg, *Alienated Affections* (New York: St. Martin's, 1981), p. 11 ff.

11. Ennis, *op. cit.*

12. Martin P. Levine, "Gay Ghetto," in *Gay Men: The Sociology of Male Homosexuality*, ed. by Martin P. Levine (New York: Harper & Row, 1979), pp. 182–204.

13. Alan P. Bell, and Martin S. Weinberg, *Homosexualities: A Study of Diversity among Men and Women* (New York: Simon & Schuster, 1978), p. 143 ff.

14. Timothy d'Arch Smith, *Love in Earnest: Some Notes on the Lives and Writings of English "Uranian" Poets, 1889–1930* (London: Routledge, Kegan, Paul, 1970), pp. 191–96.

15. Jonathan Katz, *Gay American History* (New York: Crowell, 1976), p. 573; Wallace Hamilton, "The Secret Life of Horatio Alger," *Christopher Street*, July 1981.

16. An informal estimate proposed by a number of gay professional women interviewed.
17. Jill Johnston, *Lesbian Nation: The Feminist Solution* (New York: Simon & Schuster, 1973).
18. Deborah Wolf, *The Lesbian Community* (Berkeley: University of California Press, 1980), p. 98 ff.
19. *Ibid.*
20. Bell and Weinberg, *op. cit.*, p. 234.
21. Wolf, *op. cit.*, p. 158.
22. Rita Mae Brown, "The Last Straw," in *Class and Feminism*, ed. by Charlotte Bunch and Nancy Myron (Baltimore: Crossing Press, 1974), p. 16.
23. Robin Leonard, "Lesbians in the Work Force" (unpublished paper, New York University, May 1981).
24. Robert A. Hogan, Anne N. Fox, and John H. Kirchner, "Attitudes, Opinions and Sexual Development of 205 Homosexual Women," *Journal of Homosexuality* 3 (Winter 1977), pp. 123–29.
25. Robin Leonard. Personal communication to the author.
26. Bunch, *op. cit.*, p. 71.
27. Rita Mae Brown, in Bunch, *op. cit.*, p. 21.
28. Richard Zoglin, "The Homosexual Executive" in Levine, *op. cit.*, p. 75.

CHAPTER 10

1. B. J. Widick, ed., *Auto Work and Its Discontents* (Baltimore: Johns Hopkins University Press, 1976), p. 67. See also, Bennett M. Berger, *Working Class Suburb: A Study of Auto Workers in Suburbia* (Berkeley, CA: University California Press, 1971).
2. For one of the earliest and least known analyses of sabotage in American industry, see Thorsten Veblen, "On the Nature and Uses of Sabotage," *The Engineer and the Price System* (New York: Gordon, 1921); for a recent discussion of its role in the auto industry, see Emma Rothschild, *Paradise Lost: The Decline of the Auto-industrial Age* (New York: Random House, 1973).
3. Widick, *op. cit.*, p. 70.
4. Ely Chinoy, *Automobile Workers and the American Dream* (New York: Doubleday, 1955). The careers of Bobbie Corsi Meara and two generations of male Ritchies reflect the weight of research suggesting minimal occupational mobility for unskilled labor. See Ely Chinoy's observation of auto workers as "trapped by high pay and lack of alternatives" (p. 88). In their revised classic, Peter Blau and Otis D. Duncan conclude that "men who start their working lives in manual jobs experience relatively little intergenerational mobility": Blau and Duncan, *The American Occupational Structure* (New York: Wiley, 1967), p. 55. For a dissenting view, see Sar A. Levitan, *Blue Collar Workers* (New

York: McGraw-Hill, 1971), p. 377, who notes, on the basis of a survey of eleven major industries, that "those wanting to get ahead could do so through job changes if promotion were foreclosed on the job." Also see Eli Ginzberg, *The Manpower Connection* (Cambridge, MA: Harvard University Press, 1975).

5. The high school diplomas of the Eldredge children reflect the extraordinary chapter in black mobility represented by migration from the rural south to the manufacturing centers of the Midwest. By the 1960s upward of 40 percent of Detroit's auto workers were estimated to be black. See Thomas R. Brooks, "Workers, Black and White," *Dissent* (January–February 1970). The layoffs of the early 1980s take on an added tragedy of losing hard-won ground.

6. *The Colored American*, Boston, March 6, 1841. The phrase was later— and often—used by Booker T. Washington.

7. Josef Berger, *In Great Waters* (New York: Federal Writers' Project, 1941), p. xiii.

8. Sandra Wolforth, *The Portuguese in America* (San Francisco: R. & R. Research, 1978), p. 19.

9. Berger, *op. cit.*, p. 61.

10. Note: John B. Jensen, "The Portuguese Immigrant Community of New England: A Current Look," *Studia Revista Semestral*, no. 34 (Lisbon, 1972), p. 133.

11. For prosperity of Portuguese in California see Gerald Estep, "Portuguese Assimilation in Hawaii and California," *Sociology and Social Research*, 26 (September–October 1941), p. 63.

12. Wolforth, *op. cit.*, p. 112.

13. Jensen, *op. cit.*, pp. 133–34; also, James P. Adler, *Ethnic Minorities in Cambridge: The Portuguese* (Cambridge, MA: 1972), 1:14, p. 25.

14. William Carlson Smith, *Americans in the Making* (New York: Appleton-Century, 1937), p. 22.

15. Ann Banks, ed., *First Person America* (New York: Knopf, 1980), p. 35.

16. Peter Berger, *The Social Construction of Reality* (New York: Knopf, 1976).

17. Banks, *op. cit.*, p. 35.

CHAPTER 11

1. Most researchers use the term nonideologically; see Frank Levy, "How Big Is the Underclass?" Working Paper 0090–1, The Urban Institute (September 1977). More recently, some writers have claimed the word "caricatures a segment of humanity, and serves as a way of 'writing off' those whom society is unwilling to help." See Daniel Fox, "The Underclass," review of *The Underclass*, by Ken Auletta, in *Social Policy* (Fall 1982), pp. 60–62.

2. U.S., Bureau of the Census, "Money, Income and Poverty Status of Families and Persons in the United States, 1980" (Advance Data from

the March 1981 Current Population Survey), *Current Population Reports*, Series P–60, No. 127, p. 3.

3. Arthur Spindler, *Public Welfare* (New York: Human Science Press, 1979), p. 53. See also Levy, *op. cit.*, for the discussion of the poor as a shifting population.

4. Robert C. Stone and Frederic T. Schlamp, *Welfare and Working Fathers* (Lexington, MA: Heath, 1971), p. 242. See also two classics on this subject: E. Wight Bakke, *The Unemployed Male* (New Haven: Yale University Press, 1940), p. 282; and Elliot Liebow, *Tally's Corner* (Boston: Little, Brown, 1967). All of these studies deal with the "stigma" suffered by the nonearning male in this society. There is a question as to whether the same pariah status is suffered by the "welfare mother," especially in communities where this mode of support would be the norm.

5. Kenneth E. Boulding, quoted in Herman P. Miller, "What Is Poverty—Who Are the Poor?" (paper presented for the UCLA Seminar on Poverty, Spring 1965), p. 51.

6. Spindler, *op. cit.*, p. 442.

7. Mark Green and Norman Waitzman, "Cost, Benefit and Class," *Working Papers* (May–June 1980), 39–51.

8. "In the Best of Times," aired on "*U.S. Chronicles*," Eastern Educational Network, September 15, 1980.

9. Felix Kaufman, "The Jobs That Nobody Wants: Economic Challenges of the 1980s," *Futurist*, 13 (1979), pp. 269–74.

10. Bruce S. Harvey and Rudolph L. Kagerer, "Marginal Workers and Their Decisions to Work or to Quit," *American Journal of Economics and Sociology*, 35 (1976), pp. 137–47.

11. Lester C. Thurow, "Education and Economic Equality", *The Public Interest*, 38 (1972), pp. 66–81.

12. Leonard Goodwin, *Causes and Cures of Welfare: New Evidence on the Social Psychology of the Poor* (Lexington, MA: Lexington Books, 1983), chaps. 3 and 4. See also Leonard Goodwin, *Do the Poor Want to Work?* (Washington, DC: Brookings Institution, 1972).

13. The theory that the lower-class person, without abandoning the values of the dominant culture, develops a "stretched" or negotiated version. See Hyman Rodman, "The Lower Class Value Stretch," *Social Forces*, 42 (1963), pp. 205–15.

14. Richard Titmuss, *Essays on the Welfare State* (Winchester, MA: Allen & Unwin, 1981).

CHAPTER 12

1. Among many other examples of the "make-believe" activities of the rich, see Thorsten Veblen on the rationale for servants, in *The Theory of the Leisure Class* (Boston: Houghton Mifflin, 1973), p. 59.

2. Suzanne Keller, *Beyond the Ruling Class: Strategic Elites and Modern Society* (New York: Arno, 1963), p. 262.

3. C. Wright Mills, *The Power Elite* (New York: Oxford University Press, 1956), pp. 328. See also G. William Domhoff and Hoyt B. Ballard, *C. Wright Mills and the Power Elite* (Boston: Beacon, 1968).

4. Note: *Ibid.*, pp. 163–64.

5. G. William Domhoff, *The Powers That Be: Processes of Ruling Class Domination in America* (New York: Random House, 1978), pp. 66, 97, and passim.

6. G. William Domhoff, *The Bohemian Grove and Other Retreats: A Study in Ruling Class Cohesiveness* (New York: Harper & Row, 1975).

7. Coleman and Rainwater, *op. cit.*, p. 240 ff.

8. *Ibid.*, p. 241.

9. Roger Vaughn, "Ted Turner's True Talent," *Esquire*, October 10, 1978; Harry F. Waters, "Going Super with Ted," *Newsweek*, January 1, 1979; "Terrible Ted vs. the Networks," *Time*, June 9, 1980.

10. Joan Didion, "On the Mall," *The White Album* (New York: Simon & Schuster, 1979), pp. 180–86.

11. Stewart Brand, *The Whole Earth Catalog* (New York: Random House, 1981).

12. Arthur Lubow, "Composting the 60's," *New Times*, August 5, 1977.

13. Note: David Sanford, *Me and Ralph* (New Rochelle, NY: 1976).

14. Joseph Epstein, "Running and Other Vices," *American Scholar*, 48 (Spring 1979).

15. Georgia Dullea, "Enduring the Marathon Marriage," *New York Times*, October 18, 1981, p. 72.

16. Gael Greene, "Hey, Good Lookin'—What Ya Got Cookin'?" *New York*, December 29, 1980–January 5, 1981.

17. Mark Roman, "Who's in the Kitchen with Dinah, Garland, among Others," *New York Times*, August 23, 1981, Section D, p. 16.

18. "The Marcella Hazan School of Classic Italian Cooking in Bologna" (brochure).

19. Francesca Stanfill, "Living Well Is Still the Best Revenge," *New York Times Magazine*, December 26, 1980.

20. C. Z. Guest, "Around the Garden," *New York Post*, June 12, 1981, p. 29.

21. *New York Times Magazine*, September 27, 1981.

22. Quoted in Michael de Courcy Hinds, "New Fixture in the Home: The Computer," *New York Times*, June 22, 1981, p. 73.

23. Jane Geniesse, "A 60s Echo in an 80s Loft: The Conversation Pit," *New York Times*, August 13, 1981, Section C, p. 6.

24. Joan Didion, "Many Mansions," *White Album*, p. 72.

25. The change from "Captains of Industry to Captains of Consumption and Leisure" was first described by Riesman, *op. cit.*, p. 239. Many other studies since have charted the disappearance or transformation

of the traditional "work ethic." See Joseph Veroff, Elizabeth Douvan, and Richard A. Kulka, *The Inner American: A Self-Portrait from 1957 to 1976* (New York: Basic, 1981); and Daniel Yankelovitch, *New Rules* (New York: Random House, 1981). For a summary of this change, also see Bell, *Cultural Contradictions*, p. 70.

CHAPTER 13

1. Coleman and Rainwater, *op. cit.*, p. 298.
2. Martin H. Bush, *Duane Hanson* (Wichita, Kan: University of Kansas Gallery of Art, 1976), p. 31.
3. Peter Schjeldahl, "Warhol and Class Content," *Art in America*, May 1980. See also, Andy Warhol and Pat Hackett, *POPism: The Warhol Sixties* (New York: Harcourt Brace Jovanovich, 1980).
4. David Bourdon, quoted in Schjeldahl, *op. cit.*, p. 116.
5. Course Prospectus. Dale McConathy. Personal interviews with the author and Jay Rosen.
6. George Segal. Personal communication to the author.
7. George Boudaille, *Gustave Courbet: Painter in Protest* (Greenwich, CT: New York Graphic Society, 1969).
8. Serge Guilbaut, "The New Adventures of the Avant-Garde in America," *October*, 15 (Winter 1980), pp. 61–78.
9. Hilton Kramer. Personal communication to the author.
10. Lucy Lippard. Personal communication to the author.
11. Jim Rosenquist. Personal communication to the author.
12. Kay Larson, "The Gowanus Guerrillas," *New York*, June 8, 1981.

CONCLUSION

1. Fred Hirsch, *Social Limits to Growth* (Cambridge, MA: Harvard University Press, 1981), p. 5.

SELECTED
BIBLIOGRAPHY

Baker, Russell. *Growing Up*. New York: Congdon & Weed, 1982.

Bell, Daniel. *The Coming of Post Industrial Society*. New York: Basic Books, 1973.

———. *The Cultural Contradictions of Capitalism*. New York: Basic Books, 1976.

Bendix, Reinhard and Lipset, Seymour Martin. *Class, Status and Power*. Glencoe, IL: Free Press, 1966.

———. *Social Mobility in Industrial Society*. Berkeley and Los Angeles: University of California Press, 1967.

Berger, Bennett. *Working Class Suburb*. Berkeley and Los Angeles: University of California Press, 1971.

Blau, Peter and Duncan, Otis Dudley. *The American Occupational Structure*. New York: Wiley, 1967.

Blumberg, Paul. *Inequality in an Age of Decline*. New York: Oxford University Press, 1980.

Bruce-Biggs, B., ed. *The New Class?* New Brunswick, NJ: Transaction Books, 1979.

Bunch, Charlotte and Myron, Nancy. *Class and Feminism*. Baltimore: Diana Press, 1974.

Carter, Hugh and Glick, Paul. *Marriage and Divorce: A Social and Economic Study*. Cambridge: Harvard University Press, 1970.

Chinoy, Eli. *Automobile Workers and the American Dream*. New York: Doubleday, 1955.

Coleman, Richard P. and Rainwater, Lee. *Social Standing in America: New Dimensions of Class*. New York: Basic Books, 1978.

Coles, Robert and Erickson, Jon. *The Middle Americans*. Boston: Atlantic Monthly Press, 1971.

Didion, Joan. *The White Album*. New York: Simon & Schuster, 1979.

Domhoff, G. William. *The Bohemian Grove and Other Retreats*. New York: Harper & Row, 1975.

———. *The Powers That Be: Processes of Ruling Class Domination in America*. New York: Random House, 1978.

Duncan, Greg J. and Morgan, James N., eds. *Five Thousand American Families: Patterns of Economic Progress*. Vols. 2–4. Ann Arbor: Institute for Social Research, University of Michigan, 1974–77.

Featherman, David and Hauser, Robert. *Opportunity and Change*. New York: Academic Press, 1978.

Furstenberg, Frank F., Jr. *Unplanned Parenthood: The Social Consequences of Teenage Childbearing*. New York: Free Press, 1976.

Gans, Herbert J. *The Levittowners*. New York: Pantheon Books, 1967.

———. *Popular Culture and High Culture: An Analysis and Evaluation of Taste*. New York: Basic Books, 1975.

Glazer, Nathan and Moynihan, D. P. *Beyond the Melting Pot: The Negroes, Puerto Ricans, Jews, Italians and Irish in New York City*. 2nd ed. Cambridge: M.I.T. Press, 1970.

Gouldner, Alvin. *The Future of Intellectuals and the Rise of the New Class*. New York: Seabury Press, 1979.

Hacker, Andrew. *U.S.: A Statistical Portrait of the American People*. New York: Viking Press, 1983.

Jencks, Christopher, *et al*. *Who Gets Ahead: The Determinants of Economic Success in America*. New York: Basic Books, 1979.

Keller, Suzanne. *Beyond the Ruling Class: Strategic Elites in Modern Society*. New York: Random House, 1963.

Kohn, Melvin L. *Class and Conformity: A Study in Values*. Homewood, IL: Dorsey Press, 1969.

Levine, Martin E., ed. *Gay Men: The Sociology of Male Homosexuality*. New York: Harper & Row, 1979.

Levinger, George and Moles, Oliver C. *Divorce and Separation*. New York: Basic Books, 1979.

Levitan, Sar A. *Blue Collar Workers*. New York: McGraw-Hill, 1971.

Lipset, Seymour Martin. "Whither the First New Nation." *Tocqueville Review*, vol. 1, no. 1 (Fall 1979).

Mackenzie, Gavin. *The Aristocracy of Labor: The Position of Skilled Craftsmen in the American Class Structure*. Cambridge: Cambridge University Press, 1973.

Marx/Engels: Selected Works. Edited by Lawrence and Wishart. 1 vol. London: International Publishing Co.; New York, 1968.

Mills, C. Wright. *White Collar: The American Middle Classes*. New York: Oxford University Press, 1951.

———. *The Power Elite*. New York: Oxford University Press, 1956.

Moore, Kristin A. and Wertheimer, Richard F. *Teenage Childbearing: Public Sector Costs*. Washington, DC: Urban Institute, 1982.

Packard, Vance. *The Status Seekers*. New York: D. McKay, 1959.

Patterson, James. *American's Struggle against Poverty: 1900–1980*. Cambridge: Harvard University Press, 1981.

Podhoretz, Norman. *Making It*. New York: Random House, 1967.

Rainwater, Lee. *And the Poor Get Children*. New York: Quadrangle Books, 1967.

Riesman, David. *The Lonely Crowd: A Study of the Changing American Character*. In collaboration with Reuel Denny and Nathan Glazer. New Haven: Yale University Press, 1958.

———. *Individualism Reconsidered, and Other Essays*. Glencoe, IL: Free Press, 1954.

———. *On Higher Education*. San Francisco: Jossey-Bass, 1980.

Ross, Heather L. and Sawhill, Isabel V. *Time of Translation: The Growth of Families Headed by Women*. Washington, DC: Urban Institute, 1975.

Sennett, Richard and Cobb, Jonathan. *The Hidden Injuries of Class*. New York: Vintage Books, 1973.

Spindler, Arthur. *Public Welfare*. New York: Human Sciences Press, 1979.

Steinfels, Peter. *The Neoconservatives*. New York: Simon & Schuster, 1979.

Veblen, Thorsten. *Theory of the Leisure Class*. 1919; Boston: Houghton Mifflin, 1973.

Veevers, Jean. *Childless by Choice*. Toronto: Butterworths, 1980.

Wallerstein, Judith S., and Kelley, Joan Belin. *Surviving the Breakup*. New York: Basic Books, 1980.

Warner, W. Lloyd. *Yankee City*. 5 vols. 1941–49. Abridged version, 1 vol., New Haven: Yale University Press, 1963.

———, et al. *Social Class in America: A Manual of Procedure for the Measurement of Social Strata*. Chicago: Social Science Research Associates, 1949.

Weber, Max. *From Max Weber: Essays in Sociology*. Translated and edited by Hans H. Gerth and C. Wright Mills. New York: Oxford University Press, 1946.

INDEX

Bacall, Lauren, 20
Bailey, Anthony, 109n.
Baker, Russell, 20
Bates, Alan, 306, 307 and n.
Battered wives, 262
Bell, Alan P., 207, 219 and n.
Bell, Daniel, 56, 72, 293
Bensman, Joseph, 81
Berger, Peter, 62
Bernard, Jessie, 134
Beyond the Melting Point
    (Moynihan), 67n.
Birth control. *See* Contraception
Black Child Care (Pouissant,
    Comer), 42
Blacks, 17; childless, 190 and n.;
    female, 84–86; gay, 204–205,
    206, 208–209; media identities
    of, 84–86, 94–98; middle class,
    39–44, 84–86, 95–97; teenage
    mothers, 159–165, 166 and n.,
    167 and n., 171–177, 190–191;
    unemployed, 257 and n., 260
Bloomingdale's, 197 and n.
Blue-collar workers, 229–249
Boredom, and teenage pregnancy,
    170
Breckenridge, Mary, 194
Brooks, John, 80n.
Brown, Helen Gurley, 77n.
Brown, Rita Mae, 221
Bunch, Charlotte, 223
Bunker, Archie, 55, 87, 92–94
Business: gay-owned, 224; and
    middle class, 46; and New Class,
    57 and n., 66 and n., 67, 71, 72;
    statistics on, 46; and upper class,
    274–294; women in, 76–82, 84,
    91–92. *See also* Income;
    Occupations; Self-employment
Business schools, 71, 72
Busing, 27

California, 137, 246, 247, 297–
    303, 306, 310

Campbell, Angus, 137
Campbell, Arthur, 163
Capitalism, 72
Caplow, Theodore, 35
Careers. *See* Occupation(s)
Careful and Critical Discourse
    (CCD), 54–56, 121n.
Carnegie, Andrew, 20
Carpentry, 107 and n., 108
Cassetty, Judith, 148n.
Castelli, Leo, 300
Catalogues, mail order, 284–285
Catholicism, 36–37
Central air-conditioning, 34
Chaplin, Charlie, 20
Child abuse, 166, 229–230
Childlessness, 179–195
Children: costs of, 179 and n.,
    180, 181, 184–185, 190–192;
    effects of divorce on, 129, 136–
    155; middle class, 30, 31 and n.,
    39–42, 47–48; of teenage
    parents, 165–172
Child support, 137–139, 140n.,
    141, 142, 148 and n.
Chinese, 4, 17
Chinoy, Ely, 236
Christopher Street, 225
Church, Frederick, 306
"Cinderella Complex," 148
Class convergence, 24, 89
Class definitions, 13–15
Clayburgh, Jill, 149, 150, 306–307
Cleaver, Eldridge, 205
Coleman, Richard P., 279
College, 24 and n., 25 and n.,
    160n.; business schools, 71, 72;
    children of divorced parents
    discriminated by, 151n.; and GI
    Bill, 26, 57 and n., 58; and
    1980s B.A. devaluation, 115. *See
    also* Education
Comer, James, 42
Computers, 235, 291
Conservatism, 193

Ennis, Michael, 203
Entertainment, middle class, 34–35, 47
Espenshade, Thomas, 184, 185
Essence, 84–86
Estates, 2

Factory work, 106 and *n*., 113, 230–242
Family, 15, 17–18; and downward mobility attitude, 104–107; dual-career, 24, 25, 181; effects of divorce on, 129, 135–155; media images of, 86–99; post-World War II middle class, 23–24, 28, 29–31, 34–35, 47
Family planning, 19, 29, 163, 175. *See also* Contraception
Farming. *See* Agriculture
Fashion, 84 and *n*., 289–291
Fertility statistics, 190–191, 195
Fiction, class depicted in, 19–21
Fishing, 243–246
Folk art, American, 292
Food processors, 287, 288 and *n*.
Food stamps, 171, 176, 252
Freud, Sigmund, 28*n*.
Furstenberg, Frank, 167

Galleries, art, 300, 309–315
Gallup polls, 201
Gans, Herbert J., 98
Gays, 197–225
GI Bill, 26, 57 and *n*.
Glazer, Nathan, 66
Glick, Paul C., 130
Gloucester, 243–245
Good-Bye Girl, The (film), 150
Good Times" (TV show), 95–97
Gouldner, Alvin, 55, 56
Great Depression, 26, 34, 258, 314
Great Society, 2, 191*n*., 193*n*., 253
Greeley, Andrew, 248
Greenberg, David, 152, 153*n*.
Greene, Gael, 287

Green Mountain Dykes, 225
Growing Up (Baker), 20
Guest, C. Z., 290
Guilbaut, Serge, 314
Gutmann, Peter M., 114

Haagen, Hess, 110–111
Hacker, Andrew, 70
Hampton, Robert, 135, 136
Hansen, Duane, 295 and *n*.
"Happy Days" (TV show), 89–90
Hardy, Janet, 166
Harlem, 11–12, 39
Having It All (Brown), 77*n*.
Hazan, Marcella, 288
Head Start, 19, 255
Health risks, occupational, 254
High school dropouts, 110–111, 113, 114, 152, 247, 257, 258, 267; and teenage pregnancy, 159–161, 163, 165
High school sports, 35, 47, 48
High Tech, 290–291
Hirsch, Fred, 317
Hirsch, Paul M., 93
Homeless, 251–252
Home ownership, 27*n*.; and carpenter demand, 107*n*.; discrimination in, 27; middle class, 26–28, 34, 43–44, 46–47; upper class, 283, 284
Homestead Act (1864), 26
Homosexualities (Bell, Weinberg), 207
Homosexuality, 197–225
Hornaby, John, 124
Housing: artists' lofts, 307–312; effects of divorce on, 141–144; lesbian, 218, 219–221; public, 162, 252. *See also* Home ownership
Howells, William Dean, 19
Hustling, gay, 214
Hyde Amendment (1977), 176 and *n*.

Politics (*continued*)
64–65; statistics on, 193 and *n.*;
and television, 59; union, 239–241
Pollack, Jackson, 314
Populism, 62
Portuguese-Americans, 243–248
Poussaint, Alvin, 42
Poverty, 11–13, 251–270; and
childlessness, 190–191, 193,
195; and divorce, 133–134, 139,
142–143, 147; income, 252, 253,
254, 259; lesbian, 218–221, 225;
media portrayal of, 95–98;
occupations, 252–270; statistics
on, 1 and *n.*, 252; status, 253;
and teenage pregnancy, 159–177
Pregnancy, teenage, 159–177,
190–191
Production, 13, 56
Professionalism, 44
Progressive Education Movement,
31*n.*
Property, 26–28. *See also* Home
ownership
Prostitution, 12
Public housing, 162, 252

Rainwater, Lee, 175, 279
Rauschenberg, Robert, 297
Recession, mid-1970s, 235
Religion, 30; New Traditionalism,
30, 36–38
Remarriage, 133, 148–149;
statistics, 148
Republican party, 193
Revolution, 69
Rohatyn, Felix, 289
Rosenquist, James, 315
Roth, Philip, 56
Rothko, Mark, 306
Rubyfruit Jungle (Brown), 221
Running, 286

Salary. *See* Income
Sales, 34, 35
"Sanford and Son" (TV show), 94–95
San Francisco gay community,
217, 218–219
Saturday Night Fever (film), 86,
87, 88
Savvy, 147
Schjeldahl, Peter, 296
Scientific American, 46
Sears catalog, 285
Secretarial work, 116
Segal, George, 311, 314
Self-employment, 17, 236;
agricultural, 109, 110; and
downward mobility, 108–110,
112, 114 and *n.*, 121–124, 125;
New Class, 71; statistics on, 123
Servants, 68–69
Sex and sexuality: education, 173–174; gay, 197–225; middle class,
29–30; teenage, 159–177, 190–191
Shapiro, Esther, 200
Sheehan, Susan, 3
Shopping malls, 285 and *n.*
Showing Off in America (Brooks),
80*n.*
Sinister Wisdom, 225
Smith, Jaclyn, 192*n.*
Smith, Timothy d'Arch, 208
Snowball sampling, 4
Social mobility. *See* Mobility
Social programs, 19, 191*n.*, 258,
260 and *n. See also specific
programs*
Social psychologists, 17
Social work, 201, 224
Sociologists, 17
Soho, 304, 306, 307–312
Speech patterns, 78–82
Spiegel, Sam, 289
Sports, high school, 35, 47, 48